European Commission

EUROPEAN
ECONOMY

Reports and studies

Directorate-General for Economic and Financial Affairs

1994

Number 4

EC agricultural policy
for the 21st century

Abbreviations and symbols used

Member States

B	Belgium
DK	Denmark
D	Germany
WD	West Germany
GR	Greece
E	Spain
F	France
IRL	Ireland
I	Italy
L	Luxembourg
NL	The Netherlands
P	Portugal
UK	United Kingdom
EUR 9	European Community excluding Greece, Spain and Portugal
EUR 10	European Community excluding Spain and Portugal
EUR 12–	European Community, 12 Member States including West Germany
EUR 12+	European Community, 12 Member States including Germany

Currencies

ECU	European currency unit
BFR	Belgian franc
DKR	Danish krone
DM	German mark (Deutschmark)
DR	Greek drachma
ESC	Portuguese escudo
FF	French franc
HFL	Dutch guilder
IRL	Irish pound (punt)
LFR	Luxembourg franc
LIT	Italian lira
PTA	Spanish peseta
UKL	Pound sterling
USD	US dollar
SFR	Swiss franc
YEN	Japanese yen
CAD	Canadian dollar
ÖS	Austrian schilling
R	Russian rouble

Other abbreviations

ACP	African, Caribbean and Pacific countries having signed the Lomé Convention
ECSC	European Coal and Steel Community
EDF	European Development Fund
EIB	European Investment Bank
EMCF	European Monetary Cooperation Fund
EMS	European Monetary System
ERDF	European Regional Development Fund
Euratom	European Atomic Energy Community
Eurostat	Statistical Office of the European Communities (SOEC)
GDP (GNP)	Gross domestic (national) product
GFCF	Gross fixed capital formation
LDCs	Less-developed countries
Mio	Million
Mrd	1 000 million
NCI	New Community Instrument
OCTs	Overseas countries and territories
OECD	Organization for Economic Cooperation and Development
OPEC	Organization of Petroleum Exporting Countries
PPS	Purchasing power standard
SMEs	Small and medium-sized enterprises
toe	Tonne of oil equivalent
:	Not available

Contents

Annex

Tables

Graphs

Members of the expert group

Ron Anderson, Professor, Département des Sciences Economiques, Louvain-la-Neuve, Belgium

Klaus Frohberg, Research Scholar, Institut für Agrarpolitik, Bonn, Germany

Michiel Keyzer, Deputy-Director, Centre for World Food Studies, Amsterdam, Netherlands

Ulrich Koester, Professor, University of Kiel, Kiel, Germany

Arne Larsen, Director, Institute of Agricultural Economics, Copenhagen, Denmark

Louis Mahé, Professor, ENSA, Département des Sciences Economiques et Sociales, Rennes, France

Maurizio Merlo, Professor, University of Padova, Padova, Italy

Per Molander, Ministry of Finance, Stockholm, Sweden

Alexander Sarris, Professor, University of Athens, Athens, Greece

Dominique Van der Mensbrugghe, Principal Administrator, Dr, OECD Development Centre, Paris, France

Rapporteurs:

Knud Munk, Principal Administrator, Economic Service, European Commission, Brussels, Belgium

Kenneth Thomson, Professor, University of Aberdeen, Aberdeen, United Kingdom

Foreword

A group of independent agricultural economists was asked to undertake an economic assessment of current EC agricultural policy and to consider various ways to reform the common agricultural policy (CAP). The expert group was chaired by Arne Larsen, Director of the Institute of Agricultural Economics, Copenhagen.

The results of the work of the expert group are presented in this report. The report reflects the consensus of opinion of the group of experts and contains a number of far-reaching recommendations for further reform of the CAP. These recommendations do not represent the position of the Com- mission but are, in the spirit of transparency, published together with the supporting analysis in order to contribute to the on-going discussions on agricultural policy reform.

The report draws on evidence and analysis contained in papers provided by individual experts. These papers are published in a separate volume of *European Economy* entitled 'The economics of the CAP'.

Heinrich Matthes
Chairman of the Editorial Board of
European Economy

Executive summary

Most developed countries support agriculture in order to alleviate the social strains brought about by economic change. In this respect the European Community (EC) is no exception. Under the common agricultural policy (CAP), the level of support to agriculture in the EC is generally in line with that in other developed countries, taking into account relative income levels and the net balance of agricultural trade.

The basic CAP instrument has been market price support, which encourages production but penalizes consumers, and has resulted in EC self-sufficiency or surpluses in most temperate farm products since the 1980s. This method, although always problematic, has over time become increasingly costly in terms of complicated administration, distortion of resource use, detrimental environmental effects and international trade tensions. Although high food prices mean that the economic costs of the CAP continue to be borne mainly by EC users and consumers of farm products, taxpayers have faced increasingly budgetary costs of export and other disposal subsidies, intervention storage, direct payments to farmers and administration. Moreover, market support has also become increasingly inefficient as a way of helping those in farming who are most in need of income assistance.

The 1992 CAP reforms, based on the Mac Sharry package, represent a major change in policy direction, from price support to direct payments, and will reduce some of the negative effects mentioned above. The package was essential in paving the way for a GATT settlement on agriculture. However, it is limited to about 50% of total EC agricultural output and has increased the imbalances in price support levels between commodities and has added to the administrative burden of the CAP. Also, the direct payments are still partly tied to current levels of production, rather than being completely 'decoupled', and are not sufficiently targeted towards those farmers in need of support.

For these reasons, considerations of economic efficiency alone would suggest further reform of the CAP. However, there are also compelling additional reasons for further change. The present policy seriously complicates the development of freer international trade, and the eventual enlargement of the Community to the countries of Central Europe. Furthermore, with the introduction of direct income support, a clearer separation of the responsibility for internal market unity and for competition on the one hand, and the responsibility for more localized social and environmental aims of agricultural policy on the other, is possible. Whereas the responsibility for the former should remain at Community level, the principle of subsidiarity endorsed in the Maastricht Treaty of European Union suggests that the responsibility for the latter should be allocated to Member States.

With this background, the report suggests a general and long-term perspective for the future of the common agricultural policy. The fundamental approach is to separate more clearly two aspects of agricultural policy, that of economic efficiency on the one hand, and that of social and environmental measures on the other. The use of different instruments and institutions for these two areas would make the CAP more effective in achieving these objectives.

The main elements in such a reform are:

(i) Further cuts in agricultural support prices, initially for commodities, such as milk products, fruit and vegetables, sugar, tobacco and wine which have not been affected by the 1992 reforms. These price cuts should be phased in over a reasonable time period in order not to disrupt overly the production and rural conditions. Remaining import levies and quotas should be transformed into flat *ad valorem* tariffs which would restore world market links. The objective should be a level of market protection no higher than that enjoyed by other sectors in the EC economy.

(ii) Compensation for price cuts could continue via direct payments, as in the 1992 reforms. However, these payments should be completely decoupled from current levels of production and use of production factors, for both existing and new compensations.

(iii) Initially, compensatory payments should be financed by the EC budget as at present, but gradually (over 7 to 10 years) this common financing should be phased out. Member States would be free to continue these payments on a decoupled basis, or to utilize their own funds for rural development, environmental improvement or structural adjustment purposes, in strict conformity with EC competition policy.

(iv) With support prices close to world market price levels the rationale for quantitative restrictions, such as milk quotas and set-aside would have been eliminated, and should therefore be abolished. This would facilitate the entry in the profession for young farmers and allow production and export to expand.

(v) EC regional, social and cohesion funds should be used more comprehensively as accompanying measures to aid structural developments, and could be exploited to ensure that no Member State, in particular those with low per capita income, suffer substantial financial penalties.

Along these lines, further reform would enable farm income support to be separated from farm production and allow assistance to be targeted to those most in need from a social or economic point of view. Efficiency of agricultural production and policy administration would be improved. Rural development and environmental protection could by the use of targeted instruments be promoted in a more cost-effective way.

The original principles of the CAP — market unity, Community preference and common financing — would be maintained by this approach although Community preference would be at a much lower level than now, and although the financial burden to deal with the structural adjustment problems in agriculture would be shared using general rather than agriculture-specific instruments, i.e. using the Structural and Cohesion Funds. Responsibility for trade and competition policy would remain at Community level, while the primary responsibility for social and environmental policies affecting the agricultural and rural population would be at Member State level, as for other sectors. Although total budgetary costs might increase temporarily, there would be no serious losers amongst Member States, who would all share the substantial long-term efficiency gains and would benefit from increased freedom to adjust direct income support measures to national social, rural and environmental preferences and circumstances. Sources of contention and division within the Community over agricultural policy would be greatly reduced, and the Community's flexibility towards trading partners and new entrant States would be greatly enhanced.

Chapter 1

General introduction

1.1. Motivation

With the May 1992 agreement on reform of the common agricultural policy for the period up until 1996, and the December 1993 Uruguay Round agreement on international agricultural trade during the period 1995-99, the CAP is currently undergoing the most substantial change in its history. It might therefore be thought premature to consider at this time the further reform of the policy. Moreover, there have been many past analyses, by both the European Commission and outside commentators, of the CAP's development and problems. Is there a need for yet another expert report? There are several reasons for asserting that this is a useful exercise.

First, several aspects of EC agriculture ensure its continued significance. Half the substantial EC budget continues to be allocated to the sector, representing an issue of major importance to its citizens as taxpayers. Economic interest is assured by the inherent characteristics of farming, in its variegated utilization of the Community's land and water resources, and its problems of structural adjustment to changing technology and consumer demand. Further, a number of international issues remain open even after the Uruguay Round, including relationships with countries to the east and south of the Community, links with developing countries, and the longer-term pattern of trade between the EC and the major global agricultural importers and exporters.

Second, the 1992 reforms, which although they represent a major shift in EC agricultural policy, do not cover all sectors and do not within reformed sectors imply a complete move away from market price support. The Commission itself is therefore in the process of preparing reform proposals for sectors such as wine, beef, fruit and vegetables and sugar, and is requested by the Council to formulate ideas for the policies to pursue after 1996 by that year.

Unlike many policy measures and reform proposals in the past, the present report has not been provoked by any acute crisis. In preparing the report, this has allowed the expert group to take a general and long-term perspective with a view to stimulating discussion in good time before the 1996 assessment of the remaining imbalances and of the logical implications for the future EC agricultural policy of the move from market price support to direct payments which was initiated with the 1992 reform.

1.2. Approach

The analysis proceeds from the basic assumption that agriculture shall not be treated any differently than other sectors if there are not strong reasons to do otherwise. The report therefore — using an economic perspective — considers the arguments for developing special policies to deal with the problems in agriculture.

The report recognizes that changing circumstances even with unchanged objectives may lead to new policy conclusions and therefore considers how changing circumstances over time have put pressure on the common agricultural policy as it was originally designed. It considers how the Community has responded to these pressures. Drawing the lessons from this exercise and extrapolating the experience into the future, the report provides general but concrete guidelines for further reform of the CAP with the main consideration given to the objective of economic efficiency, but with due regard to the other objectives which the CAP needs to satisfy and the need for policy changes to be adopted to receive widespread support.

1.3. Plan

Chapter 2 reviews the objectives for agricultural policy and the level of support to agricultural sectors in various developed countries. At first sight, there are striking differences in the overall level of farm support and in the policy instruments employed for channelling support to the agricultural sector. However, closer examination reveals a common pattern which offers not only interesting insights into the need for and possible direction of domestic policy reforms, but also highlights the significant international dimension of the reform process.

Chapter 3 traces the evolution of the CAP. Four periods are distinguished: from the early 1960s to the first enlargement in 1973, covering the setting-up of the market organizations and the Mansholt plan; between 1973 and 1981, the gradual build-up of pressure for change of a policy which was becoming unsustainable, largely because of a rapid increase in the degree of self-sufficiency; the years 1981-91 which are presented as years of experimentation; and finally, the years of reform marked by the 1992 CAP reform decision and the 1993 GATT Agreement. A critical assessment of these successive policy developments first helps to identify policies which, for the future, look either unpromising or even harmful. But there are also more positive lessons to be learnt for shaping a sense of the right approach to the future. By interpreting the extrapolation results of quantitative model analyses, the chapter also assesses the economic consequences of the reforms relative to alternative scenarios up to the year 2001. Against this background, Chapter 4 draws the lessons to be learnt and identifies the future challenges for EC agricultural policy.

In Chapter 5, general guidelines for future EC agricultural policy design are formulated. It starts by presenting the foundation on which the proposed guidelines are based. Recommendations are provided concerning changes to the main elements of the CAP: prices, quantitative regulations and stabilization, and supplementary measures to secure support for the changes.

Chapter 6 provides an assessment of the proposal in relation to objectives presented in Chapter 2 and from the point of view of European cohesion and integration. It is finally argued that all Member States stand to gain.

Chapter 2

Agricultural policy: objectives and approaches

2.1. Introduction

Agricultural policies in the European Community have persisted despite considerable budgetary costs and much criticism from both trading partner countries and from commentators, including some of those in agriculture itself. However, the European Community has been far from alone in protecting its agriculture: throughout the developed world, governments have implemented policies which assist the farming sector. There is evidence therefore that agricultural policy addresses substantial and widespread socio-economic issues.

The first part of this chapter discusses the major government objectives influencing agricultural policy in developed countries — concerned respectively with farm incomes, rural communities, the environment, technical efficiency and competitiveness, economic efficiency and international trade relations — and places the EC's common agricultural policy in this context. The second part recognizes differences in the level of support between developed countries, but identifies also a common pattern of this support.

2.2. Policy objectives

A. Farm incomes

The effects of the basic economic forces of supply and demand on real agricultural world market prices, which have fallen substantially, by an average of 2% per year since 1948, are illustrated in Graph 1. Following a temporary rise in the 1970s, there has been an even steeper annual decrease of around 6% during the last decade. Although these movements are affected by national agricultural policies and other factors, the long-term decline in real agricultural prices (which can be traced back to the 19th century at least) may be taken as a well-established phenomenon.

Economic analysis suggests that the impact of falling prices on farm incomes would be cushioned if there were a large enough 'flight from the land' by the farming population. However, such out migration is often regarded as socially and economically undesirable (see below). Moreover, despite the weather and other hazards of a farmer's existence, there is often a strong resistance to the idea of leaving the land, stemming from the nature of the lifestyle, the close mutual support in the agricultural community and loyalty to the local area. In many countries, despite strong economic pressures, emigration from agriculture does not seem to have been sufficient to protect the farming incomes of those who have remained in the sector. In the EC, farm employment has declined at a roughly constant rate of 3% per year, from about 10% of the total labour force 20 years ago to about 5% today. This has not been sufficient in recent years for farm incomes to increase in line with those in other sectors.

In fact, the level of income in agriculture worldwide, as recorded by value-added per person employed, is consistently lower than that in other sectors (Graph 2). This is particularly true in countries where the agricultural sector has deep historical roots, such as Japan and Europe. However, low productivity and remuneration of agricultural labour does not necessarily imply that total income levels of farm households are lower than those of other households. Increasingly, people living on farm holdings receive income from non-agricultural employment and other sources, such as pensions. In fact, recent empirical work suggests that the income of farm households in the most highly developed industrialized countries may be as high if not higher than that of non-farm households. Table 1 shows that for a number of countries in the European Community the income of farm households is indeed higher than that of other groups — in the Netherlands significantly so. Other information suggests that the distribution of farm incomes is highly skewed, with a 'tail' of low returns despite the operation of income support and stabilization policies, which may even aggravate the income-distribution problem. This may reinforce the perception of a continuing 'farm income problem'.

Thus, politicians have long considered that there is a need to support and stabilize farm incomes, arguing that, without support, farm incomes would tend to fall below those of the general population, and be unusually volatile. In the post-war world, the 'farm income problem' was believed to become more urgent when rising general prosperity did not lead to equivalent increases in demand for agricultural products, while at the same time technological changes steadily increased agricultural supply. It was considered that without

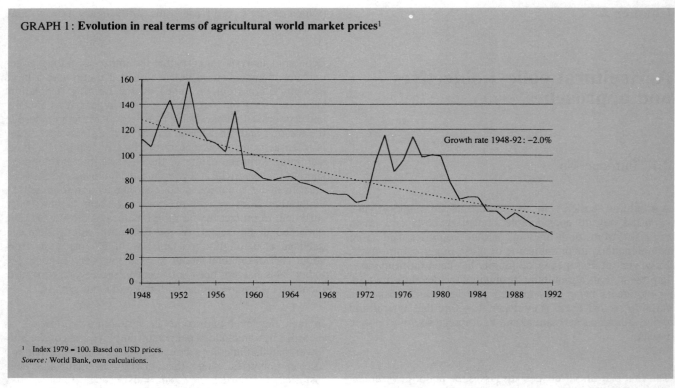

GRAPH 1: **Evolution in real terms of agricultural world market prices**[1]

Growth rate 1948-92: −2.0%

[1] Index 1979 = 100. Based on USD prices.
Source: World Bank, own calculations.

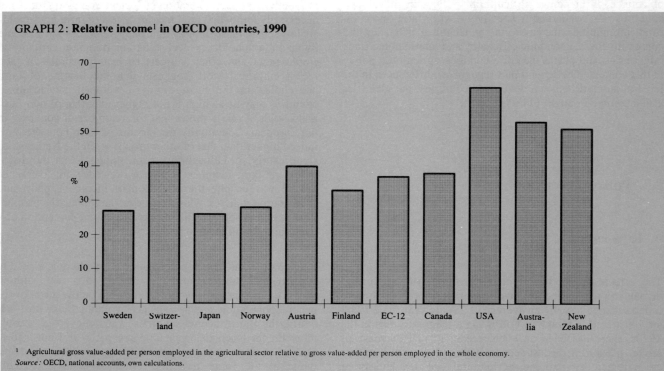

GRAPH 2: **Relative income**[1] **in OECD countries, 1990**

[1] Agricultural gross value-added per person employed in the agricultural sector relative to gross value-added per person employed in the whole economy.
Source: OECD, national accounts, own calculations.

Table 1

Relative agriculture incomes, EC[1]

Country	Total disposable income of agricultural households as percentage of that of all households	Year
Denmark	115	1988
Germany	110	1988
Greece	108	1985
France	108	1989
Ireland	112[2]	1982
Italy	145	1988
Luxembourg	143	1985
Netherlands	228	1989
Portugal	81	1986

[1] Figures for Belgium, Spain and United Kingdom are not reported.
[2] Percentage of total (disposable) income.
Source: Statistical Office of the European Communities, 'Total income of agricultural households, 1992 Report, 5C, Luxembourg.

government intervention, the downward trend in farm product prices would squeeze farm incomes, especially for certain groups such as small farmers or producers competing against cheaper external supplies. Furthermore, during certain time periods there has been marked instability on world agricultural markets, suggesting to policy-makers the need for stabilizing measures.

Governments in most developed countries have therefore set out to secure a satisfactory and equitable standard of living for farmers and to stabilize agricultural markets and farmers' incomes. For the EC, this objective is formulated in Article 39 of the 1957 Treaty of Rome: 'to ensure a fair standard of living for the agricultural community, in particular by increasing the individual earnings of persons engaged in agriculture; to stabilize markets.' To assess the pursuit of these objectives, information on general and farm incomes must be gathered and assessed; this is a complex conceptual and statistical exercise, particularly when international aspects are involved.

B. Rural communities

Many policy-makers believe that rural communities based on family farms are a form of social organization which preserves values such as social solidarity and community care. They also seem sensitive to the maintenance of service infrastructures dependent (at least originally) on farming. From an economic point of view, reductions in agricultural employment can have ripple effects which lead to the closure of schools, shops and service industries in rural areas, with

corresponding adjustment costs and under-utilization of capital. At the same time, a drift from the land to the cities can put more pressure on urban services constantly struggling to meet demands.

The maintenance of prosperous rural communities, and the preservation and encouragement of family farming, are explicit or implicit agricultural policy objectives in many countries. According to Article 39 of the Treaty of Rome, account is to be taken of 'the particular nature of agricultural activity, which results from the social structure of agriculture and from structural and natural disparities between the various agricultural regions'.

However, regional development based on agriculture alone cannot succeed in achieving these aims without unacceptable levels of economic costs. Thus regional policies in general encompass activities other than those related directly to agriculture. Nevertheless, farming forms the background for residential and other land uses, and a foundation for local culture, particularly for smaller rural settlements. Thus support for rural communities and their development remains a major policy objective to be taken into account in the context of agricultural interventions by the State.

C. The environment

The maintenance of the countryside as a source of natural resources for utilization and enjoyment is a further long-standing public objective. However, there is now no consensus that agriculture can or should be relied upon to provide a satisfactory rural environment, or even that farmed landscape should prevail over wilderness. Some modern farming practices are environmentally unfriendly, particularly in terms of loss of rare species and water quality. In fact, although many rural regions retain their traditional natural attractions, there is no doubt that changes in farming structures and techniques have had detrimental effects on the rural environment.

Government in most countries imposes obligations on farmers to prevent loss and damage to natural resources, to maintain the appearance of the countryside, and to preserve its wildlife. In fact, environmental protection is an explicit agricultural policy objective in counties like Austria, Switzerland, Norway and Sweden. In the European Community, the environment is not explicitly mentioned as an agricultural policy objective, but Article 130R of the 1986 Single European Act specifies that: 'Environmental protection requirements shall be a component of the Community's other policies'. This has important connotations for agriculture, which is the largest land user in the EC, occupying 57% of its total area, and is subject to a highly developed and significant common policy.

The welfare of farm animals and the assurance of food safety are also considered the responsibilities of modern governments. These concerns are currently undergoing rapid evolution with the development of new ways to breed and husband livestock, and to treat crops, animals and foodstuffs. Biotechnology seems likely to enlarge further the potential for yield, variety and quality of agricultural products, but the difficulty of relying on private information and markets to arrive at optimal positions for all interests points to intensified government involvement in this area.

D. Technical efficiency and competitiveness

The pursuit of technical efficiency is an important goal of agricultural policy, not only to attain higher levels and growth rates of national income (GDP), but also to achieve a greater degree of food security and international competitiveness, two common government concerns. In the Community, these aims underlie the Article 39 objectives 'to increase agricultural productivity by promoting technical progress and by ensuring the rational development of agricultural production and the optimum utilization of the factors of production, in particular labour', as well as 'to assure the availability of supplies and to ensure that supplies reach consumers at reasonable prices'.

Technical efficiency in the agricultural sector which indicates the relationship between the level of agricultural production and the amount of inputs used, depends on the technological knowledge applied in the sector and on the enterprise structure. Efficiency in this sense is an important determinant of international competitiveness, and the related government objective of food security. Support both for agriculture in general and for scientific research, investments in R&D, education in agriculture and extension services has been justified on this basis.

The technical efficiency of the agricultural sector also depends on the extent to which economies of scale are exploited. Generally, small firms are less technically efficient than are larger ones. This has provided the justification for structural adjustment programmes to support farm consolidation and enlargement in order to capture the economies of scale apparent in larger units.

E. Economic efficiency

Economic efficiency requires that capital, labour, land and other inputs are allocated to produce the highest possible level of gross domestic product. As regards agriculture, the main cause of economic inefficiency in developed countries is too many resources being used in that industry relative to

other industries. Within agriculture itself, resources may be similarly misallocated.

Economic efficiency in general requires the abolition of barriers to external trade and of government subsidies which influence production decisions. Market price support which increases domestic price relative to world market prices, hence retaining more resources in agriculture and discouraging consumption, has therefore a cost in terms of economic efficiency.

The Treaty of Maastricht obliges the European Union to maintain 'an open market economy with free competition' (Article 3a). The Treaty of Rome already specified (Article 110) that 'by establishing a customs union between themselves Member States aim to contribute, in the common interest, to harmonious development of world trade, the progressive abolition of restrictions on international trade and the lowering of customs barriers'. Inefficiencies in agriculture can result from reasons other than market price support, and may indeed be used to justify government intervention to alleviate the inefficiencies. Anti-competitive market structures have negative impacts on price, output and consumption patterns. Protecting agriculture against monopolistic trade and industry practices in upstream and downstream markets has frequently justified government intervention in agricultural markets. The role of government in providing information and in stimulating investment in R&D has already been mentioned above as a tool to improve competitiveness, but may also be justified on efficiency grounds. Such knowledge and information constitute public goods and without government support, are likely to be under-supplied, particularly in a sector consisting of many small enterprises. Inadequate information flows also obstruct the efficient functioning of markets. Given the unusual nature of information as an economic commodity, and its crucial role in market operations, government policy often aims at ensuring satisfactory levels and forms of information to producers, traders and consumers.

Perfect capital markets could accommodate the inherent risk in agricultural enterprise due to changing climatic conditions and due to instability in commodity markets. The non-existence of such markets, however, provides an argument for government intervention to stabilize agricultural prices and stimulate agricultural investments.

It may be argued that economic efficiency for policy-makers is difficult to conceptualize and is therefore not perceived as a separate objective, which explains why it has not been given much weight in agricultural policy formulation compared to other objectives. However, economic inefficiencies due to agricultural support systems, when reflected in high budget costs, in high consumer prices for food, and in trade tensions, do, clearly influence policy-makers.

F. International policy coordination

Agricultural policies have a significant international dimension through their effects on trade flows and world markets. Agricultural support not only creates domestic economic distortion, but it also creates international spill-over effects in terms of lower world market prices, essentially exporting the domestic problems of structural adjustment. By depressing world market prices, it increases the problems for farmers in other countries, though easing difficulties for low-income food-deficit countries dependent on cheap food imports.

Domestic policy-makers will tend not to take these spill-over effects into consideration, leading to a higher level of subsidization than if these effects were taken into account. Given the income objective, unilateral reduction in market price support requires policy-makers to substitute economically costly and highly-visible budget transfers for less visible transfers from consumers. Even for big countries, there is only a small positive impact on world market prices to facilitate this process. However, if developed countries act together to reduce trade-distorting support measures, the adjustment is eased by a rise in world market prices, as well as a reduction in the political pressures for higher prices by reference to those offered in other countries. This reasoning underlies the Ministerial Declaration marking the 1986 commencement of the Uruguay Round of GATT negotiations on agriculture and the OECD Ministerial Mandate of 1987, and has been implemented in the form of the 1992 GATT Agreement.

2.3. Policy approaches

A. Differences in agricultural support ...

While there is a considerable degree of similarity between agriculture policy objectives throughout the developed world, there are striking differences in the level of support to the industry and in how it is provided. Graph 3 shows that the level of total assistance as measured by the percentage producer subsidy equivalent (PSE), i.e. the transfer to producers relative to the farm gate value of agricultural production, varies from around 80% of output value in

Switzerland to only 5% in New Zealand, with the Community in a middle position at around 45%.

The most common method of assistance to the agricultural sector is market support. This system maintains internal prices above world market prices for both producers and consumers, and thus generates an economic transfer to farmers from consumers, and from taxpayers in the case of exporting countries. According to the OECD, market price support accounts for 80% of all assistance granted to agriculture as measured by the PSE, but there are big differences between OECD Member States (see Graph 4). The common agricultural policy has traditionally provided the bulk of its assistance to EC agriculture in this form, although in recent years the proportion of total transfers ascribeable to other methods has been rising fast.

Alternative methods of assistance to agriculture have been used to a much lesser extent. These include output subsidies (e.g. deficiency payments to guarantee a higher producer price), subsidies on variable and capital inputs in farming, food consumption subsidies, tax concessions, support to marketing infrastructure and research, and direct payments based on income, environmental services or other grounds. These methods usually throw the full burden of providing assistance onto the taxpayer, and often necessitate complex and costly administration. Finally, some governments combine price support with the regulation of domestic and foreign supplies, usually with the effect of reducing government budget costs and raising prices in a protected market. Important examples are the production quotas for rice in Japan, sugar in the EC and Australia, and milk in a number of OECD countries, US import quotas for sugar, and land set-aside in the EC, the US and some EFTA countries. However, the application and administration of such methods can be difficult, and economic measurement of their effects is equally complex.

B. ... but a common pattern of support

Despite these striking differences in the level and method of support to agriculture, a common pattern can be detected. The degree of public support for agriculture correlates with the disparity between agricultural and non-agricultural incomes as measured by value-added per person employed (see Graph 5). In Australia and New Zealand, parity of incomes between agriculture and non-agriculture goes hand in hand with a low level of assistance. In Japan and the Nordic countries, where value-added per person employed in farming is less than a third of that in the rest of the economy, the level of assistance is extremely high. Seen in this context, the level of agricultural support in the EC is consistent with farming's level of relative income.

GRAPH 3: **Transfers to agricultural producers[1] in OECD countries, 1990**

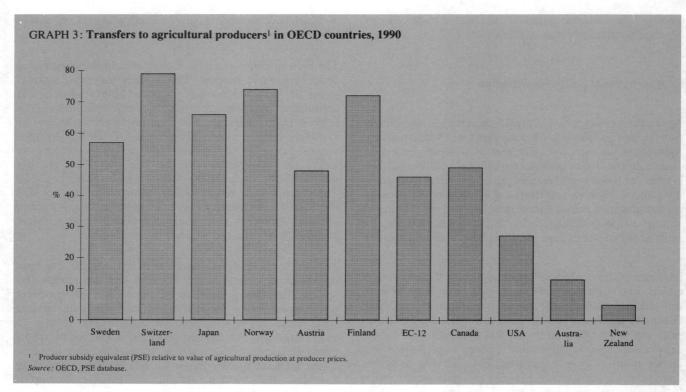

[1] Producer subsidy equivalent (PSE) relative to value of agricultural production at producer prices.
Source: OECD, PSE database.

GRAPH 4: **Consumer and taxpayer shares of transfers to agricultural producers[1] in OECD countries, 1990**

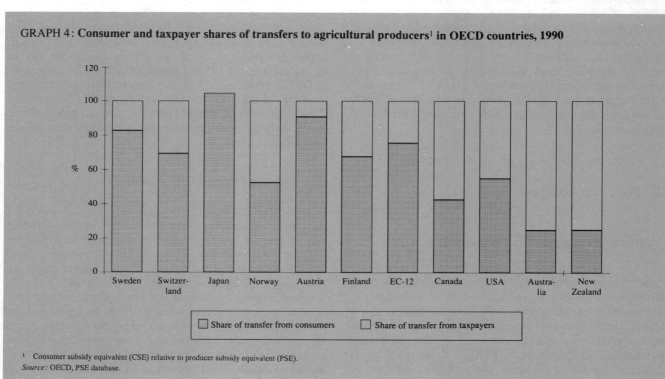

☐ Share of transfer from consumers   ☐ Share of transfer from taxpayers

[1] Consumer subsidy equivalent (CSE) relative to producer subsidy equivalent (PSE).
Source: OECD, PSE database.

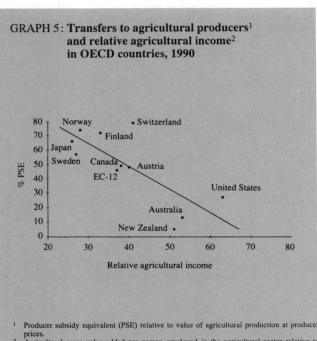

GRAPH 5: **Transfers to agricultural producers[1] and relative agricultural income[2] in OECD countries, 1990**

Relative agricultural income

[1] Producer subsidy equivalent (PSE) relative to value of agricultural production at producer prices.
[2] Agricultural gross value-added per person employed in the agricultural sector relative to gross value-added per person employed in the whole economy.

Source: OECD, PSE database, national accounts, own calculations.

Agricultural protection also correlates strongly with the extent to which a country is a net exporter of agricultural products (Graph 6). Generally speaking, agricultural importers subsidize more than exporters (Graph 7), and the share of transfers due to market price support tends to diminish the more that a country is a net exporter of its farm production (Graph 8). The New Zealand economy, for example, is heavily dependent on agricultural exports and has the lowest level of assistance to producers within the OECD, as well as the smallest share of transfers due to price support. On the other hand, Japan is a significant net importer of agricultural produce with one of the highest levels of assistance to the farming sector. The Community is a small net importer of agricultural products overall,[1] and provides a level of assistance close to the average for OECD countries as a whole.

EC decision-making, with all its inherent peculiarities, does not, therefore, seem to yield strikingly different outcomes

[1] Within the overall 'Agricultural and Food Products' group, the EC is a major net importer of fruit and vegetables, animal feed, fish, oilseeds, textile fibres and timber, and a major net exporter of cereals, milk products and alcoholic beverages. Within the smaller 'Food Products and Live Animals' group (which excludes beverages, tobacco, oilseeds, timber, fibres, etc.), it is also a net importer.

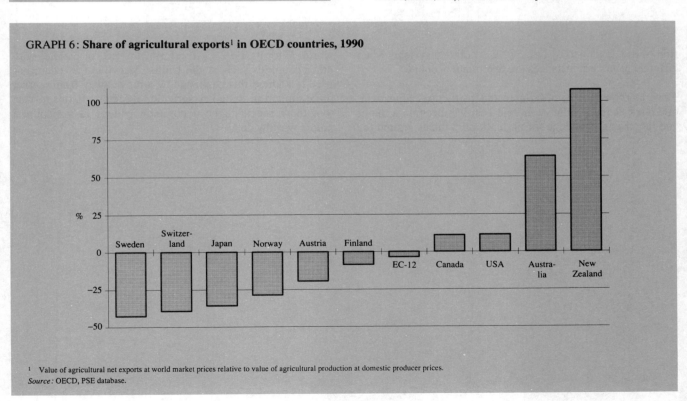

GRAPH 6: **Share of agricultural exports[1] in OECD countries, 1990**

[1] Value of agricultural net exports at world market prices relative to value of agricultural production at domestic producer prices.
Source: OECD, PSE database.

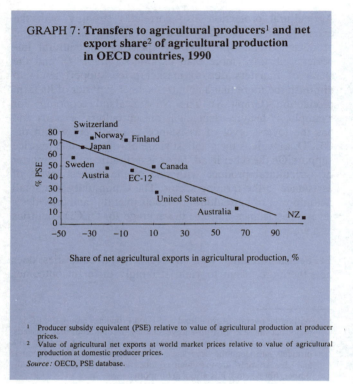

GRAPH 7: **Transfers to agricultural producers[1] and net export share[2] of agricultural production in OECD countries, 1990**

[1] Producer subsidy equivalent (PSE) relative to value of agricultural production at producer prices.
[2] Value of agricultural net exports at world market prices relative to value of agricultural production at domestic producer prices.
Source: OECD, PSE database.

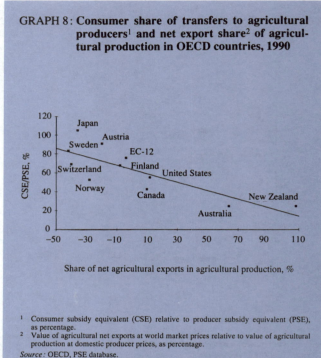

GRAPH 8: **Consumer share of transfers to agricultural producers[1] and net export share[2] of agricultural production in OECD countries, 1990**

[1] Consumer subsidy equivalent (CSE) relative to producer subsidy equivalent (PSE), as percentage.
[2] Value of agricultural net exports at world market prices relative to value of agricultural production at domestic producer prices, as percentage.
Source: OECD, PSE database.

from those generated by other OECD political systems when differences in circumstances are taken into account.

To support the income of farmers under structural adjustment pressures at reasonable economic cost has become a major and increasing challenge for agricultural policies around the world. With its 1992 CAP reform, the EC, in parallel with other countries such as the United States and Sweden, has tried to address this challenge by a move away from market price support in some key agricultural sectors. In this respect too, there seems to be a common pattern in agricultural policy worldwide.

Chapter 3

The evolution of the CAP

3.1. Introduction

The well-known Article 39 of the 1957 Treaty of Rome specifies the original objectives but not the nature of the common agricultural policy.[1] Instead, the 1958 Stresa conference did most of the initial architectural work on the CAP. It set out a system, put into place by the Commission and the six national governments during the early 1960s, for supporting market prices of farm products coupled with the dismantling of tariffs on intra-EC trade and the introduction of a common external tariff. The family farm ('the essential foundation of agriculture in Western Europe', according to the Stresa resolution) required a secure environment for which stable prices were held to be the key.

Despite successive attempts at reform, market price support has remained the main policy instrument during the three decades of the common agricultural policy. However, the number and complexity of other measures also operating within the policy have increased greatly over the years. Several phases of policy development can be summarized, and roughly dated, as follows.

From 1962, after the establishment of the CAP, national market price support systems were consolidated at Community level, and used as the predominant instrument in the common market organizations for most of the EC's main agricultural products. During the 1970s, the inherent problems of market price support were partly and temporarily overshadowed by the accession of new Member States and by the market and other instabilities of that decade. During the 1980s, as market price support came under pressure, an array of supplementary measures were tried and tested in a somewhat *ad hoc* way. Finally, the 1992 CAP reforms have marked a recognition of the need to switch from market price support to direct income support, although the extent and consequences of this move are yet to become fully apparent.

A number of economic explanations of these longer-term developments in EC agricultural policy may be put forward, depending on the approach adopted and the emphasis given to the various factors at play. A popular explanation lies in the mix of political lobbying and bureaucratic manoeuvring which surrounds the policy-making process: more formally, the system can be seen as a succession of rounds of a 'game' in which the 'players' seek to gain advantage for themselves or their supporters. Thus attention is focused on the changing structure of the Community's political and institutional make-up, and the historical context within which particular decisions were taken and pursued.

An alternative explanation is based on 'social rationality', by which governments seek, successfully or otherwise, to achieve policy 'objectives' such as those set out in the previous chapter. It is not necessary for governments to be conscious about this process of multivariate optimization as long as the process is driven by fundamental economic forces. These forces would include changing technological and market conditions such as the costs of farm production and of administration, and social trade-offs involving the relative level of farm incomes and the balance of agricultural trade. Since these parameters have altered over the last three decades, it follows that the CAP itself has adapted in order to enable the Community to satisfy its goals more efficiently.

The second of these approaches underlies the way in which this chapter, in the next three sections, deals with the four CAP phases identified above. This short history demonstrates how the adverse consequences of market price support, which were recognized from the start of the CAP and have given rise to continuous discussion of its reform, have increased in importance relative to the benefits. A final section (3.6) outlines the current structure of agriculture in the EC.

3.2. 1962-72: the early years

A. Market price support

In devising a policy to meet the objectives of the common agricultural policy, the six founding Member States had no hesitation in selecting market price support. No fundamental change in policy operation was involved since this type of policy already formed the basis of the national agricultural policies of the Six and merely required adjustment to the same regulatory conditions in all Member States. Alternative forms of intervention, such as deficiency payments (which

---

[1] Article 3 of the Rome Treaty requires 'the adoption of a common policy in the sphere of agriculture'. Article 38 defines 'agricultural products', and relates the common agricultural policy to the establishment of the common market in general. Article 40 requires a 'common organization of agricultural markets', excluding 'any discrimination between producers or consumers within the Community', and imposing 'common criteria and uniform methods of calculation' on 'any common price policy'. Articles 42 to 47 concern the evolution and transition towards CAP common market organizations. Article 110 states that, in establishing a customs union, 'Member States aim to contribute, in the common interest, to the harmonious development of world trade, the progressive abolition of restrictions on international trade and the lowering of customs barriers'.

compensate farmers for market prices below pre-determined levels), would have been much more costly to the initially modest Community budget. Neither did the Six then have the administrative infrastructures to make direct payments to farmers a realistic option for policy-makers.

Thus, by the mid-1960s, the Community had established a system of market protection for nearly all farm products, based on fixed Community-wide 'target prices'. At the relatively high levels agreed, the economic burden on consumers was heavy but consumers were then used to expensive food and had vivid memories of its scarcity during and after the Second World War.

The system of market price support was (and is) implemented by three basic instruments:

(i) Import levies, varied as often as daily according to import price levels, force external producers to sell inside the Community above a 'threshold' price. Essentially, these insulate the Community against fluctuations in world market prices which are widely held in Europe to be somewhat artificial and conditioned by the

hegemony of the United States. The other virtue of import levies was that they raise EC revenue to offset the costs of market support.

(ii) Export refunds, similarly variable according to world market conditions, compensate EC exporters for the difference between the internal Community price (usually somewhat below the threshold price) and the lower world price. These subsidies are a charge on the EC budget, though due to the uncertainties of harvests and exchange rates, expenditure is very hard to predict more than a short period ahead.

(iii) Intervention prices become the trigger for the purchase of EC farm products by Community authorities when oversupply pushes Community market prices below predetermined ('intervention') levels. The costs of purchase (net of revenue from stock disposal sales) and storage again fall on the EC budget, giving rise to a difficult policy trade-off between export subsidization and domestic intervention.

These instruments were operated through national customs authorities and intervention agencies, and were financed via the EC budget (see Box 1).

Box 1: Agriculture and the EC budget

Agricultural spending under the common agricultural policy is very largely financed from the Community budget, which itself is financed from the EC's so-called 'own resources', mainly direct contributions from Member States.

Agriculturally derived revenues are provided by levies on imported agricultural products and also from producer ('co-responsibility') levies. CAP revenue of this kind (some of which is treated as 'negative expenditure') grew from below ECU 1 billion per year in the early 1970s to over ECU 4 billion in 1991 and 1992, but with CAP reform (see Box 2) has now fallen by about ECU 1.5 billion.

Expenditure is covered by the European Agricultural Guarantee and Guidance Fund (EAGGF, or FEOGA from the French equivalent). Total annual outlays increased in nominal terms from about ECU 3 billion for the EC-9 in 1974 to ECU 30 billion for the EC-12 in 1990, in real terms an average annual rate of increase of 7.6%. In addition, around ECU 3 billion is spent on guidance (structural) and other agricultural schemes.

The three components of EAGGF Guarantee Section spending have varied in importance through time. In terms of real 1985 ECU, the main developments have been as follows:

(i) Storage costs increased relatively gradually during the 1970s from ECU 1 billion to ECU 2 billion, and then rapidly to over ECU 5.5 billion in 1985, before falling back to ECU 3 billion in 1990;

(ii) Export refunds grew swiftly from 1974 to 1980 when they reached ECU 8 billion. They then dipped somewhat, before a new peak of ECU 9 billion in 1988;

(iii) 'Other' spending — mainly direct price supports such as producer and consumer subsidies — fluctuated around ECU 6 billion from 1974 to 1983. In the following eight years, it doubled to ECU 13 billion, once again dominating the other two categories.

Other taxpayer transfers are made to EC agriculture through national government expenditure inside and outside the CAP. The OECD ('Agricultural policies, markets and trade', *Monitoring and Outlook,* 1993, p. 160) estimated that total public spending on agriculture in EC Member States in 1992 was ECU 51.8 billion.

B. Emerging problems

Stimulated not only by relatively generous support prices but also by technical changes affecting the raising of livestock and crops cultivation, EC farm output leapt ahead — by 30% in the 10 years after 1963. The Community became self-sufficient in most products, except for those such as beef, fresh fruit and vegetables which were in increasing demand because of rising household incomes. However, general consumer food demand by no means kept pace, resulting in rapidly growing Community expenditures on intervention purchases and export subsidies for wheat, dairy products and sugar.

The annual price fixings by Community agriculture ministers became steadily more difficult, under pressure on the one side from the limited room allowed by the Community's budget for generous awards, and on the other from the demands of the farming lobby. By 1972, Agricultural Fund spending accounted for about two thirds of the Community budget, while revenue from agricultural levies covered less than half the Fund expenditures. Moreover, while farm incomes increased in real terms, they did not keep pace with the rest of the economy, with the result that producers were felt unfairly treated.

Moreover, decision-making in the CAP was not conducted along the lines originally planned. Resistance to majority voting on 'very important' issues in 1965-66 left decisions vulnerable to national veto. This complicated the management of the common organization of the agricultural markets at a time when its smooth operation was also being disrupted by currency instability. In 1969, further realignments of the French franc and the German mark led to the invention of artificial 'green' exchange rates for converting CAP support prices into national currencies and stabilizing national farm prices against currency fluctuations. However, at least in the short term, the green rates effected different support prices in certain countries, while monetary compensatory amounts (MCAs) were needed as taxes and subsidies at Member State borders in order to prevent the distortion of trade to which these differentials might have led. Green rates and MCAs were a departure from the principle of market unity, and introduced a new element of national discretion into the operations of the CAP, as well as considerable possibilities for both arbitrage and fraud.

C. Structural policies and a first attempt at reform

The original financial plan for the CAP envisaged the allocation of one third of the budget to the so-called Guidance Section for structural measures. Essentially, these were to aim at creating the larger units widely seen as necessary out of the small-scale pattern of much European farming, and at promoting the efficiency and viability of remaining farms. The process was to be aided through CAP funds for retraining and capital investment. However, apart from a limited 1964 Directive, little was achieved in this area in the first phase of the CAP.

The realization that the CAP was not working as originally hoped led to the first of many reform proposals in its long history. The Mansholt Plan (Commission, 1968) attempted to use prices more flexibly to achieve a better balance between demand and supply. Under the plan, five million hectares of land and five million people would have left EC-6 agricultural production during the 1970s. It also sought to convert dairy herds to beef production, which at that time was much lower than consumption. However, the plan proved too radical to be politically acceptable. It was seen as destructive of too many family farms and too great a departure from the policy of market price support.

Structural objectives were finally embodied in three socio-structural directives derived from the abortive Mansholt Plan, and adopted in 1972. These directives dealt respectively with farm modernization, with cessation of farming and land reallocation, and with the supply of guidance and training in new skills. However, the subsidies for farm modernization, the most successful of the directives, were mainly taken up in the better-structured farming areas in the northern part of the Community, and thus added to the problems of market disequilibrium.

3.3. 1973-83: a missed opportunity for reform

A. The first enlargement

When the Community was enlarged in 1973, there were three reasons for expecting that the CAP could be put on a sounder footing. First, as a large net importer of foodstuffs, it was clear that the United Kingdom would be a net loser in budgetary and in more general economic terms from agricultural market price support. It was therefore reasonable to expect that the UK would exercise its influence to lower price support. Because majority voting in the CAP was still not common practice, and unanimity was generally required for decisions on prices, one country could hope to restrain the others.

Secondly, the 1973 enlargement altered the economic character of agriculture in the Community. While it enlarged the productive area by nearly 50%, the number of farms increased by only 15%, so that the average farm size was raised by some 30%. This might have led to considerations of efficiency being given greater weight in relation to the redistributive objectives in favour of the agricultural sector.

Thirdly, the enlargement made the Community a much more important player in world markets for agricultural products; the Nine accounted for about one third of world trade in farm produce and foodstuffs. The CAP's impact on longstanding patterns of agricultural trade was one of the reasons which had prompted the United Kingdom, as a major agricultural importer, to stay outside the original Community. Its eventual accession in 1973 required some major concessions in order to accommodate the UK's special trade relations with a number of Commonwealth countries, such as New Zealand (butter and sheepmeat), and African, Caribbean and Pacific (ACP) States (sugar).

At first, the expectations that enlargement would bring significant change to the CAP seemed to be justified. Soon after the accession of the three new Member States, the Commission was asked to consider and bring forward proposals for its improvement. The Commission duly presented the 'Stocktaking of the common agricultural policy' report (Commission, 1975) to the Parliament and to the Council. This report remains to this day a bold work of analysis, and its evaluation of the effectiveness of the CAP's various instruments is still generally valid today.[1]

B. Increasing support and CAP spending

However, the proposals for policy changes were not as far-reaching as the rigour of this analysis might have suggested, even if there was a recognition that 'the manner in which this policy is implemented must accord with the need to maintain and — in certain cases — re-establish the structural equilibrium of markets'.[2] The agricultural sectors of the three new Member States — Britain, Ireland and Denmark — were significantly boosted by higher EC support

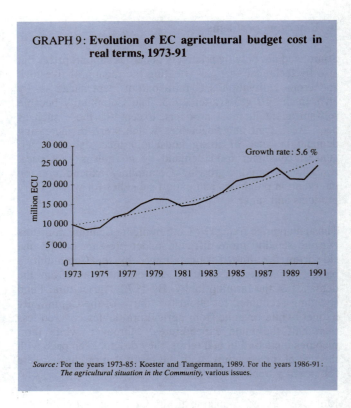

GRAPH 9: **Evolution of EC agricultural budget cost in real terms, 1973-91**

Growth rate: 5.6 %

Source: For the years 1973-85: Koester and Tangermann, 1989. For the years 1986-91: *The agricultural situation in the Community,* various issues.

---

[1] Points 74, 75 and 76 are particularly worth recalling:
   '74. Interventions which tend to dissociate farmers' receipts from the prices paid by consumers falsify economic calculation; they prevent the price system from correctly informing producers of consumer preferences, and consumers of the relative costs of the various products. The use of production or consumption subsidies cannot be considered low-cost solutions in relation to income or living-cost objectives except over short periods for the purpose of correcting the effects of accidental surplus situations (meat) or shortages (sugar) in the internal supply of a given product.
   75. Production quotas limit competition between producers and therefore tend to enable production to be continued in farms or in regions where costs are higher; the corollary is higher prices for consumers and a bonus for better-situated producers.
   76. Income subsidy implies that optimum use is not being made of the labour factor in the farms considered. It can therefore only be justified economically as a provisional solution pending the modernization of the farms or the retraining of farmers for other types of activity.'
[2] See point 92 of the stocktaking paper.

prices,[3] while the UK market became virtually closed to many non-EC suppliers. As a result, the 1973 enlargement was only a very temporary palliative for the CAP's growing surpluses. The policy remained largely unchanged, and EC degrees of self-sufficiency in a broad range of products increased rapidly. Surpluses increased, and the Community had to resort more and more to subsidized exports for their disposal.

As a result, CAP spending doubled in real terms between the mid-1970s and the mid-1980s (see Graph 9). Additional pressures on costs came from rising MCA expenditures prompted by repeated currency instability, and after 1980 from the accession of Greece. Real agricultural incomes fell by 10% between 1978 and 1980, despite a 3% per year decline in the total number of EC farms between 1975 and 1980. Neither did schemes to encourage people to leave the land help much to resolve the underlying problems of an over-large agricultural labour force (expanded by the accession of Greece in 1981), particularly since high unemployment levels rendered such schemes steadily less effective.

---

[3] UK self-sufficiency in temperate farm products rose from 65% in the mid-1960s to 75% at the beginning of the 1980s.

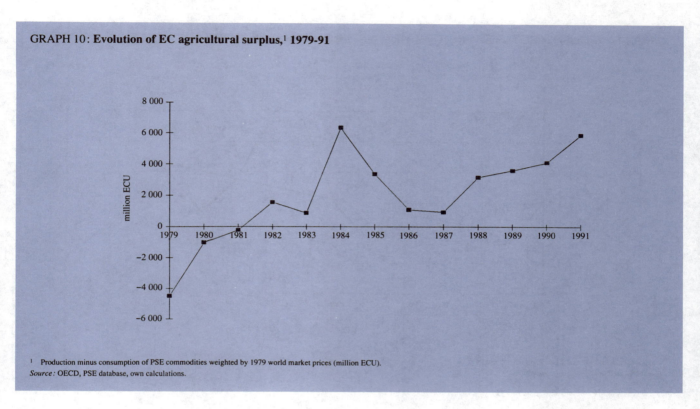

GRAPH 10: **Evolution of EC agricultural surplus,**[1] **1979-91**

[1] Production minus consumption of PSE commodities weighted by 1979 world market prices (million ECU).
Source: OECD, PSE database, own calculations.

Between 1978 and 1980 some of the pressure from surpluses did ease because of relatively poor harvests, and a short-lived general economic recovery. Further help came from a recovery in world markets — partly due to a strong rise in the US dollar — which temporarily lowered the cost of export subsidies. As a result, the need to tackle the CAP's structural problems of commodity surpluses and budget expenditures appeared to be less urgent. However, after 1980, the former problems of the CAP for the Six began to re-emerge for the Ten.

3.4. 1983-91: years of experimentation

A. Crisis unrelieved

The 1980s were years of almost unrelieved crisis for the CAP, with:

(i) rapid growth in budgetary costs incurred through intervention purchases of product surpluses and their subsidized export (Graph 9);

(ii) growing surpluses in all main crop and livestock sectors (Graph 10);

(iii) a variety of uncoordinated attempts to discourage overproduction.

As the EC's budgetary crisis deepened, the Community responded with smaller and smaller rises in nominal support prices, representing significant decreases in real terms. Intervention rules were tightened, weakening the effectiveness of market support. However, with world market prices falling further, this did not prevent the growth of nominal protection over the decade as a whole (Graph 11). Nevertheless, discontent grew among producers increasingly squeezed by stagnant prices and rising costs.

B. A variety of measures

It was clear that the 'rigorous' pricing policy was not curing the growing budgetary and political pressures on the CAP. At different times, but at an accelerating tempo, the Community brought in a variety of measures which sought to curb growing costs and surpluses:

(i) Co-responsibility levies were a form of producer marketing tax, existing from the start of the CAP regime for sugar, then (in 1977) imposed on milk, and later (in 1986) on cereals. They made some contribution to covering the costs of the milk and cereal regimes — about 20% in the case of cereals, and about half for sugar, between 1989 and 1991. A Commission proposal to impose an extra tax on milk from high-output

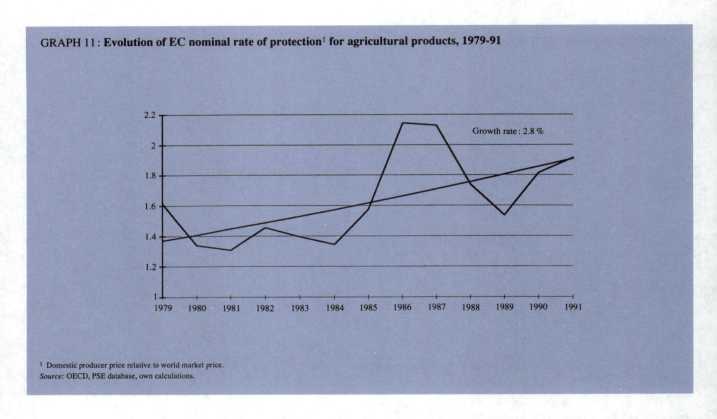

GRAPH 11: **Evolution of EC nominal rate of protection[1] for agricultural products, 1979-91**

Growth rate: 2.8 %

[1] Domestic producer price relative to world market price.
Source: OECD, PSE database, own calculations.

'intensive farms' was not adopted. Co-responsibility levies have led to cuts in production and thus perhaps slightly higher world price levels after a fall in exportable surpluses. However, in practice they have mainly constituted an additional tax on consumers, and an incentive to evasion and avoidance.

(ii) Guarantee thresholds were applied to a range of products including cereals, some oilseeds and certain fruits. Under this system, support prices for the forthcoming marketing year were to be reduced automatically if aggregate production exceeded a pre-set level. Obviously, effectiveness turns on the setting of these levels, and the degree of reduction in support prices for 'excess' output. In practice, the Council of Ministers tended to be generous in setting maximum production levels and there was often controversy over actual production levels.

(iii) Stimulation of domestic consumption was tried for several commodities through consumer subsidies or by marketing campaigns financed by Community funds. However, administrative costs were often high, as was the incidence of fraud. Neither was there much certainty that subsidized demand did not replace normal consumption of the same or other products.

(iv) Marketing quotas had been a feature of the sugar regime since its inception in the 1960s, and together with co-responsibility levies limited the net budgetary cost of that regime. Extension of the system to other commodities was long resisted because of its inherent complexities and inefficiencies. However, the rapidly worsening situation in the dairy sector in the early 1980s led to the application, virtually overnight in April 1984, of quotas for individual milk farms or cooperatives. In subsequent years, this system has been the subject of a number of adjustments, arising partly from the original, rather generous, level of quota awards, and partly from legal settlements relating to special groups of producers.

(v) Diversification of production was occasionally encouraged as a means of relieving pressures in mainstream commodity markets. Several schemes encouraged the switching of cattle enterprises from milk to beef production, but with limited success. Following the 1973 US embargo on soyabean exports, oilseeds were given strong EC support as a substitute crop for cereals because the Community was a substantial importer of this source of protein for animal feed. But the regime, based on subsidies for processors and producers, became increasingly expensive and a source of major political

GRAPH 12: **Evolution of EC domestic producer prices and world market prices for agricultural products in real terms, 1979-91**[1]

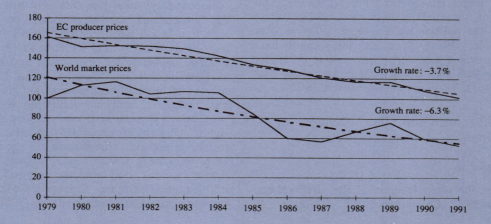

[1] Both series weighted by value of EC production at domestic producer prices, and deflated by ECU deflator. World market price index in 1979 = 100. EC producer price index in 1979 = 100 (EC domestic producer prices/world market prices).

Source: OECD, PSE database, own calculations.

tension with the US.[1] Since the 1980s, increasing interest has been shown in bio-mass and bio-energy from traditional and novel crops, and a number of experimental programmes of set-aside and rural development were initiated in certain Member States.

C. Continued problems

Despite their number and variety, these measures did not solve the fundamental problems of the CAP. Farm incomes remained static, and budgetary concerns persisted despite some relief after the US drought in 1988, and the institution of an expenditure ceiling from that year onwards. The invention of the 'green ecu' in 1984 was an attempt to avoid some of the difficulties of monetary compensatory amounts, but probably blurred the transparency of the policy. Weak world markets resulted in a growing differential in the movement between EC and world market prices during the decade (Graph 12).

Surpluses, which had been reduced during the later 1970s, reached chronic levels in some sectors, with cereals joining dairy as a major problem sector. By 1988-89, net cereal exports had grown to 27.5 million tonnes whereas in the early 1970s the EC had been a net importer of 10 million tonnes. Also in the later 1980s, a CAP 'beef mountain' emerged as a new object of public ridicule. Further, the 1986 accession of Spain and Portugal threatened new burdens of support for Mediterranean products. At the end of 1990, there were 14.4 million tonnes of cereals, 600 000 tonnes of dairy products and 530 000 tonnes of beef in public stores.

While food self-sufficiency had been largely attained and markets had been stabilized, a further 30% rise in CAP spending from 1989 to 1991 did not prevent a fall in farm incomes, driving a significant number of farmers towards exit. The CAP's image was further sullied by increasing complaints of fraud and inefficiency.

By the end of the decade, external pressures for CAP reform were becoming intense. The Community was faced with tough and determined demands for changes in the Uruguay Round negotiations in the GATT (see Section 3.5.C) below). These broke down in December 1990, at least in part because

[1] In 1962, the Community agreed to GATT bindings of zero or very low tariffs on oilseeds and other non-cereal animal feed products such as manioc. Thus the normal market price support regime could not be adopted for oilseeds, and deficiency payments ('variable premiums') were paid to crushers in order to guarantee producer prices well above world market levels. Guarantee thresholds (levels of aggregate production at which co-responsibility mechanisms are triggered) were introduced for certain oilseeds in the early 1980s.

of the Community's refusal to go far enough to satisfy other agricultural exporting countries, notably the US and the Cairns Group.

Under pressure from the deteriorating budgetary legacy of the 1980s, the Commission produced in February 1991 a set of *Reflections* on the CAP (Commission, 1991a) which recognized that the policy's existing approaches were no longer sustainable. This analysis and the Commission's subsequent proposals of July 1991 (Commission, 1991b) led eventually to the May 1992 Council agreement on the 'Mac Sharry' package of CAP reforms (Commission, 1992a).

3.5. The 1992 reform and other recent developments

A. The 1992 reforms

Box 2 specifies the main features of the CAP reforms agreed in May 1992 (Commission, 1992). Most of the changes involve a three-year transition over the marketing years 1993/94, 1994/95 and 1995/96. Following the lines of the 1991 recommendations (Commission, 1991), these centre on a substantial reduction in the support prices for cereals, alongside a system of regionally calculated 'compensatory' area payments tied to a set-aside scheme for 'professional' producers. Lower cereal prices permit reduction in aid payments for oilseeds and protein crops, and lower support prices for milk and beef, with regional headage payments for male cattle and beef cows. Other changes involve simplification of the tobacco regime, a halving of 'normal' beef intervention purchasing, standard and 'extensive' stocking limits on eligibility for beef premiums, a two-tier system of transferable sheep premium rights, and a set of 'accompanying measures' for environmental protection, afforestation of agricultural land and early retirement. Commission proposals have or will be drawn up for non-rotational set-aside, dried fodder, milk, sugar, fruit and vegetables, wine, agri-monetary arrangements and the administration of the new systems.

Box 2: The 1992 CAP reforms

The main features of the measures agreed on May 22 1992 were:

Arable sector:

(i) a reduction of about one third in the cereal intervention price, which is to fall by 1995-96 to 100 green ECU per tonne, in three steps. An important degree of protection remains through the threshold price of 155 green ECU per tonne;

(ii) elimination of price support for oilseeds and protein crops;

(iii) compensation through direct area payments based on historical base areas and regional yields, subject to 15% rotational set-aside[1] for such crops grown by all except small farmers (under 92 tonnes of cereal equivalent).

Livestock sector:

(i) a 15% reduction in intervention prices for beef from July 1993, in three steps;

(ii) compensation through direct headage payments (premiums) subject to a maximum stocking rate (two livestock units (LU) per fodder hectare by 1996);

(iii) increased male bovine and suckler (beef) cow premiums subject to individual limits per holding and to regional reference herd sizes which, if exceeded, reduce the number of eligible animals per producer. There are extra 'extensification' headage premiums if a producer reduces the stocking rate below 1.4 LU per fodder hectare;

(iv) a reduction in the ceiling for normal beef intervention buying from 750 000 to 350 000 tonnes by 1997.

Accompanying measures:

(i) implementation through Member State programmes with 50% of the cost (75% in Objective 1 regions) borne by the CAP budget;

(ii) an agri-environmental package aimed at more extensive means of production and the use of land for natural resource protection and public leisure;

(iii) aid for forestry investment and management with up to 20 years' compensation for income loss;

(iv) various forms of compensation for early retirement, including lump sum or annual payments, for farmers and farm workers over 55.

---

[1] In 1993, non-rotational set-aside, at 18 or 21%, was introduced on an optional basis.

In some respects, the reforms fall short of the Commission's proposals. The Commission had proposed a cut in the cereal target price to ECU 110 per tonne, with the intervention price 10% below this and the threshold price 10% above. In the event, the Council set a new target price of ECU 110 per tonne, with intervention at ECU 100 per tonne and the threshold at ECU 155 per tonne, thus preserving a strong measure of Community protection against imports. The existing stabilizer arrangements for cereals, including the coresponsibility levies and maximum guarantee quantities, were withdrawn at once rather than at the end of the transitional period. There were no immediate cuts in the milk quotas, and support price cuts for milk products were small.

From an economic point of view, the significance of the price reductions depends largely on the remaining gap, if any, between markets inside and outside the Community. Although the Commission aimed at eliminating this gap by the end of the transitional period (allowing for some recovery in world market prices), it seems unlikely that this will be fully achieved, and continued budget expenditure and efficiency losses will therefore occur. However, lower cereal prices will encourage greater use of cereals in animal feed, thus reducing the need for quantitative restrictions and subsidized disposal. Similar points can be made about the smaller changes in the beef regime.

Introduction of the reforms has so far proceeded more or less to plan, with the notable exception of the 1992-93 crisis in the European Monetary System. This has resulted in substantially higher support prices in the United Kingdom since that country left the arrangement in September 1992, and imposed strains on the 'switch-over' mechanism after the widening of the exchange-rate bands in summer 1993. The application of strict controls at regional and farm levels (reference herd and flock sizes, set-aside percentages, etc.) have necessitated the introduction of large and complex national systems of administrative control, particularly in the initial year 1992/93. Continuing efforts in updating and modifying these systems are to be expected.

Modelling results

In order to assess the potential impact of agricultural policy reforms in the European Community, the Expert Group commissioned a number of special analyses. Existing models of the CAP were exploited in order to simulate developments over the next decade with and without changes in policy parameters. These models contain considerable commodity and in some cases country detail of EC agriculture. However,

no economic model can incorporate all relevant variables — in particular, the administrative costs of the CAP are not addressed by current models, nor much of the detail of the regional and farm-level mechanisms.

As with all such exercises, it is important to determine a common and acceptable set of basic assumptions about external conditions such as inflation and world market trends. Taking into account that the benefits of the 'green revolution' have been largely realized, and that consumption in developing countries is picking up after the debt crisis of the 1980s, the model runs assume that world market prices will continue to decrease in real terms, but at a much less rapid rate than in the 1980s, i.e. by less than 1% per year instead of about 6% per year. Under the base scenario (see below), real domestic EC farm prices are also assumed to continue to decrease less rapidly than in the recent past, but only by about 1% point more slowly. Thus the 'wedge' between EC and world market prices for agricultural commodities is therefore expected to decrease rather rapidly over the 1990s even without CAP reform; this has significant implications for the comparisons with the alternative scenarios.

The main policy scenarios simulated were (a) continuation of pre-1992 CAP developments, including continued decline in real price support (the base scenario); (b) the 1992 reforms themselves; and (c) the reforms with full 'decoupling' of the compensation payments from current production levels. The May 1992 reform package was the first truly important recognition by EC governments that the price support system could no longer square the circle of maintaining farmers' incomes and at the same time bringing markets into better balance. Without the reform, one model simulation presented in Chapter D demonstrates that cereal production would have made further leaps from 164 million tonnes in 1992 to nearly 200 million tonnes in 2001 while farm incomes would have declined by 0.9% a year in real terms.[1] The increase in cereal production would lead to a near doubling of net exports, from 35 million tonnes in 1992 to 66 million tonnes in 2001.

The model results suggest that the 1992 reform is not only beneficial for the economy as a whole, but also for the agricultural sector. The decline in farm incomes is reduced from 0.9% to 0.5% a year in real terms. The real income of the economy as a whole is more than ECU 5 billion higher by the year 2001. A decline in cereal production would more

---

[1] In Chapter D, the continuation of pre-reform policies is represented principally by an extrapolation, over the period 1993-2001, of changes in producer prices observed during the 1980s. In real terms, these changes are all negative, with the largest decreases for cereals (-3 %), oilseeds (-2.5 %) and beef (-2 %). World market prices are assumed to decline with a long-term trend of between 0.5 % to 1.5 % in real terms.

than halve net exports of this key commodity group to 15 million tonnes in 2001, instead of nearly doubling it under the no-change scenario. In addition, cereals would considerably increase their share in feed use, thereby achieving the objective of so-called 'rebalancing' which has long been an important point on the EC agenda for international trade negotiations.

Thus the 1992 reform will yield tangible economic improvements. Even so, the reform does not remove the need to face up to further economic and political challenges in the re-organization of the Community's agriculture. Not only has structural change been retarded in some sectors, leaving a legacy of 'catching-up' to be accomplished, but the post-1992 CAP regime will not remove the need to address future pressures for structural adjustment. Furthermore, the post-1992 CAP may turn out to be administratively very costly.

B. The Uruguay Round agreement

Consideration of the CAP in the second half of the 1980s and in the early 1990s was frequently influenced by the development of the multilateral Uruguay Round trade negotiations under the General Agreement on Tariffs and Trade (GATT). Pressure to open these talks started soon after the completion of the 1973-79 Tokyo Round, which left agricultural policy largely unaffected. In 1982, the OECD Ministerial Mandate called for 'an analysis of the approaches and methods for a balanced and gradual reduction of protection for agriculture, and the fuller integration of agriculture within the open multilateral trading system, while taking into account the specific characteristics and role of agriculture'. In 1985, the US Food Security Act (Farm Bill) included provisions for retaliation against other countries accused of unfair trading.

In July 1986, the Uruguay Round was launched, with the opening declaration that 'Contracting parties agree that there is an urgent need to bring more discipline and predictability to world agricultural trade ... Negotiations shall aim to achieve greater liberalization of trade in agriculture and bring all measures affecting import access and export competition under strengthened and more operationally effective GATT rules ... by: i) improving market access, ii) increased discipline on the use of all direct and indirect subsidies affecting directly and indirectly agricultural trade, and iii) minimizing ... phytosanitary ... barriers'.

More than 100 countries took part in the negotiations, which included trade in services, intellectual property rights and several other issues as well as agriculture, but attention naturally focused on the positions of the United States, the European Community (for which the Commission acted as negotiator), the Cairns Group of 14 farm product exporting countries, and Japan. Throughout the negotiations, the Community was determined to preserve the essential nature of the CAP, as well as seeking 'rebalancing' of protection between cereals and oilseeds. However, until the CAP reforms of 1992, compromise appeared impossible.

The agricultural issues addressed and eventually resolved during the Round included the following, as they affected the three main areas of market access, domestic support and export subsidies:

(i)   'credit' for policy measures taken prior to the final agreement;

(ii) the classification of policies into 'red', 'amber' and 'green', corresponding respectively to those to be fully dismantled, those subject to monitored reduction, and those permitted to continue as not significantly distorting trade;

(iii) 'tarification', i.e. the conversion of all import barriers not explicitly provided for under the GATT, such as variable import levies and minimum import prices, into simple tariffs, eventually to be 'bound' at lower rates;

(iv) specified percentage reductions required in the three main areas.

After seven years of intensive and often very difficult negotiations, especially between the Community and the United States, final agreement was reached in Geneva on 15 December 1993. The outcome (which at time of writing is still subject to ratification by legislatures around the world) can be seen as a partial success in terms of the original governmental goals described above. At the least, the dangers of sliding into mutually damaging trade disputes, and export-subsidy competitions in third-country markets, have been lessened. A fixed timetable for the measured reduction of protectionist policies over six years has been established, under the scrutiny of a new World Trade Organization to replace the GATT itself. Some detail of the EC's commitments in December 1993 are shown in Box 3.

Box 3: The EC Uruguay Round agreement on agriculture

The final December 1993 agreement of the Uruguay Round in Brussels[1] included the following provisions for EC agriculture, to take effect from the first half of 1995:

Market access

(i) Border protection measures other than ordinary customs duties are to be converted into tariff equivalents (TEs) for all agricultural products. Customs duties and TEs are to be reduced on a simple average basis by 36% over six years with a minimum reduction of 15% for each. A safeguard provision consisting of a variable element added to the basic tariff may be triggered if import prices fall below or import volumes exceed a base-year level.

(ii) Minimum access opportunities are to be established representing at least 3% of domestic consumption at the start and 5% by the end of the implementation period. Current access opportunities on terms at least equivalent to those existing are to be retained.

Domestic support

(i) A total aggregate measure of support (AMS) for agriculture is to be calculated as the sum of such measures for all agricultural commodities. Total AMS is to be reduced in equal instalments, and bound at a level 20% below the base-period level by the end of the implementation period.

(ii) Direct payments under production-limiting programmes such as those in the May 1992 CAP reforms are *not* to be subject to the AMS reduction commitment if based on fixed

---

[1] Except for some 'front-loading' of subsidized exports to enable existing EC stocks to be reduced, the final agreement largely replicated the Blair House 'pre-accord' between the EC Commission and US Government in November/December 1992. In turn, the pre-accord represented marginal changes in the framework and provisions of the Draft Final Act prepared by the GATT Secretary-General Artur Dunkel in 1991.

area and yield or fixed number of head, or made on 85% of base-level production.

Export subsidies

(i) On a 1986-90 base, direct export-subsidy spending must be reduced, product by product, by 36%, and subsidized export volumes by 21%, over six years.

The EC and US also came to bilateral agreement on the following outstanding issues:

Rebalancing

If EC imports of non-grain feed ingredients rise above the 1990-92 average imports of these products, the US and EC are to seek a mutually acceptable solution.

Peace clause

Internal support measures and export subsidies that conform fully to reduction commitments are to be exempt until 2003 from GATT actions such as countervailing duties and actions based on non-violation nullification or impairment.

Oilseeds

The EC is to introduce a separate base area for producers benefiting from the specific oilseeds payments system. This base area is to be reduced by at least 10%. Non-food production is to be allowed on set-aside land up to a volume of by-products not exceeding 1 million tonnes of soya meal equivalent.

Other products

The EC is to open a tariff-rate quota of 500 000 tonnes of corn imports to Portugal, and establish a zero-duty tariff quota of 120 000 tonnes of malt sprout pellets. A solution has been agreed for screenings, steep water, microscopic analysis and certification, to enable normal customs clearance procedures.

C. The Europe Agreements

Until the dramatic political events of 1989, eastern enlargement of the Community, to include countries of Central Europe, was difficult to conceive. Up to that time, the significance of the Comecon bloc to the development of the CAP was confined mainly to strictly controlled quantities of EC imports — most importantly of live animals and meat — from Poland, Czechoslovakia, Hungary, Romania, Bulgaria, Yugoslavia, Albania and the USSR, and to occasional subsidized exports of product surpluses — most often of cereals and ex-store butter to the Soviet Union.

In 1989-90, food aid was granted to Poland and import quotas were introduced or increased within the Community's PHARE programme. Negotiations also began on Association Agreements with Poland, Czechoslovakia and Hungary. However, the main event of 1990 was the integration on 3 October of the territory of the former German Democratic Republic into a unified Germany and the Community itself. To the 127 million hectares of utilized agricultural area in the EC-12, this added a further 6 million hectares, three quarters arable, and nearly all within some 4 750 highly specialized State and cooperative holdings. Given the diversified nature of the large workforce on these units, the inadequacies of the food processing sector and the problems of land and firm privatization, the incorporation of this region into the CAP posed severe problems, necessitating special regulations which still persist.

The Europe Agreements eventually agreed with Poland, Hungary, the Czech Republic, Slovakia, Romania and Bulgaria cover five years, from 1992 to 1996, and provide for the consolidation of concessions already made under the EC's Generalized system of preferences, as well as new concessions for several other agricultural products.[1] Most of the new concessions involve a 3-year staged reduction of import levies or duties, with 10% increases each year in the maximum quantities for commodities which are subject to levy. The quantities involved are based on actual amounts traded in the reference years 1988-90.[2] They mainly reflect the more traditional and specialized products of the supplier countries, and are small or zero in the case of products in severe structural surplus in the Community. Minimum import prices must be observed for soft fruit for processing, where EC producers are particularly sensitive. A 'safeguard clause' in each agreement provides for consultation in cases of market difficulties, and the Community retains the right to impose health and safety checks at its borders.

It is too early for a firm judgment to be reached on the success of these agreements, and indeed on the success as a whole of the extensive internal and external efforts to transform the agricultural sectors of the Central and East European countries from a situation of State domination to one of private ownership and market orientation. Such a judgment depends, amongst other things, on the extent to which expectations — amongst economic observers and amongst the citizens of the countries concerned — are confirmed or otherwise. Some of these expectations have certainly been frustrated in the initial stages of the agreement period, partly because of the selectivity of the concessions granted, and partly because many of the preferential tariff quotas have not been fulfilled. Reasons include preventative health measures introduced at very short notice by the Community in 1993, and a lack of information, flexibility or profitability in the exporter countries' agricultural sectors. The nature of the Europe Agreements means that much depends on the ability of Central European suppliers to compete on quality and other non-price grounds with EC produce.

---

[1] Meanwhile the 'Visegrád' Central European Free Trade Agreement between Czechoslovakia, Hungary and Poland was signed in December 1992 and came into force on 1 March 1993; however, this agreement has a very limited agricultural role.

[2] For Romania, 1988-89 and for Bulgaria, 1989-91.

D. Completion of the internal market

A previous section in this chapter mentioned that 'green' rates and monetary compensatory amounts (MCAs) were introduced in 1969 in order to avoid the unacceptable repercussions of immediately basing effective CAP support prices on re-aligned Member State currencies. This 'agrimonetary' system necessitated internal border checks for the required tax and subsidy payments, and constituted a breach with the fundamental Community principle of common markets. It also led to ever-increasing policy complexities, as efforts to phase out undervalued and overvalued green rates (corresponding to positive and negative MCAs respectively) were thwarted both by the reluctance of the higher-priced countries to lower support to their farmers, and by the occurrence of further exchange-rate changes and hence a catching-up process.

From 1984, when efforts to phase out positive MCAs for strong currency countries proved fruitless, currency re-alignments within the EMS involved the use of the 'green ecu', or a 'correcting factor' coefficient which revalued the standard ecu so as to compensate partly for the price-reducing effects on such countries. This new 'switch-over' system avoided new positive MCAs, while new or increased negative MCAs could be gradually removed without such great unpopularity, or the need for substantial compensatory direct payments. At the same time, adjustments were also made in the 'franchise', or margins within which MCAs or changes in these were regarded as unnecessary. Over the years, the effect of the 'switch-over' system has been to raise gradually the effective 'common' support price, and the average of all support prices in national currencies, by an amount now exceeding 20% of the level indicated by the 'real' or central-rate ecu.

In 1988, following ratification of the Single European Act, the goal of a single European market was adopted by the Commission as the '1992' initiative.

For agricultural products, border checks for the payment not only of MCAs, but also for value-added tax (VAT) and excise duties, as well as veterinary and food-safety controls have now been removed. A full set of common standards for such matters has been established, and alternative control systems set up to deal with cases of crop or livestock disease and food problems. The implementation of these health and safety systems continues to throw up difficulties from time to time, but the Community can be said now to have completed the internal market in these respects.

As far as the agri-monetary system is concerned, the absence of border administration has abolished MCAs, and central rates of the European Monetary System are now used for converting ecu-determined support prices and direct payments into national currencies. However, the green ecu and switch-over systems are retained, with little reduction in complexity. In cases of currency re-alignment, immediate or speedy adjustment of the conversion rates is to be enforced, with the possibility of temporary compensatory aids.

Thus, at time of writing (spring 1994), agriculture has largely taken part in the completion of the EC's internal market, with the major and important exception that support prices and direct aids are still determined in national currencies in terms of a 'green ecu' system which builds in or permits compensation to neutralize the negative farm-income effects of currency adjustments. The importance of this can be seen in the fact that some ECU 1.7 billion was added to the Guarantee Section of the EAGGF by the monetary re-alignments that occurred between September 1992 and February 1993. A further extension of the single market for agricultural products will take place with the accession of the EFTA countries, scheduled for 1995.[1] While the Commission is to bring forward proposals for further agrimonetary reform, the counter-attractions of price stability and upward creep in agricultural support levels remain to be overcome.

3.6. The structure of EC agriculture

A. The size of the sector

With final production worth just over ECU 200 billion, the share of agriculture in Community GDP is just under 3%, and the sector has a similar proportion of total gross fixed capital formation. However, agriculture accounts for over 6% of the employed civilian working population. Moreover, food, beverages and tobacco account for about 20% of average EC household consumer expenditure. Thus, although the sector now plays a relatively small direct role in the income-generating activities of the Community, it still occupies a significant share of employment in rural areas, while food and related products form a substantial proportion of international (and intra-EC) trade and of EC consumers' living costs.

Agriculture's low share of Community GDP may be explained in terms of value-added; consumption of intermediate inputs such as fertilizers, manufactured animal feed, etc. accounts for nearly half total output. Depreciation

(consumption of capital) and adjustment for direct taxes and subsidies further reduces net value-added at factor cost to about ECU 100 billion. However, other measures of agriculture's significance in the overall economy are implied by its utilization of 56% of the Community's total area, and by the fact that total expenditure on agriculture occupies about 60% of the total EC budget, as well as much smaller but still significant proportions of national government expenditures. Also, EC farming itself is intimately connected to the important agribusiness sectors of farm input supply, and the processing and distribution of farm products. In some areas, the extent or nature of farming operations are important for other land users, e.g. local residents, or tourists in mountain areas. Especially in certain localities, therefore, the size and prosperity of the farming sector can play a crucial role in the general economy.

B. International trade

With production continually outstripping consumption in many products, EC agricultural exports have steadily increased. By 1990/91, the Community had become self-sufficient in all its main food commodities except oils and fats and fresh fruit. Production of cereals and sugar was more than 20% above domestic consumption, followed by butter at 15% higher. These three products alone accounted for more than USD 9 billion of exports.

However, farm products are not a very significant proportion of EC exports (8.5%), less than the corresponding figure (12%) for the world as a whole. Agriculture does have a somewhat larger profile in the Community's total import bill (11.5%) because of purchases of rubber, timber and natural textile fibres, coffee, tea, cocoa and fish. Together, these make the Community the world's largest importer of agricultural products, with net imports worth more than USD 26 billion in 1990-91.

While agriculture may contribute only a modest share of EC exports, the Community remains the second largest agricultural exporter after the US, with trade based on cereals, particularly wheat, wine, sugar, milk powder, butter, cheese and meat. The Community's exports of beef are now greater than those of Argentina and Australia, while its sugar sales almost match those of Cuba.

C. Farm size and labour

Community agriculture is particularly varied in terms of farm structure. While the average area of an agricultural holding in the EC is 13 hectares, the United Kingdom figure is nearly five times as great at 64 hectares, while Greece, Italy and

---

[1]　The European Parliament has approved the Accession Agreements for Austria, Finland, Sweden and Norway. Referendums are to be held in all these countries in late 1994, with accession (and consequential adjustments to the Uruguay Round agreements) taking place in the first half of 1995.

Portugal have averages around 5 hectares. In the southern Member States, around 80% of all holdings are less than 10 hectares in size (and thus many will not provide a farming livelihood), while in France, Denmark and Luxembourg, at least 17% of agricultural holdings are over 50 hectares in extent; in the United Kingdom this rises to 33%.

Agricultural labour in the EC amounts to over 8 million persons mainly employed in the sector, and is equally varied between countries. For example, agriculture's share of employment is 22% in Greece and 18% in Portugal. On the other hand, the equivalent shares in Belgium, Germany, Luxembourg and the United Kingdom are around 3% or less. Overall, nearly 40% of those employed in agriculture have another main gainful activity; about 2.2 million farmers are classified as full-time. Also, the age of many farmers means that many are receiving pension and investment income.

D. Agricultural production

Overall, final EC agricultural output is almost equally divided between crop and livestock production. However, except for France and Portugal, EC Member States can be divided into two rather distinct categories in this respect. In the northern countries, especially Ireland and Luxembourg, livestock farming predominates, with around 60% of total (final) output on average, while crop products account for the remaining 40%. By contrast, in the southern countries, the proportions are reversed, crops accounting for at least 60% of total production, and livestock the rest. However, land-use patterns are not closely correlated: for example, Denmark has under 10% of its agricultural area in permanent pasture, while the United Kingdom share is nearly 65%.

Five product groups — cereals, fresh vegetables, milk, beef and veal, and pigmeat — each account for over 10% of total EC agricultural output. However, about a third of grown cereals and nearly all grass (roughage) is fed directly to animals, and therefore does not appear as output. Other important EC agricultural products are wine and must, and poultrymeat (each about 5%).

In terms of output level, France and Italy are the leading Member State producers, with about 20% of the EC total each, followed by Germany, Spain and the United Kingdom. In relation to domestic consumption, agricultural production is particularly important in Denmark, Ireland and the Netherlands. As a share of GDP, agriculture is particularly important in Greece (14%) and Ireland (10%); for all other Member States, the sector does not account for more than about 5% of GDP.

E. The CAP budget and transfers

In recent years, CAP expenditure has accounted for about 60% of the total EC budget, or around 0.6% of EC GNP. Box 1 above outlines the main features of the CAP budget, including its financing. In nominal terms, the CAP budget has, grown from ECU 3 billion in 1974 to over ECU 30 billion in 1990. Guarantee Section expenditure on market support and direct payments has now risen to ECU 35 billion (budget 1994), due to increased spending on cereals and several other commodity groups. The full implementation of the 1992 CAP reforms will bring additional demands to finance the direct compensatory payments included in those reforms. There is therefore strong upward growth in the CAP budget, and a danger of encountering the 'guideline' ceiling which has been imposed since 1989 on most Guarantee expenditure and is linked to a fraction of GNP growth.

As outlined in Box 1, CAP expenditure can be classified into 'market support' — essentially storage costs and export refund subsidies totalling some 15 billion in the early 1990s — and 'other' Guarantee expenditure on direct producer and consumer subsidies, accounting for most of the rest. This second category has always been relatively important, if not so easy to classify and analyse, and is scheduled to grow further as a consequence of the current reforms. Market support expenditure depends on a mixture of climatic, commodity-market and exchange-rate factors, and is inherently less easy to predict.

As between commodity sectors, crops account for about two thirds of total Guarantee spending, and livestock about one third. This corresponds to an approximately equal division of final agricultural production in the Community as a whole. The difference is largely accounted for by the heavy budgetary support afforded to arable crops such as cereals, sugar and oilseeds, and to tobacco, while pigmeat and poultrymeat attract relatively low Guarantee spending. As yet, additional and accompanying measures, such as non-annual set-aside payments and special environmental and rural development schemes, account for relatively limited amounts (about ECU 1 billion in 1994).

Budget costs arising from the CAP can be divided between transfer expenditures provided to farmers as income support or to consumers and processors as partial or selective compensation for the high EC domestic prices. Non-transfer expenditures represent the purchase of goods and services by the EC authorities for their own purposes, mainly the storage of agricultural products for the purpose of stabilizing (rather than supporting) domestic market prices, and for rural development and environmental purposes. Analysis along these lines (see Chapter B) shows that about half the net budget costs of the CAP in recent years has been production-related transfers to producers, while about a sixth is directed to consumers and the remaining third to stabilization and other 'public good' activities.

It needs to be emphasized that these budgetary costs and transfers to not correspond to real income effects, since they do not take into account the costs imposed on the EC economy through the CAP's distortion of production resource use and of consumer choice. Also, the inefficiency losses of tax-raising and administration are not included. Nor, of course, are costs imposed on third countries or non-marketed goods and services such as the environment taken into account. Nevertheless, they are important as an obvious determinant and outcome of agricultural policy-making in the EC, particularly since the CAP accounts for such a large proportion of the Community's budget.

A wider concept of policy transfers has been employed by the OECD, which has extended its well-known PSE calculations to take account of all commodities (PSEs covers only 74% of EC agricultural production in 1992), of public storage costs, and of certain schemes (such as the milk production cessation premium) which the PSE method ignored. Table 6 shows these 'total transfers', defined as 'the sum of all transfers from taxpayers, plus all transfers from consumers, less estimated budget receipts from tariffs on agricultural imports', and expresses them in various ways. The burden of support falling on consumers rather than taxpayers is well shown, as is the large transfer per full-time farmer. However, the EC ranks about the middle of all OECD countries for most such calculations (for further detail, see Chapter B).

The OECD transfer calculations may be interpreted as providing an upper limit estimate of the yearly direct payments which would compensate farmers for the removal of the CAP. However, the longer the time horizon for such an operation, the easier it would be for the capital and labour employed in EC agriculture to find a new employment equilibrium, and thus the need for such compensation would lessen accordingly.

Table 2

Agricultural shares of value-added and employment, and labour productivity growth, EC 1991

	GVA/GDP%	Emloyment (FTEs)
Belgium	2.9	2.7
Denmark	3.7	5.5
Germany	1.5	3.3
Greece	13.9	21.6
Spain	4.6	10.7
France	3.3	5.8
Ireland	9.5	13.8
Italy	3.6	8.5
Luxembourg	2.2	3.1
Netherlands	4.0	4.5
Portugal	5.3	17.5
United Kingdom	1.4	2.2
EC-12	2.9	6.2

Source: The agricultural situation in the Community, 1993.

Table 3

EC agricultural trade and self-sufficiency, 1990-91

	Self-sufficiency %	Net exports (+) imports (−) 1 000 t	1990 USD Mio
Cereals	120	24 981	4 519
Sugar	128	3 615	1 074
Butter	115	3 362	(3 575)[2]
Wine	103	5 500 hl	(7 055)[3]
Fresh fruit	85	−4 417	−9 054
Fresh vegetables	106	1 861	
Meat	120	1 218.4	236
Eggs	103	81.3	2
Oils and fats	70[1]	not available	—
All agricultural and food products	—	—	−26 366[4]

[1] Rapeseed and sunflower seed only.
[2] Milk and eggs together, figure for butter not available.
[3] All alcoholic beverages.
[4] In addition to the deficits shown for fruit, vegetables, and oils and fats, the major contributions to this overall net import figure come from fish (USD −6 611 Mio), coffee, cocoa, tea and spices (−4 174), animal feed (−4 211), oilseeds (−4 198), rubber, timber and natural textile fibres (−14 277).

Source: The agricultural situation in the Community, 1993.

Table 4

Agricultural production, 1991

(a)   Crop and livestock shares, by Member States

	Crops (%)	Livestock (%)
Belgium	38	62
Denmark	34	66
Germany	37	63
Greece	68	32
Spain	61	39
France	55	45
Ireland	14	86
Italy	63	37
Luxembourg	15	85
Netherlands	44	56
Portugal	51	49
United Kingdom	41	59
EC	52	48
— (million ECU)	(105.9)	(98.5)

(b)   Shares of individual products in final production

	Crop (%)		Livestock (%)
Wheat	6.9	Milk	15.8
Barley	2.3	Beef/veal	11.2
Maize	2.2	Pigmeat	10.4
Sugarbeet	2.2		
Olive oil	2.4		
Fresh fruit	4.7		
Fresh vegetables	10.1		
Wine and must	5.2		

Source: The agricultural situation in the Community, 1993.

Table 5

EC farm structure, 1987

	Utilized agricultural area per holding	% of holdings with less than 10 ha	% of holdings with more than 50 ha
Belgium	14.8	45.8	5.8
Denmark	32.2	18.0	17.2
Germany	16.8	47.0	6.1
Greece	4.0	89.4	0.5
Spain	13.8	72.3	6.0
France	28.6	29.9	18.1
Ireland	22.7	31.3	9.0
Italy	5.6	84.8	1.9
Luxembourg	30.2	28.8	26.2
Netherlands	15.3	43.3	4.4
Portugal	5.2	87.5	1.9
United Kingdom	64.4	25.9	33.3
EC-12	13.3	66.0	6.8

Source: The agricultural situation in the Community, 1993.

Table 6

Total agricultural policy transfers, EC, 1990-92 (billion ECU)[1]

	1990	1991	1992	OECD average 1992
From taxpayers	39.3	47.5	51.8	
From consumers	66.1	71.4	69.3	
Budget revenues	0.7	0.5	0.6	
Total transfers	104.8	118.4	120.5	
share in total GDP (%)	1.9	2.0	2.0	2.1
per head of population (ecu/hd)	300	340	350	340
per full-time farmer equivalent (ecu/FFE)	11 900	13 400	13 700	16 900
per hectare of farmland (ecu/ha)	750	850	870	240

[1] Includes ex-GDR.

Source: OECD secretariat estimates, 'Agriculture policies, markets and trade', *Monitoring and Outlook*, 1993.

Chapter 4

Lessons and future challenges

4.1. Introduction

Following the previous chapter's description of the past and present situation of EC agriculture, this chapter assesses the future economic prospects for EC agricultural policy, as these appear shortly after the beginning of the implementation of the May 1992 CAP reforms and the major shift from market price support to direct income support. Following a number of general 'lessons' which may be drawn from experience to date, the structure of analysis follows the list of policy objectives identified in Chapter 1 of this report. The aim is to identify a set of challenges which any future policy changes, such as those outlined in the following chapter, will have to address.

4.2. Lessons

The development of the CAP up to the 1992 reforms suggest a number of lessons to be learnt:

1. Market support measures such as those of the traditional CAP tend to become less and less transfer-efficient as the price elasticity of agricultural production in the process of economic development implying the increased use of purchased input become more elastic. Benefits to producers are eroded by higher land and other input prices, while consumers pay high food costs and rising surpluses lead to ever-higher taxpayer costs. Indeed, the circle becomes a vicious one, with taxpayer-financed export subsidies helping to depress world prices which then require more subsidies to dispose of surpluses on world markets.

2. CAP-type support is not distributed satisfactorily amongst producers. One estimate (CEC, July 1991) is that 80% of CAP spending goes to only about 20% of farmers, overwhelmingly the bigger and richer ones. This is partly the result of tying spending to production and of biasing it towards 'northern' products. Attempts to fine-tune CAP support in favour of different groups of farmers have proved difficult and expensive.

3. Despite CAP support, a large number of EC farm households can no longer realistically expect adequate incomes from farming in the longer term, particularly in comparison with non-agricultural alternatives available to many of their younger members. The economic survival of many farm enterprises run by these households thus remains doubtful, even for those which might succeed in achieving greater cost efficiencies, in creating larger farming units, or in diversifying into non-farming activities.

4. Rural communities continued to suffer a number of economic and social problems which cannot be addressed by further CAP-type support to agriculture (CEC, 1988, Rural World). While the 1988 reform of the EC Structural Funds and other initiatives goes some way towards addressing this issue, the greater part of CAP expenditure still does little to promote broader rural development.

5. Price support places the Community's ability to compete in industries where the agricultural products are used as inputs at risk. The development of new crop-based industries, such as bio-energy and materials manufacturing, is made difficult without expensive subsidies.

6. The administration of the CAP has become increasingly complex and fraud-ridden because of numerous modifications to the original price supports and the introduction of experimental and *ad hoc* schemes. The enlargement of the Community from Six to Twelve, and probably more, and attempts to introduce national features into common policy regimes has worsened such problems in inconsistency and complexity.

7. CAP supply control mechanisms have been unable to prevent an overall increase in agricultural surpluses. Farmers have been proved adept at avoiding such restrictions, and at finding alternative production avenues. The controls themselves were often introduced too loosely, but negotiating the necessary changes with farmers and Member States proves increasingly lengthy and expensive.

8. The negative environmental impact of the CAP's production-stimulating measures has become more severe, such as ecological decline induced by crop-growing methods, and by water and air pollution caused by agri-chemicals and animal waste. Agriculture's growing environmental problems cannot be satisfactorily dealt with by voluntary schemes.

4.3. Future challenges: policy objectives reconsidered

A. Farm incomes

Even though future decline in real world market prices for agricultural commodities is expected to be less severe than in the 1980s due to trade liberalization and high income growth in developing countries, the downward pressure on prices is likely to continue for most traditional agricultural products. At individual level, the consequent fall in farming income can only be limited if employment in agriculture falls significantly around the world. However, this does not mean that there is a straightforward trade-off between the income and employment objectives of governments in rural areas in the sense that lower employment leads to higher incomes, or that higher income requires lower employment.

Patchy evidence suggests that the real incomes of farm households, as opposed to farming income per person employed, have generally risen over recent years, partly because many EC farming families have developed other sources of income. The general recession of the early 1990s and slower growth thereafter than in the 1980s, may also mean a less difficult task for farmers to maintain relative incomes at least for a period. Furthermore, the CAP reforms mean that many farmers will now benefit from secure and direct income support which is independent of market and climatic fluctuations.

The growth of social security safety nets has eased the hardship suffered by those leaving agriculture due to business failure. The CAP was never intended to be a social insurance against the failure of a farming enterprise, although some of its mechanisms have been dedicated to keeping scarcely viable activities in business. The EC now has other instruments, including substantial rural development policies, available to ease the transition for individuals.

The decline in the number of middle-sized farms has been accompanied by a rapid growth in the number of large farms which now account for a high proportion of output. The decline in numbers of small farms, however, has been much slower. This means that farm structures are now much more clearly divided between large and small. This is evidence that price support is missing its target of transferring income to producers with low relative incomes.

The increases in the size of farm units and in the value of the output of each unit is prompting larger producers to employ the services of financial and insurance markets. A variety of means are now available to cover against crop failures and unexpected blows to livestock production. The price-fixing mechanism is thus relatively less important as an income stabilizer.

Within the Community, exchange-rate changes have in the past caused great difficulties for many farmers in countries with strong currencies while provoking inflationary pressures in countries with devaluing currencies. In comparison to other industries, however, EC agriculture was partly cushioned by monetary compensatory amounts and other policy measures. Nevertheless, exchange-rate changes will continue to pose a threat and a challenge to the CAP. The 1993 decision to enlarge the exchange-rate mechanism bands to 15% has already created new difficulties and tensions as national EC currencies continue to vary against each other. The problems associated with currency changes will not in fact be resolved until the EC has a common currency as foreseen by the Maastricht Treaty.

The future challenges for EC agricultural policy in the area of farm incomes are thus to target a lower aggregate level of essential income support to farmers whose continued occupation in activities is endangered but is deemed to be of general social, environmental and cultural benefit, and to promote the development of institutions which will allow agriculture to cope with market and exchange-rate risk in a similar way as other sectors.

B. Rural communities

Rural communities obviously threaten to die without rural employment and as a result of continuing agricultural change, as well as technical changes in manufacturing and business transport and services, some (but not all) rural communities in the EC are likely to continue to pose problems of economic development or at least substantial and perhaps undesirable changes in their occupational and social character. It has become clear that many of the current problems of rural communities cannot be addressed by further CAP-type support to agriculture (CEC, 1988), and the challenge here is to continue to develop the various rural development initiatives under the 1988-reformed EC Structural Funds.

It can of course be questioned whether such communities, especially those in remote areas, should be maintained by policy subsidies or special regulations, or whether free-market forces should be allowed to operate with little interference. From an economic point of view, this question depends in a complex way on the opportunity costs of public expenditure on rural development and social assistance, on economies of scale and capital utilization in rural services, on the transition costs that would be imposed on individuals if a fast rate of change were enforced, and on externalities valued by the general population, such as the maintenance of traditional environment and way of life. The importance of these concerns varies greatly from place to place.

What is however clear is that modern agriculture will no longer be labour-intensive and will employ only limited numbers of people directly or in many cases (e.g. off-farm handling of bulk production) indirectly. Even with high levels of price and direct support, some areas of the Community suffer problems of social 'desertification' and a serious run-down in farming activity. With still lower price support, there may be quite serious problems of whole regions losing competitiveness in the production of traditional, mainstream commodities such as cereals and sheepmeat due to lower productivity growth than in the more developed regions. The continuous fall in employment is obviously undermining the belief that agricultural price support is essential to the maintenance of rural communities. It is also provoking a search for other more cost-effective methods of keeping rural communities alive. Evidence in some parts of the Community for a 'rural renaissance' based on grass-roots and income activity suggests that such a search is not fruitless.

C. The environment and related issues

Public opinion is increasingly aware that the search for higher production, stimulated by price support, is having negative consequences for the quality of natural resources. Unwanted effects include pollution from such inputs as nitrate fertilizers, aesthetic damage caused by practices such as field enlargement and intensive stocking, and highly artificial methods of livestock husbandry. Simple market support cannot deal satisfactorily with these problems, and may even contribute to them despite environmental and animal-welfare regulations, while voluntary and experimental schemes have not yet been shown capable of addressing the complexity, variety and time-scales of the issues involved.

The current CAP market reforms are unlikely to change dramatically the level of externalities, both positive and negative, produced by EC agriculture, although there should be a better balance towards more extensive crop and livestock production. However, regions and Member States already facing structural problems of under-utilized and poorly rewarded agricultural resources are likely to face the greatest difficulties of adjustment to the new conditions. Much will depend on the conceptual elaboration and practical implementation of the reform's accompanying measures for the agri-environment, particularly the extent to which they contribute towards a 'global' local strategy of conservation of desirable natural and vernacular features, and their utilization for economic purposes (Merlo and Manente, 1992).

Higher consumer incomes have created an increasing demand for high-quality products to which the market price support system of EC agriculture is poorly adapted. As with animal welfare, the CAP has proved inappropriate in addressing modern demands relating to product origin and production methods; these have had to be addressed by other policy means, or by the private sector, often in contradiction to the price signals set by the CAP.

D. Technical efficiency and competitiveness

Fundamental technical and economic forces will continue to pose inescapable challenges to which the political process will have to adjust. Although the lower EC prices now being introduced may have a longer-term effect of slowing down the pace of invention, development and adoption of new methods, technological progress such as genetic manipulation and electronic controls will continue to raise the productivity of even the most advanced production systems. There is also still considerable scope for productivity gains through structural change (larger farms). In addition, hitherto less efficient regions of the world such as Eastern Europe have a catch-up potential which will need to be accommodated. Substantial supply increases in agricultural products worldwide must, therefore, be expected. On the other hand, demand for agricultural products will remain stagnant in the Community while increases in effective worldwide demand will be limited.

To be sure of being able to feed itself, the Community does not need to increase production further. Supply of most main products exceeds 100% of consumption. Moreover, these consumption levels could be adjusted if, for whatever reason, Member States found themselves forced to use their own resources to feed their populations more efficiently in nutritional terms, as long as a certain level of production capacity is preserved.

The ending of the Cold War and the melting away of political tensions in Europe have made a future threat to food supplies even less plausible than before. The only factors justifying concern about future supplies of food are the Community's dependence on imported inputs which have so boosted productivity, and possibly the consequences of a Chernobyl-type nuclear accident in a wide and crucial area of Western European agriculture. However, the appropriate responses to these threats lie elsewhere than in the continuation of market price support for current food production.

The challenges for future EC agricultural policy in this area therefore lie in the encouragement (without undue public expenditure) of high-quality and low-cost production and marketing of farm commodities for domestic and external markets, and the reform of CAP mechanisms which discourage or complicate this approach.

E. Economic efficiency

As regards agricultural policy, the pursuit of overall economic efficiency relates to the EC's balance of broad political goals, both internal and external. Internally, the continuing exploitation via the single market of regional comparative advantage in farm production will throw up problems of structural and personal adjustment for those areas and farmers placed at relative disadvantage in traditional occupations. The pace and scale of re-allocating physical, financial and human resources away from unprofitable farming activities and towards more rewarding (in commercial or public-good terms) ones will involve difficult searches and choices amongst available options. However, such difficulties should not be ignored by policy-makers, both because re-allocation is necessary if the EC as a whole is to improve its economic efficiency (which determines overall output and hence the amounts available for income redistribution), and because policies can reduce the private costs and coordinate the path of adjustment in many areas.

Externally, economic challenges are posed by the competitive producers and potential customers in the Community's trading partners, particularly the industrialized countries of North America, Eastern Europe, South-East Asia and elsewhere. Not only will the technical and marketing efficiency of the EC farm sector be under increasing pressure (on food, fibre and other markets at home and abroad) as a result of the Uruguay Round agreement, but the worldwide development of macroeconomic performance is at least influenced by the efficiency of the agricultural sector and its role in international trade policy formulation (see next subsection).

F. International trade relations

Future challenges for EC agricultural policy also lie in wider issues of trade and political relationships with other countries. As in the past, questions of enlarging the Community will involve adoption of the current CAP as part of the *acquis communautaire,* and such problems will become easier to deal with if the CAP (a) avoids high distortion of farm product markets, and (b) contains a greater degree of internal differentiation and flexibility in direct support payment systems.

Another important question to be resolved in the next decade is the compatibility of current CAP reforms and the EC's Uruguay Round commitments on export subsidies. Whether or not difficulties can be avoided during the period of the agreement, longer-term questions remain, particularly if

world market commodity prices maintain their long-run decline in real terms.

G. Central and Eastern Europe

An important consideration for EC agricultural policy will be how to develop agricultural trade relations with Central and Eastern Europe prior to accession and how to integrate the agricultural sectors in these countries into the CAP during the usual transitional period after accession. It is in the EC's overall interest to support the political and economic development of the countries of Central and Eastern Europe. Normally, an important aspect of this support would be opening up to their trade and, in fact, the Community's bilateral agreements with these countries address this need. The Europe Agreements[1] in particular grant them privileged access to the EC market, although a restrictive attitude prevailed in some sectors, especially agriculture.

An across-the-board preference for exports from Eastern Europe would be an expensive and distortive method of assistance as long as agriculture in the EC is highly protected. It would be expensive because it would replace imports from other countries or increase EC exports by an amount corresponding to the higher imports from the East. Subsidies for these exports would have to be financed from the EC budget. Privileged access would thus amount to a special-purpose grant from the EC budget to Eastern Europe linked to agricultural exports whose value to these countries would be less than the budgetary cost incurred by the Community. A direct grant to these countries would be less expensive.

In addition, privileged access would have a distortive effect, in that CAP protection would be extended eastward. Farmers there would be receiving price signals which were not oriented to the world market. This would lead to distorted supply responses, as it does in the EC. Farmers in Eastern Europe would produce more than they would do under less artificial market regimes, in the process aggravating problems in the Community and worldwide.

Agriculture is more important to the eastern economies than it is to the EC, but the Community can effectively help them only if it reduces its level of price support and external protection. The inefficiencies in the income maintenance system, even after the 1992 reform and the GATT Agreement, are not only an obstacle to assisting Community

---

[1] With Poland, Hungary, the Czech Republic, Slovakia, Romania, Bulgaria and Albania.

farmers in an economically sound way, they are also a major stumbling block to a supportive relationship with Eastern Europe.

The CAP in its present form is not only a complication to the development of free trade with Eastern Europe, it would also be a source of great difficulty to any eventual attempt by the EC to honour its commitment to take the Visegrád Four (the Czech Republic, Slovakia, Hungary and Poland) into membership. If they were to apply market price support at the present EC level, they would be transferring resources from consumers to producers in volumes which may be thought politically undesirable. In the long run, they might also be stimulating production to reach levels far in excess of their domestic requirements.[1]

---

[1] However, it does not appear that the direct impact of eastern enlargement on EC agricultural expenditure would pose major problems, contrary to the recent estimates of some economists. Most of the Central and East European countries are net agricultural importers and they would thus contribute to the Community's budget (through duties on imported farm products) rather than cause a significant increase in spending. This is unlikely to change dramatically while they are still outside the Community.

Chapter 5

Guidance for future policy

5.1 Introduction

This chapter offers a general and long-term perspective for the future of the CAP. The fundamental aim is to make the CAP more consistent with the principles on which EC policies generally are based through a clearer separation of responsibilities for the efficiency and income aspects of the present policy. This implies a further re-orientation of the CAP away from price support and towards direct income support, allowing the allocation of tasks between the Community and the Member States to be made more in accordance with the principle of subsidiarity.

This basis for the analysis is first of all an assessment of the possibilities for achieving the objectives underlying agricultural policies pursued worldwide, as identified in Chapter 2. Emphasis is put on the objective of economic efficiency reflecting the general tendency for more weight to be given to such considerations in current government decision-making.

However, guidelines for reform of the CAP also need to take into account a number of constitutional principles which characterize the Community at its present level of development. These are:

(i)   fair competition,

(ii) subsidiarity,

(iii) consensus.

The principle of 'fair competition' finds its expression in Article 92 of the Maastricht Treaty which lays down the general principle that State aids which threaten to distort competition among firms in different Member States are forbidden. There are certain exceptions, for example aid to facilitate the development of certain activities or of certain economic areas may be permitted where such aid does not adversely affect trading conditions to an extent contrary to the common interest. Article 93 sets out the procedure by which the Commission can exercise its control and impose specific obligations on Member States. In performing this task, the Commission has in each case to decide whether the harm done to competition in the Community is outweighed by the contribution that the aid may make towards other Community objectives. This policy may be interpreted as implying that agriculture should be treated in the same way as other sectors of the economy, unless reasons can be advanced why it deserves special treatment in terms of government support.

The principle of 'subsidiarity' is expressed in Article 3b of the Maastricht Treaty: 'in areas which do not fall within its exclusive competence, the Community shall take action ... only if and in so far as the objectives of proposed action cannot be sufficiently achieved by the Member States and can, therefore, by reason of the scale or effects of the proposed action be better achieved by the Community'. When it comes to social and incomes policies, there is in general little, if any, *a priori* evidence that better results can be achieved with responsibility placed at the Community level.[1] Even at the increased level of integration achieved with the Maastricht Treaty, the responsibility for achieving an equitable income distribution still remains largely with the Member States. This not only reflects the relatively low level of cohesion in the European Union compared with that in the individual Member States, but is also justified because it allows measures, for example, to deal with structural adjustment problems to be differentiated according to their severity and according to differences in social security institutions in the Member States. This suggests that, in a reformed CAP, there should be convincing evidence that agricultural policy measures adopted at Community level would be an efficient method to achieve social or income redistributional objectives. It is important here to emphasize that the question to what extent the financial burden of social and structural adjustment problems in agriculture or in general should be shared between Member States is a separate, essentially political issue, which may be dealt with independently of the allocation of the responsibilities for dealing with these problems.

The principle of 'consensus' is embedded in both the constitutional rules and in the practice of the Community. The Treaty on European Union requires that political decisions be taken either by qualified majority or by unanimity, and it is reasonable to expect that decisions which will affect important national interests will only be adopted if a consensus can be achieved. For a CAP reform proposal to be adopted, it is therefore important that the distribution of costs and benefits between Member States does not change dramatically as a result of its implementation and also that it is perceived in each Member State not to do so. Widespread analysis and open discussion of the effects and implications of proposals for further reform of the CAP is therefore important.

---

[1]   See 'Stable money — sound finances' *European Economy* No 53, 1993.

5.2. Guidelines for further CAP reform

A. Further cuts in agricultural support prices

A main objective for further reform of the CAP should be for agricultural support prices eventually to provide a level of protection no higher than that enjoyed by other sectors in the economy.

The 1992 CAP reforms represented a major stride towards a more market-oriented EC agricultural policy, but also created important new imbalances in the level of market protection afforded to different farm products, in particular on the demand side. Initial price reductions, beyond those already agreed, should therefore be concentrated on commodities such as milk and sugar whose regimes were not significantly affected by the 1992 reform. This would mean a substantial move in the direction of world market prices for most products other than cereals and oilseeds, whose prices will be reduced to close to world market level already as a consequence of the 1992 reforms.

The price decreases should be phased in over a relatively long period, in order to limit the budget cost due to compensation payments and to avoid causing too much disruption in rural areas and in industries depending on the agricultural sector. However, the price cuts should be implemented in full, without weakening of their effect due to monetary or national adjustments.

The planned reduction in domestic EC farm product support prices should be clearly announced in advance. However, domestic price adjustments should take reasonable account of world market price developments with the conditions for deviations from the planned developments clearly spelt out.

B. Reform of stabilization measures

Reductions in price levels do not, in themselves, imply a reform of the market price system, although, as EC prices approach world levels, there might be a reduced need for direct price stabilization if, as a result of the internal reform in the EC and in other countries, world market prices became more stable. In order to strengthen these market links and thus their price-stabilizing effects, the remaining EC levies and import quotas should be transformed into flat *ad valorem* tariffs as required by the Uruguay Round agreement. There may be some scope for maintaining variable levies as a stabilizer against unacceptable fluctuations in internal prices, and to prevent these falling below certain levels. In any case, alternative means of stabilization including forward contracts, insurance and possibly mutually operated income stabilization funds should be encouraged.

C. Elimination of quantitative restrictions

Quantitative restrictions in the form of production quotas for milk and sugar, reference levels of regional cattle herds and sheep flocks, and land set-aside proportions may have desirable effects in reducing budget expenditures, but also create production inefficiencies and administrative costs. Reduction in prices will reduce the incentive to expand production and thus the pressures on the EC budget. All such quantitative restrictions should therefore ultimately be eliminated.

In particular, the provision in the 1992 reform package for set-aside in the crop sector should be gradually eliminated. The modelling analysis carried out for this report suggests that likely price developments over the next few years will lead to cereal prices approaching world prices quite closely, so that no set-aside would then be needed to comply with the Uruguay Round agreement. If, in fact, subsidized cereals exports threatened to conflict with the EC's international commitments, further cuts in cereal prices with corresponding income compensation should be made to eliminate export subsidies, to allow set-aside to be abolished and EC exports to expand. The objectives of preserving social and landscape features in rural areas should be achieved by other instruments.

D. Direct income support: a Member State responsibility

The need for compensation for decreases in prices will differ very much between Member States depending on the severity of the structural adjustment problems, and according to differences in pension schemes, unemployment benefits and other social provisions. Political support with respect to the degree and time-scale for such compensations is also likely to differ among Member States. Providing compensation to all farmers in the Community according to the same rules might therefore imply under-compensation in some Member States and over-compensation in others, according to national preferences.

In line with the subsidiarity principle, the responsibility for direct income support, i.e. for deciding on criteria of eligibility, on size and on duration of such payments, should therefore be allocated to the Member States, on condition that the payments do not distort competition.

E. Temporary transfers to Member States from the EC budget.

Providing compensation to farmers for the price decreases under the 1992 reform and for further price decreases will increase the burden on the national budget in the Member States, particularly in those countries where pre-reform transfers from the EC budget and from consumers have been particularly large.

In order to ease the transition process, the Community should therefore provide compensation to the Member States on a temporary basis. This compensation would be financed in part from the payments which during the three-year implementation period under the 1992 reform are paid directly to farmers from the EC budget and in part from savings following the further reform of the CAP in terms of reduced export subsidies and other costs. The transfers will be limited in time and provided on a degressive basis, and should be used only for direct compensation to farmers or for rural development, environmental or structural adjustment purposes. Community financing for this purpose should be phased out over a pre-determined period, say seven to 10 years.

F. Rules to ensure fair competition

National agricultural policy measures must of course always conform to EC competition policy. In general, therefore, support linked to current production will not be allowed, although payments to achieve rural and environmental objectives, not affecting trading conditions contrary to the common interest, should be permitted. It has to be accepted that some rural regions in the Community are still highly dependent on agricultural and closely related activities for the occupations and incomes of their inhabitants. For this reason, certain agricultural measures may continue to be appropriate. However, these should be funded and assessed on the same basis as assistance to other sectors of the rural economy, e.g. tourism, forestry, small-scale manufacturing, etc., according to the principle that agriculture should be treated in the same way as any other sector if there are no strong reasons to the contrary.

'Decoupled' income payments, i.e. payments which satisfy similar conditions as specified in the so-called 'green box' of non-trade-distorting measures agreed in Uruguay Round negotiations, would be allowed. Member States will therefore in general be free to provide compensations based on historical levels of production because such payments do not provide an incentive to increased production.

As in other sectors of industrial policy, the Community's responsibility is and will be to set the ground rules in line with its disciplines on State aids in general. Governments, therefore, have to satisfy the Commission, as the custodian of the Community's responsibility in this area, that the support they give to farmers does not distort competition in the EC's internal market. During the transitional period, before prices are reduced to world market price level, high rates of export subsidies and tariffs in case of increased production still create significant spillover effects in terms of increased costs to the common budget. A common organization to reinforce the Commission's general authority in this area should therefore be envisaged. Such an organization could involve the obligation on Member States to produce, for approval at Community level, multi-annual plans for direct income support to farmers.

G. Other measures

The above guidelines maintain the Community's financial solidarity for the operation of the common agricultural policy, but imply that financial responsibility for the structural adjustment problems in agriculture and rural areas after the transition period will be shifted away from the CAP. The Structural and Cohesion Funds need therefore to be used more comprehensively as a source of accompanying measures to aid structural adjustment than those available under the 1992 reform package. The reform proposal outlined here would cover many more commodities and policy areas, and additional measures should be targeted specifically at rural development and environmental objectives. Local markets for environmental services could be supported by public funds, subject to Community regulation and monitoring to avoid unfair competition.

There is also a case for partial compensation being paid to Member States for the cost of installing the administrative structures necessary to switch from the present system to the new one, and possibly for the maintenance of these systems where this would make for improved overall economic efficiency in the Community. The Community could provide special help to those Member States with relatively weak administrative capabilities and large numbers of small farms. Such States are likely to find the implementation of direct income support programmes relatively costly.

Stockpiling and external trade arrangements should be explored as alternative methods of ensuring food security, which in any case is a less important objective than at the inception of the CAP. Such measures should also be used to ensure that the Community is able to provide emergency food aid.

Finally, arrangements should be made to assure continued public funding — at Community level where appropriate — of scientific research, technological development, extension services and education systems for the agricultural sector.

Chapter 6

Assessment

6.1. Introduction

This chapter provides an assessment of the guidelines for reform outlined in Chapter 5. The guidelines are evaluated according to the general policy objectives identified in Chapter 2. Finally their impact in terms of European cohesion and integration is discussed.

The guidelines are assessed using basic economic reasoning. Given the long-term nature of the suggestions for further reform of the CAP and the limitation of the available models in this respect, the expert group decided not to undertake a quantitative assessment. This remains a challenge for future work.

6.2. Policy objectives

A. Farm incomes

In the long run (i.e. after full adjustment has taken place), one would expect only the price of land, as the fixed factor of farm production, to fall as a consequence of a reduction in farm prices. The employment of capital and labour in the agricultural sector will decline in response to the reduced level of market price support as some fraction of these factors is diverted to other sectors, but their remuneration will not fall because it will remain linked to the capital rents and wages obtained in other sectors of the economy.

In the short term, however, price cuts lead to drop in income for farm capital and labour as well as for land. It takes time for existing capital to be depreciated and for labour to find alternative employment. To avoid the negative impact on farmers' income Member States may, however, subject to Community competition rules, provide direct income support as compensation and as payments for environmental services. Under the new system, support may be more efficiently targeted to those most likely to be in need from a social or economic point of view.

In the long run, farm household incomes will, when non-farm income is taken into account, stabilize at a level similar to that enjoyed by households employed in other industries. After the sharp reduction in farming population which has taken place and which continues to take place in most

Member States, the task of absorbing a further reduction of agricultural employment in the economy will be less and less difficult. For most Member States it will therefore be sufficient and administratively convenient to extend to farmers the national social security net, job-training programmes, pre-pension schemes and other social and employment measures. These would allow social problems in the farming industry created by structural adjustment to be dealt with in the same way as is done for other industries. In some Member States this is already the case, which limits the need for special compensation schemes following the proposed price reductions.

Under the reformed CAP, domestic agricultural prices will be subject to increased fluctuation. With the development of capital markets stimulated by government encouragement and regulation, it will however be possible for new futures markets and other financial instruments to smooth excessive variability in farmer returns.

B. Rural communities

The decrease in agricultural prices will in itself have a depressive effect on economic activities in rural areas, especially those highly dependent on agriculture. The effects on food-processing industries and industries supplying input and capital to the agricultural sector also need to be taken into account. A significant part of the direct income support provided in compensation to farmers is, however, likely to generate private investment activities in rural areas which will counteract this depressive effect. Furthermore, in general, the proposed increase in support for rural economic activities will also compensate for the decline in agricultural production. Agriculture has become an increasingly capital-intensive industry. A more balanced support to rural activities is therefore likely to provide relatively more employment in rural areas and hence more support to rural communities. National policies could be adjusted more easily than at present to accommodate strong public preferences for supporting rural communities which exist in certain Member States. Such measures might stimulate agricultural production, causing a problem from the point of view of EC competition policy. However, the effect would be rather limited if the measures are properly targeted. Small farms in rural areas in need of development account for only a small part of total EC production. But, of even greater importance, the costs imposed on other Member States would be much reduced after reduction of agricultural prices to world market levels, because the negative effects on the EC budget would have been eliminated, or at least reduced very significantly.

C. The environment

Under the kind of approach advocated here, protection of the environment in the Community would be cheaper and easier. Reduction in farm prices would both lower the incentives for farmers to intensify via higher levels of purchased inputs and higher stocking rates, and enable alternative land uses such as forestry, low-density housing and environmentally-friendly production systems to compete more effectively for space. Subject to Community rules of fair competition, there would also be greater freedom for Member States to operate national or regional systems to provide compensation to farmers for the production of environmental services or to reduce the negative impact of agricultural production. Again, should this stimulate agricultural production, then the negative spillover effect would be far less important than under the present market price support system.

D. Technical efficiency and competitiveness

Lower agricultural prices and less stable agricultural prices are likely to reduce the incentive for research and development in new agricultural products and techniques. The guidelines therefore suggest targeted public support for agricultural research and development at local, national and Community levels. Such support should limit itself to offsetting significant market failures, e.g. excessive transaction costs involved in gathering contributions from many small farmers, and positive externalities unrecognized by the markets.

The move from administratively-determined prices to prices which reflect better supply and demand conditions will provide increased incentives for the development of quality products. This will provide a stimulus to the agricultural sector because these are the products where increasing consumer income is likely to expand demand most in the coming years.

Removing quantitative restrictions will improve technical efficiency by making it possible for farmers to use the most efficient production techniques and to exploit economies of scale.

Food production will become less intensive in the use of purchased inputs after the implementation of the proposals and will therefore depend less on imported inputs. Food security will therefore decrease less than the decline in self-sufficiency would suggest. Anyway, food security is not likely to be an important issue in the future.

E. Economic efficiency

Reducing agricultural prices to world market price levels will provide significant economic efficiency gains.

In the long run, the resource allocation in the Community will be improved by the transfer of labour, capital and other resources from agriculture to other more competitive sectors, and also the costs of administration will be significantly reduced. The 1992 reform has already created an administrative infrastructure which may be used for providing direct income support, and, with decreasing subsidies, the need for strict control of agricultural production and trade will decline. The gain in aggregate real income from these two factors will represent a sizeable share of the present large transfers to Community agriculture from consumers and taxpayers. Budget expenditures to pay for export refunds, intervention purchases and administration will be significantly reduced and consumers will experience a significant real income gain due to lower prices, whereas the loss in income to the owners of the primary factors currently employed in the agricultural sector will be modest.

However, in the short run, benefits compare less favourably with costs. The loss in earned income for farm households will be relatively more significant in the short run than in the long run, as the transfer of labour and capital from the agricultural sector to other sectors takes time and may create some unemployment among those previously employed in agriculture. Budget liabilities, partly borne by national governments, which are always costly to finance, will increase as the transfer from consumers are replaced by direct payments, and as the administrative costs for providing direct income support may also increase.

With price changes being decreased over a reasonably long period, and with compensation from the EC budget to Member States being gradually phased out, there need not be any increase in the EC budget. At the end of the transition period, expenditures for agricultural purposes would in fact have been significantly reduced. A revision of the EC agricultural budget guidelines may therefore not be required, whereas Member States may need, at least temporarily, to increase budget appropriations to provide compensation to farmers.

The reduction of farm prices may also create some macro-economic benefits. In an environment of general unemployment due to 'sticky' real wages, there will be some general short-term benefits as a decrease in food prices raises real wages and thus stimulates employment.

F. International trade relations

Following implementation of reform according to the guidelines suggested here, the Community's relations with trading partners should further improve. The EC will eliminate its subsidized exports, easing relations with the United States and other food-exporting countries. The Central and East European countries and many developing countries will be helped by a less restrictive EC import regime. For poor countries dependent on food imports whose price may be increased by EC or multilateral policy reform, there will be a need to continue food aid in emergencies and to design longer-term economic development programmes financed by the Community.

Particularly if agreements are made in the context of the GATT, lower EC agricultural prices will induce other developed countries to reduce their level of support to agriculture and hence increase world market prices. As the Community is increasingly becoming an exporter of agricultural products, such worldwide coordination is therefore particularly attractive for the Community.

Lower agricultural protection will also make it possible to ensure, by increased imports, the supply of raw materials to the EC food processing industry. This will avoid an over-severe structural adjustment in this sector as a result of reduced agricultural production by quantitative restrictions, which, in the absence of further reform, may be needed to fulfil the EC's obligations under the 1993 Uruguay Round agreement.

6.3. European cohesion and integration

A. Unity of the market, Community preference and financial solidarity

The implementation of the proposed guidelines will facilitate relations between the existing Member States as well as simplifying accession and integration of new Member States, hence contributing to European integration.

The common agricultural policy has played a key role in establishing and maintaining the European Community by assuring fair competition in agricultural markets. Although on several occasions during its history it has been the cause of fierce disputes among the Member States, it is still considered by many to provide an essential contribution to Community cohesion. It is therefore important to demonstrate that the proposed guidelines in essence are consistent with the three well-known principles on which the CAP was originally based: unity of the market, Community preference

and financial solidarity. The guidelines maintain the unity of the market. There will still be a common agricultural policy: responsibility for the internal market and for external protection will remain at Community level. Nor will State aids be allowed to distort competition on agricultural commodity markets. The Community's competition rules, which have been adequate in regulating State aids in other sectors, can be expected to be similarly effective in agriculture, although special provisions, as proposed, may be needed during the transitional phase when external protection for some products will still remain at a high level.

Also CAP, reformed according to the guidelines proposed here, will still be consistent with the principles of Community preference and financial solidarity. Community preference will be maintained, although at a lower level than today. Financial solidarity will also be maintained with respect to the expenditures and revenues of the EC's general budget which follows from the operation by the Community of agricultural trade and competition policy. However, after the transitional period, there will not be financial solidarity, in the context of the common agricultural policy, with respect to the costs of dealing with the income problem caused by the structural adjustment pressure on agriculture. This, however, does not exclude financial solidarity within the Community for structural adjustment problems in general using policy instruments appropriate for this purpose.

B. Changing circumstances and Community responsibilities

At the time the European Economic Community was founded, market price support systems with the objective of supporting farmers' income already existed for agricultural products in the original Member States. Creating an internal market for agricultural products could only be achieved by harmonizing these systems, thus creating a common price support scheme. In other words, although the responsibility for achieving an equitable personal income distribution was the responsibility of the Member States, the responsibility for maintaining farm incomes was allocated to the Community as it would otherwise have been impossible to create an internal market for agricultural products.

Today, with the introduction of direct payments in the 1992 reforms as an instrument to secure an appropriate level of farm income, the situation is fundamentally different. It is now possible to separate the responsibility for the administration of the internal market from that of maintaining farmers' incomes (or more generally incomes in rural areas) at an acceptable level. It is possible to leave the responsibility for maintaining the unity of the market for agricultural products, and for ensuring that competition is not distorted, to the Community, re-allocating the primary responsibility for maintaining income in rural areas to the Member States.

Furthermore, at the time the CAP was formed, the transfers between Member States were much smaller and far easier to justify than today. The degree of self-sufficiency between Member States was much less unequal, and the transfers due to the CAP were therefore not a major source of political tension. CAP benefits to those Member States which had a comparative advantage in agriculture balanced the benefits enjoyed by other Member States due to the creation of a customs union for industrial products. Today the transfers between Member States due to the CAP are a much more divisive issue. Particularly after the 1973 enlargement, the difference in the degree of self-sufficiency between Member States for agricultural products has become much more significant while the differences in benefits derived from the internal market for industrial products are far less significant than they were in the 1950s. In successive GATT rounds, the tariff rate for industrial products has been almost eliminated, and industry has become the dominating sector in the economy in all Member States. The transfers between Member States due to the CAP cannot therefore be justified to the same extent by reference to differences between Member States in size of their industrial sectors. Nor can the existing transfers between Member States due to the CAP be justified with reference to differences in income positions, since most of the net beneficiaries are high income countries.

Finally, other instruments have been created which may be used within the Community to share the burden of structural adjustment pressure in rural areas. These instruments are more cost-effective in helping those countries which in this respect have a particularly heavy burden, than are agricultural policy measures.

C. Costs and benefits for Member States

Although further quantitative work will be needed to prove the point, it seems that by appropriate timing of decreases in support prices and in the compensation from the EC budget, and by adjustment in the payments from the Structural Funds, all Member States stand to gain from the implementation of the guidelines, or at least to experience only modest losses.

The reasons for this may be summarized as follows:

In the long run, following reform according to the proposed guidelines, the removal of the inefficiencies and the depressing effect on international prices inherent in the present support system will provide benefits to all Member States in terms of lower budget contributions to the EC and lower consumer prices in the Member States, which will outweigh the losses in land rent.

During the implementation period, the transitional cost will be divided and evenly shared. Administrative costs due to the full implementation of direct income support schemes will be limited given the already established recording and monitoring system covering a large part of agriculture, as part of the 1992 reform. Community cofinance will reduce the costs in those countries where there will be a particular burden due to a large number of farms and a relatively weak administrative infrastructure. The transfers from the EC budget to the Member State governments, which are only gradually to be reduced, will limit the financial burden for those countries where the compensation to farmers for reductions in agricultural prices imposes a disproportionate burden on taxpayers. The gradual decrease in agricultural prices will provide time to transfer the resources released in agriculture and related industries to other sectors, and hence limit the need to provide income compensation. The adjustment in the food processing industries will be facilitated by access to imported raw materials due to reduction in tariff barriers.

D. Community enlargement

Finally, the proposal also offers advantages in relation to further European integration by enlargement of the Community, where agriculture also risks being a difficult issue.

The EFTA countries could, for example, maintain nationally financed direct income support at a higher level than in the rest of the Community, thereby allowing these countries to maintain high levels of support in climatically disadvantaged areas.

Making farm income support a national responsibility will also facilitate the integration of Central and East European countries into the Community. It will allow transfers from the Community budget to these countries to be directed to sectors where support will provide a greater contribution to growth, and hence to convergence, than will market price support to their agricultural sectors. The implementation of the proposed guidelines will also eliminate the potential barriers which the prospect of high budget transfers could constitute for the accession of the Central and East European countries to the Community.

Annex

Chapter A: EC agriculture past and present[1]

[1] This chapter was prepared by Ken Thomson, based on tables and graphs prepared by the Economic Service of the European Commission. Karen Lind and Søren Nielsen provided helpful technical assistance.

Chapter A

EC agriculture past and present

1. Introduction

In order to provide a historical background to the main report, this chapter describes, from an economic point of view, the major features of the structure and evolution of Community agriculture since 1973, the year of accession by Denmark, Ireland and the United Kingdom, marking the first enlargement of the EC from the Six. Statistical problems arise from the accession of Greece in 1981 and of Spain and Portugal in 1986, but these must be accepted.

The chapter is structured as follows. Developments in the EC production of agricultural commodities are first described, followed by analysis of trends in real product prices and the implications for farming incomes and related aspects of agricultural structure. Next, patterns of EC consumption and trade with third countries are dealt with, and the consequences for the Community's agricultural self-sufficiency and level of protection are treated. Finally, a brief overview of the development of CAP instruments is provided.

2. Production

After the Second World War, with assistance from domestic governments and US Marshall Plan aid, agricultural production in Western Europe was quick to recover, reaching 50% above pre-war levels by the end of the 1950s (Tracy, 1982, pp. 232-4). This trend continued for most products and in EC-9 Member States throughout the 1960s and early 1970s (CEC, 1976, p. l87).

The overall growth of EC agricultural output (measured by final production, i.e. gross production less wastage and on-farm use) since 1973 is shown in Graph 13. Over the 18-year period 1973-90, output rose by an average 2.0% per year, but only at 1.2% per year during the later sub-period 1983-90. These figures indicate a notable absolute and relative slackening of growth in the EC agricultural sector

over recent years, compared with EC-12 GDP growth rates of 2.3 and 2.9% per year over the same periods.

Within the farm sector, output levels of different commodities have changed at rather different rates. Over the whole period 1973-90, output of the major subsectors of crops, livestock (animals for slaughter) and animal products (primarily milk) grew at 2.6, 1.8 and 1.0% per year, respectively. After 1983, these rates fell to 2.3, 1.1 and – 1.3%. Consequently, the proportion of total EC agricultural output accounted for by crops rose from 45 to 48% between 1973 and 1990, while the share of animal output remained roughly unchanged at about 33%, and that of animal product output fell from 22 to 19%.

2.1. Input use

Amongst production factors, there have been striking differences in trend within the EC. Agricultural land use has remained remarkably stable with a virtually constant arable area of 36 million hectares (Mha) in the EC-6, and nearly 68 Mha for the EC-12. Total utilizable agricultural area (UAA), which includes grazing and other areas (e.g. orchards) has declined only very slowly, from 67.2 Mha in 1973 to 64.2 Mha in 1988 for the EC-6, compared to around 129 Mha for the EC-I 2.

This rather static picture disguises a more dynamic process in certain localities, as well as the operation of urbanization policies in several Member States. Studies of land use change (e.g. Whitby, 1991, for England and Wales) have shown that loss of (mainly arable) land to urban and other (e.g. transport) uses has been largely compensated for by improvement and conversion of other land from grass to crops. Afforestation and land abandonment have been largely confined to the poorer regions of the Community. Some Member States with large-scale industrial change, e.g. Germany (West) and Italy, have lost farmland at rather greater rates than agricultural countries such as Greece and Ireland, where largely, accession to the Community appears to have brought about an increase in cultivated land (CEC, 1987, p. 119).

In contrast to the steady overall level of agricultural land, the use of labour in EC-12 agriculture has declined strongly, by an almost-constant average of 3% per year between 1973 and 1989, to under 10 million agricultural work units (standard man years) (Graph 14). The only noticeable deviation from trend is an apparent slight dip during 1981-82. For the Community as a whole, the decline has virtually halved the share of agricultural employment in total civilian employment, from 13.8% in 1970 to 7.4% in 1988, and has reduced 'persons employed' (i.e. with their main occupation) in

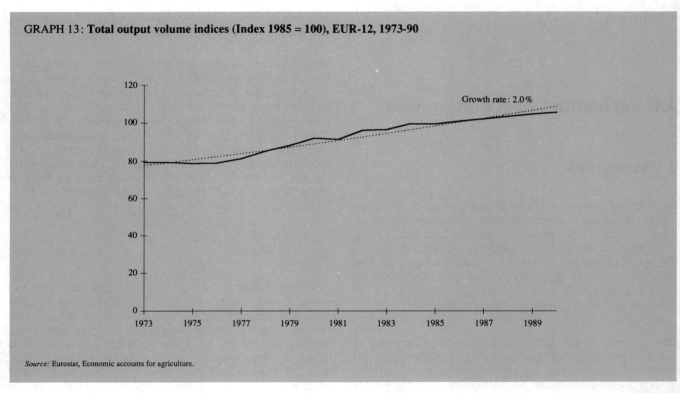

GRAPH 13: **Total output volume indices (Index 1985 = 100), EUR-12, 1973-90**

Growth rate: 2.0%

Source: Eurostat, Economic accounts for agriculture.

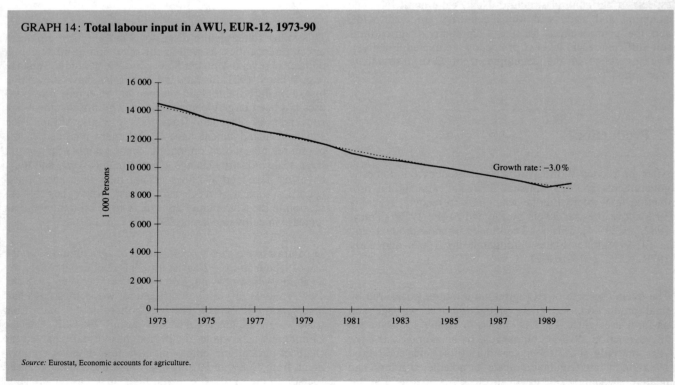

GRAPH 14: **Total labour input in AWU, EUR-12, 1973-90**

1 000 Persons

Growth rate: −3.0%

Source: Eurostat, Economic accounts for agriculture.

agriculture to 8.7 million in 1990. This decline has obvious implications for trends in crude labour productivity, and for the maintenance of real value-added and income over this period.

Again, however, this rather gradual overall pattern of development hides a number of different components. High rates of decline (over or around 4% per year) in farm labour have been observed in Denmark, Spain, Italy and Luxembourg, with some acceleration in most of the Mediterranean

countries since 1980 (Table 7 and Frohberg, 1993). The fall has been much slower in the United Kingdom and the Netherlands; in the latter, at 0.77% per year between 1980 and 1990. Statistics for the E-7 (Germany, France, the Benelux countries, the United Kingdom and Ireland) indicate annual rates of decline in farm labour slowing from 4.4% during 1967-73 to 2.1% during 1980-87, with an 1974-87 average of 2.2%. Labour reduction was faster in the other five Member States, although there too the fall approximately halved in pace during the 1980s.

Table 7

Changes in the agricultural labour force 1970-90

Country	Agricultural labour force				Share of agricultural employment in total civilian employment		
	equivalent full-time workers (AWU)		average annual change		shares		average annual change
	1970	1990	1970 to 1990	1980 to 1990	1970	1988	1970 to 1988
	in 1 000	in 1 000	in %	in %	in %	in %	%/year
B	181.2	93.2	− 3.27	− 2.10	4.8	2.7	− 3.15
DK	216.1	96.1	− 3.97	− 3.49	11.5	6.3	− 3.29
D	1 527.0	762.5	− 3.41	− 2.54	8.6	4.3	− 3.78
GR	1 192.4	781.8	− 2.09	− 2.00	40.8	26.1	− 2.45
E	3 566.5	1 400.7	− 4.57	− 4.94	29.5	14.4	− 3.91
F	2 369.0	1 473.8	− 2.35	− 2.16	13.5	6.8	− 3.74
IRL	365.2	238.4	− 2.11	− 1.92	27.1	15.4	− 3.09
I	3 653.8	2 156.7	− 2.60	− 3.04	20.2	9.9	− 3.88
L	14.6	6.0	− 4.37	− 3.97	9.4	3.4	− 5.49
NL	303.3	235.1	− 1.26	− 0.77	6.3	4.8	− 1.50
P	1 630.5	867.6	− 3.11	− 3.21	30.0	20.7	− 2.04
UK	615.0	456.4	− 1.48	− 1.47	3.2	2.2	− 2.06
EUR-12	15 634.6	8 532.3	− 2.98	− 3.00	13.8	7.4	− 3.40

Source: EC-Commission, *The agricultural situation in the Community,* various issues, Brussels.

Fixed capital in EC agriculture increased at an average rate of 1.1% per year during 1974-87 for the EC-10. Again, the 1980s showed a significant slowdown in adjustment with the EC-7 figure falling from 2.9% during 1967-73 to 0.3% during 1980-87. In recent years, renewal of facilities and equipment accounts for a very high percentage of gross asset formation in agriculture, as in the rest of the EC economy (CEC, 1987, p. 23). As between countries, over the period 1974-87, the Netherlands, Belgium and Ireland all indicated rates over 2% per year, while these were less than 1% in Germany and Italy (0.6 and 0.8% per year, respectively).

The volume of intermediate consumption (variable inputs) has increased during 1973-90 at almost the same rate as total output (1.9 compared to 2.0% per year), though with a similar drop to around 1% per year since 1983 (Graph

15). Due to the decrease in intermediate input prices, the proportion of intermediate costs in total against inputs has thus fallen back during the 1980s to 43% in 1990 for the EC-12 (CEC, annual).

There have been notable differences between specific input volume trends, especially since the mid-1980s. Fertilizer usage, which rose particularly strongly over the 1960s/70s (over 13% per year; see Bowler, 1985, calculating from Behrens and de Haen, 1980), has almost stabilized since 1980 (Graph 15), as has energy usage, while use of plant protection products has continued to increase in volume, averaging 6.4% per year between 1973 and 1989. Use of purchased feedingstuffs averaged growth at 2.4% per year between 1973 and 1990 but slowed to only 0.6% per year after 1983.

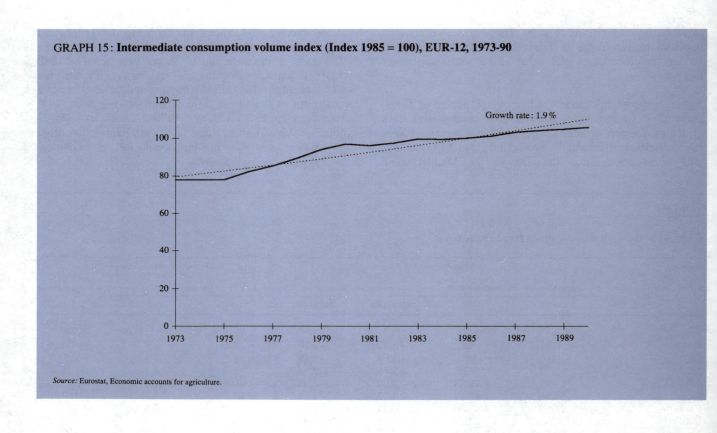

GRAPH 15 : **Intermediate consumption volume index (Index 1985 = 100), EUR-12, 1973-90**

Growth rate : 1.9 %

Source: Eurostat, Economic accounts for agriculture.

2.2. Technical change

Technical change has been significant in the development of most parts of the EC farming sector, often 'embodied' in various inputs such as seeds and machinery, but sometimes reflected in the development of technical systems of a simplified or large-scale nature. Adoption of technological improvements brings advantages in cost or (if output quality is improved) price. However, in the absence of policy measures, the 'treadmill' of market forces will eventually bring about a lowering of output price to eliminate the profit-increasing effect (and pass on the economic benefits to users and consumers), although 'early adopters' can gain a temporary advantage. The CAP has slowed down the 'treadmill', enhancing the financial attractiveness of tech-nology-enhancing investment to input suppliers and farmers by raising and stabilizing product prices. In addition, since the war, national EC governments, and latterly the Com-munity itself, have had major programmes of agricultural research and development (as well as extension and education systems) which have accelerated the invention and adoption of new agricultural methods.

Crop and grass production has been favoured mainly through yield-increasing (land-saving) innovation in variety develop-ment and labour-saving on field operations. For example, over the period 1973-90, cereals, sugar beet and oilseed rape have increased EC-12 yields by 1.9, 1.7 and 2.1% per year, respectively, enabling output on a fixed area to increase by 33 to 42% over this period. However, while the area of cereals and sugar beet have remained fairly static, that of oilseeds has nearly quadrupled, mainly by extending the geographical range over which these crops are be produced, e.g. oilseed rape in the United Kingdom, and soya beans in Italy.

In dairy production, yields per cow have increased by about 1.6% per year between 1974 and 1989, while carcass weights per adult beef animal have increased by around 0.5% per year over the same period. At the same time, faster growth rates and higher fertility levels have been achieved, accelerating the rate of output per breeding animal in these sectors, and others, notably pigs and poultry.

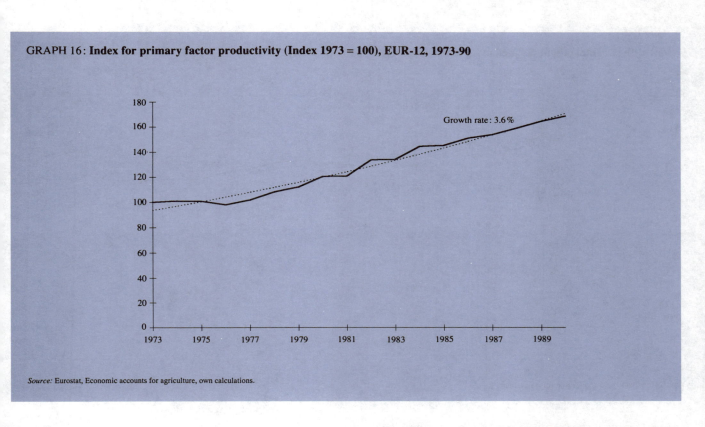

GRAPH 16: **Index for primary factor productivity (Index 1973 = 100), EUR-12, 1973-90**

Growth rate: 3.6%

Source: Eurostat, Economic accounts for agriculture, own calculations.

2.3. Productivity

The outcome of these various output and input developments can be observed in aggregate gross value-added (GVA, i.e. final output less intermediate consumption) and in productivity measures. At constant prices (i.e. in volume terms), EC-12 agricultural GVA increased by 2.1% over the period 1973-89, or at the same rate as output volume.

Other authors (Behrens and de Haen, 1980; Henrichsmeyer and Ostermeyer-Schloder, 1988) have indicated that differences in the levels and productivities of factors used in EC-9 agricultural production over the period 1963-76 differed widely between countries, due mainly to national 'dynamics' of structural change and specialization rather than product composition. Although labour and land inputs declined, this was offset by increased use of capital and variable inputs, so that total factor use remained fairly constant overall. Thus both production and factor productivity increased at the same average rate of 2% per year over this period. Total input (of primary factors and intermediate inputs) was virtually stagnant over the period analysed, so that productivity improvements account for the increase in output. However, the productivity gap amongst Member States widened rather than narrowed over this period.

Graph 16 indicates that primary factor productivity in EC-12 agriculture rose at an annual average rate of 3.6% between 1973 and 1990, suggesting significantly stronger increases in productivity in EC agriculture than in other sectors — average real GDP growth was 3.0% 1971-80 and 2.3% 1981-90. Moreover, there was little sign of slackening of productivity growth during the 1980s.

3. Prices and incomes

3.1. Price trends

According to Eurostat figures (Economic accounts for agriculture), real EC agricultural output prices (i.e. unit values averaged all production sold) fell at an average annual rate of 1.5% during the period 1973-90. For crops, the rate of fall, at 0.6%, was considerably slower than for animal output, at 2.7%, while real animal product prices fell at an average annual rate of 1.4% (Table 8 and Graph 17).

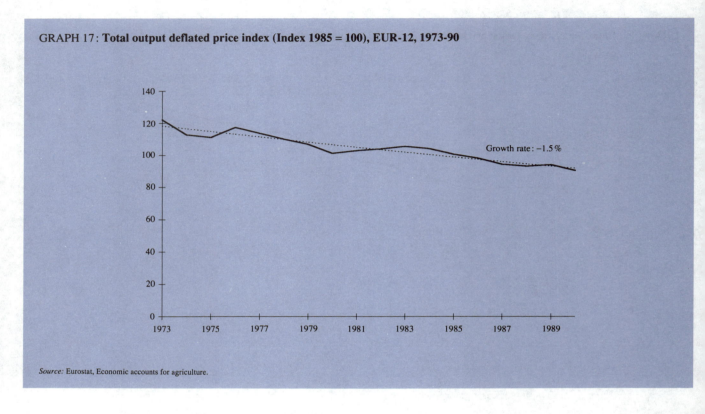

GRAPH 17: **Total output deflated price index (Index 1985 = 100), EUR-12, 1973-90**

Growth rate: −1.5%

Source: Eurostat, Economic accounts for agriculture.

Table 8

Annual rate of change for real domestic agricultural prices EUR-12[1] 1973-90 and 1983-90

	Growth rates (%)	
	1973-90	1983-90
Total output	− 1.5	− 2.1
Crops output	− 0.6	− 1.5
Cereals excluding rice	− 2.2	− 4.4
Oilseeds	− 2.3	− 6.9
Fresh vegetables	0.9	0.6
Final animal output	− 2.2	− 2.7
Animals	− 2.7	− 3.6
Cattle (including calves)	− 1.9	− 2.8
Pigs	− 4.6	− 4.8
Animal products	− 1.4	− 1.3
Milk	− 1.1	− 1.0
Intermediate consumption	− 1.2	− 3.1
Fertilizer and soil improvers	− 2.4	− 3.1
Feedingstuffs	− 2.6	− 4.2

[1] Before 1980 EUR-11 (− Portugal).

Source: Eurostat, *Economic accounts for agriculture,* and own calculations.

Weighted averages of national prices in real terms (rather than EC unit values deflated by an EC index, as above) indicate that between 1973 and 1990 EC-10 producer prices fell at an average rate of 2.7% per year, while crop and animal prices fell by about 2.5 and 2.8% per year, respectively (Tangermann, 1992, pp. 7-8).

The 18-year trend rates of real prices calculated from the agricultural accounts conceal substantial changes within the period as a whole. Over the subperiod 1983-90, the overall average rate of decline in real EC agricultural output prices accelerated to 2.1% per year, with crop prices dropping by 1.5% per year over these years, and animal output prices by 3.6% per year. Animal product prices (mainly for milk) maintained their rather slower rate of real decline (about 1.4%) throughout. Within the crops subsector, there were particularly marked differences in the rate of fall in real prices. Cereals and oilseeds prices fell at 2.2 and 2.3% per year over 1973-90 as a whole, but at 4.4 and 6.9% per year after 1983), while fresh vegetable prices actually rose in real terms.

Compared to these rates of change in farm output prices, real levels of prices of intermediate consumption commodities fell by 1.3% per year over the period 1973-90 (Graph 18). This average conceals a number of detailed features,

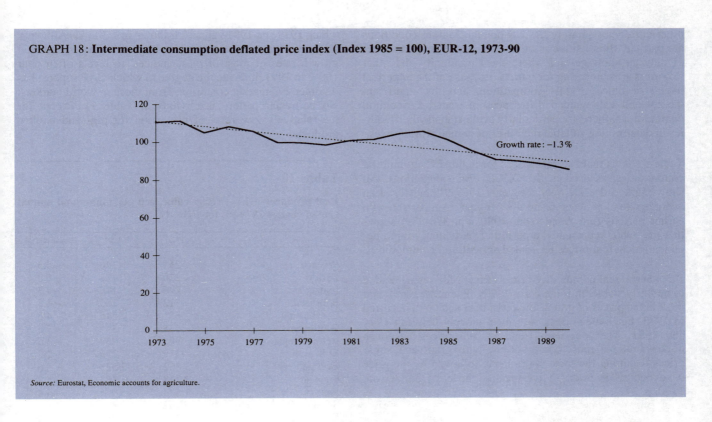

GRAPH 18: **Intermediate consumption deflated price index (Index 1985 = 100), EUR-12, 1973-90**

Growth rate: −1.3%

Source: Eurostat, Economic accounts for agriculture.

including a marked rise in real energy prices in the 1970s (+ 1.1% over the whole period) and an increase in plant protection product prices in the 1980s, while real fertilizer and feedingstuffs prices fell by 2.4 and 2.6%, respectively, during 1973-90. After 1983, real intermediate consumption prices fell by a high 3.1%.

It can thus be concluded that, over the whole period 1973-90, the EC cost-price squeeze in agriculture (the ratio of the price index of final agricultural output to that for inputs, i.e. the sectoral terms of trade) shows the expected decline, but not at a particularly rapid or consistent rate. Overall, the price relationship between outputs and intermediate consumption commodities tightened at an average rate of 0.3% per year (1.5 minus 1.2), but, after 1983, real prices of intermediate inputs fell faster than those of farm products, led by marked falls in fertilizer prices.

Moreover, this movement was not equally strong for all Member States: the Netherlands' ratio dropped by only 1% per year between 1975-79 and 1983-87, while the United Kingdom's rate was 1.9% per year. Both Spain (rise of about 15% 1975-79) and Portugal (fall of 20% 1980-87) show different patterns from those for the EC-10. Tangermann (1992), with a cost-price squeeze estimate of 0.6% per year

for the EC-10 over 1973-90, also finds that the decline in sectoral terms of trade was significantly less than that of real prices deflated by real GDP, and that in two Member States (Italy and Greece) sectoral terms of trade have even improved.

The balance of forces generating agricultural output trends over the past two decades has therefore differed between subperiods, countries and commodities. Overall, as expected, technical change has outweighed the price squeeze in offsetting relatively more expensive inputs and enabling farmers to expand production throughout the period as a whole. Crop output has expanded substantially and steadily (though with a varying mix) under a relatively slow decline in product prices, while livestock production has risen more slowly under greater cost-price pressure. In the later 1980s, milk quotas and more severe output price declines have actually stabilized livestock output.

The level of world market prices are both an important determinant of CAP expenditure and are affected by the Community's surplus disposal practices. On the other hand, EC border prices for agricultural cormmodities are also significantly affected by other influences, ranging from harvest conditions and policy decisions elsewhere in the world, to fluctuations in exchange rates between EC and

49

other currencies (mainly the US dollar). Market conditions are particularly sensitive in other parts of the world at times of unusual shortage and where the Community and other exporters are competing for outlets. Because of the imperfect nature of much of this competition, and the significant quality and value-added differences in traded agricultural commodities, there are particularly acute statistical difficulties in determining suitable measures of annual world prices.

Table 9 shows real external prices for major EC agricultural commodities, as used in the OECD PSE calculations. All show marked decline over the years 1979-91, mostly at an average rate of between 6 and 9% per year. Comparison with earlier periods (e.g. Sanderson, 1990, pp. 370-379) shows that the 1980s represented a period of particularly rapid decline in most real prices for traded agricultural commodities:

'In general, real commodity prices (except for sugar) tended to be fairly stable until the early 1970s. The most significant peak in the prices of grains, oilseeds, beef and lamb occurred in 1973, but butter prices rose most steeply between 1974 and 1981. The long-term trend in real prices has been downwards for most commodities, with grain and sugar prices declining the most since 1960, followed by the price of soybeans. The prices of livestock fell the least' (Sanderson, 1990, p. 372).

Table 9

Real external prices (1986 value, ecu per tonne) and annual rate of change 1979-91, for EUR-12[1]

	1979	1991	Growth rate (%)
Wheat	190	64	− 8.6
Barley	124	58	− 8.3
Maize	143	76	− 6.9
Soyabeans	334	153	− 6.4
Rapeseed	343	116	− 9.0
Sunflower	387	128	− 9.4
White sugar	297	194	− 6.7
Milk	136	85	− 5.4
Beef and veal	2 385	1 317	− 4.3
Pigmeat	1 722	873	− 6.3
Poultry	1 321	797	− 5.8
Sheepmeat	2 103	1 341	− 6.6
Eggs	961	703	− 5.5

[1] EUR-10 until 1986.
Source: PSE database, OECD.

The ratio between EC producer prices (Table 10) and external prices (Table 9) gives the nominal rate of protection, for

which 1979 and 1991 values are shown in Table 11. Although single-year data can be misleading, the very substantial growth rates of most of these indices, to levels often over 100% in 1991, indicate the degree to which CAP support has divorced EC market conditions from those in world markets. No particular pattern is obvious in Table 11, except for the relatively low rates of protection for pig- and poultry products.

Table 10

Real producer prices[1] (1986 value, ecu per tonne) and annual rate of change 1979-91, for EUR-12[2]

	1979	1991	Growth rate (%)
Wheat	261	140	− 5.3
Barley	230	123	− 5.3
Maize	236	149	− 4.3
Rapeseed	512	285	− 4.5
Soyabeans	635	346	− 4.8
Sunflower	635	345	− 3.8
Refined sugar	378	239	− 3.5
Milk	319	239	− 2.2
Beef and veal	3 862	2 523	− 2.6
Pigmeat	2 118	1 164	− 5.2
Poultry	1 628	955	− 4.4
Sheepmeat	5 102	3 800	− 1.4
Eggs	1 356	858	− 4.3

[1] The producer price is equal to the adjusted producer price, i.e. the producer price plus direct payments less levies.
[2] EUR-10 until 1986.
Source: PSE database, OECD.

Table 11

Nominal rate of protection (%) and annual rate of change 1979-91, for EUR-12[1]

	1979 (%)	1991 (%)	Growth rate (%)
Wheat	42	118	9.0
Barley	86	111	2.1
Maize	65	95	3.2
Soyabeans	90	125	2.8
Rapeseed	49	145	9.5
Sunflower	64	169	8.4
Milk	135	179	2.4
Beef and veal	62	92	3.3
Pigmeat	23	33	3.1
Poultry	23	20	− 1.2
Sheepmeat	143	183	2.1
Eggs	41	22	− 5.1

[1] EUR-10 until 1986.
Source: PSE database, OECD.

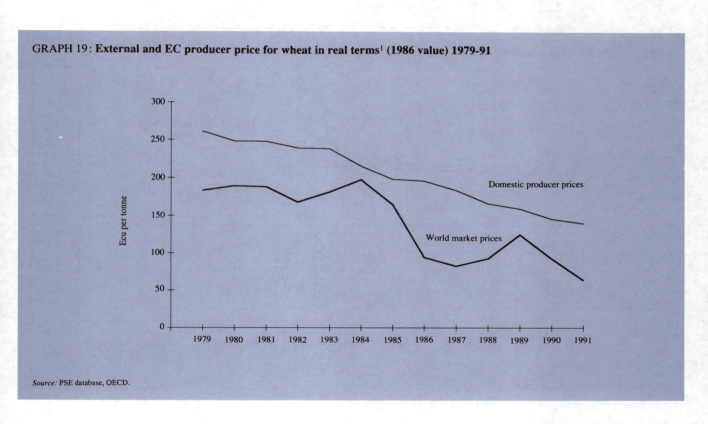

GRAPH 19: **External and EC producer price for wheat in real terms**[1] **(1986 value) 1979-91**

Domestic producer prices

World market prices

Source: PSE database, OECD.

Examination of trends in selected products shows that both EC and world prices have generally moved downwards, though with occasional peaks in the latter graphs barely reflected in the former. However, since these declines have been roughly parallel in absolute terms, the relative degree of protection as measured by the ratio has increased. Thus EC farm gate prices have followed a similar trend to world market prices as exemplified by the price of wheat (Graph 19), but they have not matched the rate of real decline, nor the short-term fluctuations (representing relative extra-EC shortages and gluts) in the latter.

3.2. Farming incomes

Sectoral income in EC agriculture is commonly measured by net value-added (NVA, or net product) per agricultural work unit (AWU, equivalent to a standard work year). Real NVA per AWU in EC agriculture increased by 1.4% per year over the period 1973-90 (Graph 20). For the EC-9, there was a slight decline between 1974 and 1978, followed by a fall of about 4% to 1980 (CEC, 1982, p. 101). After a recovery of 15% between 1980 and 1982, real NVA per AWU then stayed almost constant until 1988, and rose a further 10% in

1989 to a three-year plateau (CEC, 1993, p. 39). Since then, there has been some erosion, by 5% between 1991 and 1992, and a further 1.5% by 1993 (CEC, 1994, as reported in *Agra Europe*, 18 March 1994, p. E/8).

Overall, therefore, the NVA per AWU measure indicates that, at least until the 1990s, decline in the agricultural workforce has been just sufficient to keep real agricultural incomes on a slight and rather unsteady upward trend over the last 20 years, at an average rate of about 1% per year. Alternatively, it may be said that the level of farm incomes under the CAP has encouraged the displacement of farm labour at a rate only just fast enough to avoid a constant or declining trend. However, during the 1980s, average real GNP per person employed increased by around 2% per year, so that incomes from farming per person employed in agriculture have fallen in relative terms.

A recent study for the European Commission (Hill, 1992) has examined data and methods for estimating the incomes of agricultural households, i.e. those where the household head's main income source is independent activity in farming or his/her main occupation. This definition excludes many households whose farm holdings are included in other

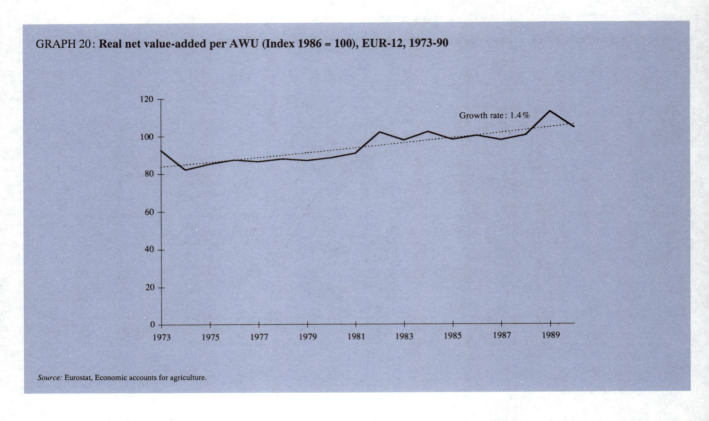

GRAPH 20: **Real net value-added per AWU (Index 1986 = 100), EUR-12, 1973-90**

Growth rate: 1.4%

Source: Eurostat, Economic accounts for agriculture.

agricultural statistics. For these 'agricultural households', the study concludes (Hill, pp. 30-31) that:

'Though typically only about two thirds of the total (income) comes from farming, there are substantial differences between Member States... . For those countries in which comparisons are possible, agricultural households appear to have average disposable incomes which are typically higher than the all-household average. The relative position is eroded or reversed when income per household member or per consumer unit is examined. In ... Germany and France, ... the relative disposable income situation of agricultural households seems to have been deteriorating over time. There is evidence that total household income is more stable than the income from independent agricultural activity (though) no clear relationship seems to hold between the relative stability of disposable income and farming income' (emphasis added).

Similar work over a longer period in the United States (reported in, e.g., Gardner, 1992, p. 77-78) indicates that any significant gap between farm and non-farm income disappeared during the 1970s (and has not reappeared for long since). Gardner concludes that, for the US, 'a sector-wide farm income problem no longer exists'. All this evidence makes trends in income from farming an unreliable

guide to the total personal income of farm households, with obvious policy implications.

4. Farming structures

4.1. Farm size

The numbers of EC agricultural holdings of various area sizes have shown markedly different trends when analysed by size group (Table 12). Within the EC-10, the total number of holdings over 1 hectare of utilizable agricultural area (UAA) — a cut-off point which eliminates over a million tiny holdings which barely qualify as 'farms' — fell from 6.6 million in 1970 to 4.8 million in 1987, a drop of 27%, or 1.8% per year on average (considerably slower than total labour input, AWU). The number of holdings between 5 and 20 ha UAA nearly halved in number from 2.4 to 1.3 million over the same period. However, the number of holdings between 20 and 50 ha in size fell by only 7%, while those over 50 ha UAA rose in number by 28% from 291 000 to 373 000, an annual growth rate of 1.5%. Very small holdings between 1 and 5 ha UAA fell in number by 25%, or 1.7% per year, with a slight rise after 1985.

Table 12

Number of holdings by size (in 1 000's), 1979-87

	Total	< 1 ha	1-5 ha	5-10 ha	10-20 ha	20-50 ha	> 50 ha
EUR-10							
1970	7 667		3 087	1 244	1 115	850	201
1975	7 100	703	2 728	1 044	938	867	325
1977	6 802		2 632	1 012	895	865	330
1979	6 820	1 362	2 494	923	847	852	338
1983	6 515	1 338	2 342	866	762	830	355
1985	6 359	1 321	2 275	826	751	816	367
1987	5 005		2 312	813	719	780	373
EUR-12							
1987	6 920		3 411	1 163	936	946	473

Source: EC-Commission, Agricultural situation in the Community, various issues.

There are therefore clear signs of differential structural effects along the area spectrum of EC farm size, with enlargement of larger holdings, which now occupy more than half of total EC UAA and relatively constant numbers (not necessarily identities) of very small holdings, while small to medium-sized farms of under 20 ha are disappearing at a relatively fast rate. The same pattern is evident in the statistics for cattle, dairy and pig herd size distributions in recent years, with growth in the numbers in the largest size categories, and decline in most of the smaller size groups.

The reasons for these developments are bound up with the maintenance of economic and technical viability, as farm businesses attempt to keep up household incomes and undertake necessary capital re-investment which in many cases is justifiable only with enterprise units of substantial size. 'Intermediate' farms (CEC, 1988, p. l9) are in continuous danger of financial failure through inadequate incomes or excessive debt burdens. Many of the CAP's structural measures over the last two decades have been directed at identifying those of such farms as may be helped towards renewed viability by temporary income supplements or investment assistance. Other farms have been seen as posing a 'social problem' to be tackled by various means, including pre-pensions for the Community's many elderly farmers (Table 13) (Frohberg 1993, Table S).

4.2. Specialization

Another aspect of structural development is the tendency towards greater specialization on EC farm holdings. Table 14 (Larsen 1992, Table 11) shows that the percentages of EC-9 farms containing a specified enterprise declined between 1975 and 1985 for all activities except sheep. Falls

were particularly marked for potatoes (34 to 18% of all holdings), root crops (22 to l0%) and pigs (13 to 7% for breeding sows), while only sheep maintained their dispersion amongst 10% of all holdings.

Table 14

Indication of production specialization in EUR-9

Percentage holdings with	1975	1985	Index 1985 on 1975
Crops			
Cereals	61	52	0.85
Potatoes	34	18	0.53
Sugar beet	6	5	0.83
Forage roots and tuber	22	10	0.45
Wine	31	30	0.97
Livestock			
Cattle	51	38	0.75
Dairy cows	37	24	0.65
Sheep	10	10	1.00
Pigs	38	22	0.58
Breeding sows	13	7	0.54
Poultry	55	36	0.65

Source: Statistical yearbook of agriculture, Eurostat, reported in Larsen 1992, Table 5.

Factors underlying the different rates of these developments may include the growing importance of locational advantage (wine and sugar), equipment capacity (cereals), and scarcity of management labour (farmers having less manual assistance). The technical ease or importance (in income terms) of

Table 13

Age distribution of farm holders by farm size and by Member State in 1987 (percent of farm holder in age class)

country	farm size	below 35	35 to 55	55 to 65	above 65	above 55
B	... < 10 ha	11.0	36.3	31.4	21.3	52.7
	10 ≤ ... < 30 ha	15.4	47.3	33.2	4.0	37.2
	30 ≤ ... < 100 ha	17.5	54.2	25.9	2.5	28.4
	... > 100 ha	14.3	57.1	28.6	0.0	28.6
DK	... < 10 ha	10.3	33.9	24.2	31.5	55.7
	10 ≤ ... < 30 ha	10.3	37.4	30.0	22.3	52.3
	30 ≤ ... < 100 ha	14.4	53.8	21.7	10.0	31.7
	... > 100 ha	12.9	61.3	16.1	9.7	25.8
D	... < 10 ha	12.3	48.3	28.9	10.6	39.5
	10 ≤ ... < 30 ha	17.7	54.2	26.3	1.9	27.2
	30 ≤ ... < 100 ha	17.4	59.1	22.1	1.4	23.5
	... > 100 ha	13.2	58.5	24.5	3.8	28.3
GR	... < 10 ha	5.6	37.5	27.7	29.2	56.9
	10 ≤ ... < 30 ha	5.5	49.1	29.8	15.5	45.3
	30 ≤ ... < 100 ha	6.5	53.3	28.3	12.0	40.3
	... > 100 ha	11.1	55.6	22.2	11.1	33.3
E	... < 10 ha	3.9	35.0	32.2	28.9	61.1
	10 ≤ ... < 30 ha	6.1	42.3	33.8	17.8	51.6
	30 ≤ ... < 100 ha	7.7	47.8	31.9	12.6	44.5
	... > 100 ha	8.1	47.7	28.7	15.5	44.2
F	... < 10 ha	5.8	31.4	33.9	28.8	62.7
	10 ≤ ... < 30 ha	11.1	40.6	38.1	10.1	48.2
	30 ≤ ... < 100 ha	14.6	53.0	28.6	3.8	32.4
	... > 100 ha	11.0	60.4	24.3	4.3	28.6
IRL	... < 10 ha	4.2	38.5	28.5	28.8	57.3
	10 ≤ ... < 30 ha	6.5	44.0	28.1	21.4	49.5
	30 ≤ ... < 100 ha	7.9	48.4	26.8	16.9	43.7
	... > 100 ha	8.8	47.1	26.5	17.6	43.1
I	... < 10 ha	5.3	34.2	31.6	28.8	60.4
	10 ≤ ... < 30 ha	6.8	39.4	32.8	21.0	53.8
	30 ≤ ... < 100 ha	8.2	42.9	30.1	18.8	48.9
	... > 100 ha	7.6	41.9	29.5	21.0	50.5
L	... < 10 ha	6.9	33.3	28.5	31.3	59.8
	10 ≤ ... < 30 ha	6.0	34.5	34.5	25.0	59.5
	30 ≤ ... < 100 ha	18.8	53.0	22.7	5.5	28.2
	... > 100 ha	28.6	57.1	14.3	0.0	14.3
NL	... < 10 ha	13.1	45.2	26.3	15.3	41.6
	10 ≤ ... < 30 ha	8.7	48.5	30.9	11.9	42.8
	30 ≤ ... < 100 ha	9.2	56.5	26.1	8.2	34.3
	... > 100 ha	0.0	66.7	33.3	0.0	33.3
F	... < 10 ha	5.2	36.2	28.8	30.3	59.1
	10 ≤ ... < 30 ha	5.8	38.2	32.1	24.0	76.1
	30 ≤ ... < 100 ha	7.4	39.5	32.1	21.0	53.1
	... > 100 ha	9.4	43.8	25.0	21.9	46.9
UK	... < 10 ha	7.5	42.3	23.0	27.2	50.2
	10 ≤ ... < 30 ha	7.0	39.2	28.3	25.5	53.8
	30 ≤ ... < 100 ha	7.8	46.0	28.5	17.7	46.2
	... > 100 ha	8.2	49.2	27.0	15.7	42.7

Source: Frohberg, 1992, Table 5.

combining farming enterprises with non-farm activities, whether on a continuous or seasonal basis, may also have altered. The reduction of market instability under the CAP might have been expected to encourage specialization due to the lessened attraction of diversification to counter commodity price risk. However, with potatoes still a non-CAP product and with the sheepmeat regime being introduced only in 1980, the pattern of specialization over the period analysed does not suggest that this has been a very strong influence.

4.3. Pluriactivity

In recent years, much attention (e.g. Arkleton Trust, 1988) has been paid to the phenomenon of pluriactivity (or multi-occupation) by farm households, i.e. the engagement by household members in activities additional to independent farming itself. Some investigators stress informal, social and cultural activities, as well as those which are remunerative, but the official statistics confine themselves to 'other gainful activities' (OGAs). Such activities may include:

(i) employment on other farms, as farm labourers or as farming contractors;

(ii) para-agricultural activities such as on-farm food processing (e.g. wine-making);

(iii) on-farm leisure enterprises, handicrafts, small-scale manufacturing or consultancy services carried out on or from the farm; and

(iv) off-farm activities ranging from part-time office work nearby to permanent 'full-time' employment or engagement in non-farming enterprises.

The importance of pluriactivity and/or part-time farming is indicated in Table 15, which shows that almost a third of all holders of agricultural holdings in the EC-10 have other jobs. More detailed data show that the percentage is highest in (West) Germany (42%) and lowest in the Netherlands (20%) and the United Kingdom (21%). Perhaps not surprisingly, the percentage of all holders with OGAs falls by farm size, from 35% in the (most numerous) category under 5 ha in area (Belgium and Germany highest at about 60%; Italy lowest at 29%), to 15% for the group over 50 ha in area (highest in Denmark at 25%; lowest in Belgium, Germany and the Netherlands at about 4%).

For the EC-10 as a whole, about 16% of spouses of farm holders have OGAs, but this proportion varies widely by country, from 55% in Ireland to 1% in the Netherlands. However, the proportion does not vary much by area size of farm.

Table 15

Dual activity by farm households, EUR-10, 1985

	Farmers	Spouses	Other family
Numbers ('000)			
Total	6 181	3 201	2 647
With other gainful activity (OGA)	1 882	514	819
Share with OGA (%)	30	16	31
— by size of holding			
< 5 ha	35	16	
5-20 ha	30	15	
20-50 ha	17	17	
50+ ha	15	19	
— by proportions of worktime on holding (%)			
< 50	44	19	
50-99	23	12	
100	10	9	

Source: Farm Structure: 1985 Survey: Main Results, Eurostat (1987) Vol. 5C Luxembourg, (Table X, pp. 122-3).

4.4. Rural labour markets

It is not sufficient to consider simply the development of farming incomes, even at household level, to understand the changes that have been at work on the occupational patterns of EC agricultural population. First, there are the adjustments in labour patterns on farms themselves. In addition to the farmer, labour can be supplied by his/her spouse and by other family members or by non-family workers, employed on a regular (full- or part-time) or irregular basis. The share of regular farm employment in the Community varies widely between Member States, from 0.4% of the total labour force in Greece, to 16% in Denmark, France and the Netherlands, and 33% in the United Kingdom. Though patchy, the official statistics (CEC, 1987 and 1992, Table 2.5.1.5) suggest a rise in these proportions over the last 15 years, while family contributions (generally the larger component) have fallen slightly.

The reasons for these developments are unclear. First, regular employees can provide a high level of skill and reliability, but involve the farm business in substantial fixed cash costs. Smaller family sizes, and increases in secondary and tertiary education, may reduce the number of younger people involved in farm activities. The use of machinery and more advanced technology discourages the participation of children who might later enter the regular workforce.

Second, there has been adjustment in off-farm employment. Improvements in communications have widened the horizons of farm people and generally reduced the segmentation of the rural labour force. Better roads and greater car ownership significantly increase the travel-to-work radius available to rural people. They also enlarge the areas of operation of agricultural services (input supply or output transport and processing), and thus affect farm-related sectors of employment, in addition to economies of scale in many of these services. Wider coverage of the electronic media (telephones, television, etc.) also lessens the effect of distance on rural employment patterns, partly by altering the industrial structure, and partly by putting rural people more closely in touch with urban standards and modes of living.

Both these factors suggest that immobility of the farm labour force, as a major underlying cause of the 'farm income problem' (where it exists), is likely to be of lessening importance. Farm work is always likely to possess its own special characteristics, attractive to some (but not all) in terms of its open-air nature, variety or responsibility, and experience. However, such a case can be made for many other occupations, and the increased content of technology and marketization involved in modern farming suggests that interflow of labour between farming and non-farming may increase.

5. Consumption

The consumption of agricultural products in the European Community involves substantial off-farm economic activity in the food processing and distribution sectors. The agri-foodstuffs industry has a turnover almost double the value of EC agricultural production, and employs some 2 million people (CEC, 1987, p. 43). Some parts of this industry (e.g. milk processing) are substantially in the hands of farmers in the form of cooperatives, etc., but others, especially further 'downstream', are run by independent concerns, both small and large, including multinational enterprises with oligopolistic characteristics. There is also a considerable amount of national and Community government regulation relating to food preparation and content.

The main features of EC food consumption patterns may be characterized as follows:

(i)   static or slowly growing aggregate consumption of major food products;

(ii) higher degrees of processing and added value in food products;

(iii) growing intra-Community trade in agricultural products;

(iv) convergence of national food purchase patterns;

(v)   increasing variety of available foods.

Table 16 shows consumption quantities per capita in the Community for about 20 farm products and product groups between 1979 and 1991, along with annual average rates of change. Apart from high growth rates in certain oilseeds, most rates of change in per capita consumption are low or negative. Rice and poultrymeat show relatively high rates of growth, while some coarse grains, and beef and veal, have declined per head over this l2-year period by over 1% per year.

Table 16

Consumption quantities (kg per head) and annual rate of change 1979-91, for EUR-12

	1979	1991	Growth rate
Total cereals[1]	432.6	405.1	− 0.5 %
Wheat	161.7	192.2	1.4 %
Common wheat	144.9	177.8	1.6 %
Durum wheat	16.8	14.46	0.9 %
Coarse grains	271.0	212.9	1.8 %
Barley	133.2	122.5	− 0.8 %
Maize	107.8	75.3	− 2.3 %
Oats	29.9	15.2	− 6.0 %
Rice	4.8	7.1	4.8 %
Oilseeds	57.5	85.1	4.1 %
Rapeseed	6.7	23.2	10.6 %
Soyabeans	45.4	48.3	1.0 %
Sunflowernt	5.4	13.5	11.0 %
Refined sugar	37.4	36.1	0.3 %
Milk	310.8	296.9	− 0.6 %
Beef and veal	26.0	23.0	− 1.2 %
Pigmeat	36.3	41.1	1.2 %
Poultry	13.6	19.1	3.1 %
Sheepmeat	3.5	4.4	1.9 %
Eggs	14.2	13.7	− 0.2 %

[1] Excludes rice, includes feed use.
Source: PSE database, OECD.

The share of food in total Community household expenditure has fallen steadily, from 20.4% in 1984 (in EC-12) to 15.1% in 1990. Taken together with low (and sometimes negative) rates of population change, these features account for the somewhat static overall aggregate consumption situation. Within the retail expenditure levels, the value share of farm products in food has fallen as a result of two factors: higher degrees of processing, and a fall in agricultural product prices relative to those of processing techniques and services.

These features are explicable in terms of low elasticities of demand. Price changes have a relatively small effect on the aggregate amounts of food purchased by EC consumers. Second, most foodstuffs exhibit low income elasticities: that is, as personal (household) incomes rise, the quantity of most foods bought increases by only a fraction of the proportional rise in incomes. For some 'inferior' foods, purchased quantities may even fall, as consumers switch to preferred commodities. However, within the European Community, sluggish growth in consumed quantities is especially noticeable as income levels, especially in the northern Member States, reach high levels.

The creation of the single market, with reduction in physical, economic and bureaucratic barriers to trade, has greatly encouraged internal trade in the Community. Between 1973 and 1985, intra-EC-9 trade in agricultural and food products (excluding fishery and forestry products) increased in current value from ECU 14.4 to 56.1 billion, a real rise of about 40%. After 1980, the real value of intra-EC-12 agricultural trade increased from ECU 67 to 88 billion by 1990, though with a slowdown in the later part of this period. Such rapid growth rates help to explain the behavioural developments in food consumption and variety noted above.

6. Trade and budget

6.1. Self-sufficiency

The more or less continuous rise in EC agricultural production over the post-war period has outstripped trends in consumption despite the positive demand factors of rising population and consumer income levels. Thus, over time, imports have been reduced, sometimes to virtually zero, and EC exports of some commodities have reached very substantial levels.

This changing balance of supply and demand has been primarily due to a combination of (a) strong market support via the common agricultural policy, (b) striking progress in farm technology, and (c) weak growth in aggregate consumer demand. These are not of course independent factors — high and stable output prices encourage the origin and adoption of technical change, and to some extent limit consumer demand.

Table 17 shows EC self-sufficiency indices for 1979 and 1991. Generally speaking, the lower the 1979 self-sufficiency figure, the faster the subsequent growth in the index. Most of the major commodities show self-sufficiency index values over 110 by 1991, with the exceptions of oilseeds (45 overall, with rapeseed and sunflowers over 90 and soyabeans at 10) and sheepmeat (82), which are both still in deficit.

Table 17

Degree of self-sufficiency for selected commodities, EUR-6, 1956/60, 1971/72-73/74 and EUR-12, 1989/90

	1956/60	1971/72 1973/74	1989/90
All cereals	85	97	110
Sugar	104	116	123
Wine	89	101	104
Butter	101	120	124
Beef and veal	92	86	107

Source: EC Commission, *Agricultural situation in the Community:* various issues, Brussels, pp. 187-9.

6.2. Exports and storage

Rising EC self-sufficiency has naturally led to increasing net Community surpluses of many agricultural commodities. Table 18 shows the surplus tonnages for most of the main temperate agricultural products between 1979 and 1991. In almost all cases, there has been an increase in potential net export quantities. As might be expected, the levels of and trends in net exports over the 1979-91 period as a whole more or less follow the pattern of the self-sufficiency indices (Table 18 above), though percentage rates of change are generally higher in magnitude. There are however the (important) exceptions of oilseeds, with a slight rise in imports of soybeans, and of milk, with a reduction in exports under quotas. Graph 21 shows the pattern of net export quantities for a few major commodities over the period 1979-91. There has been a fairly steady upward movement in total cereal surplus from zero at the start of the period to over 30 million tonnes in 1991, with beef also increasing, but unsteadily and at much lower tonnage levels). On the other hand, the trend in both milk product exports and oilseed imports reversed around 1983-84.

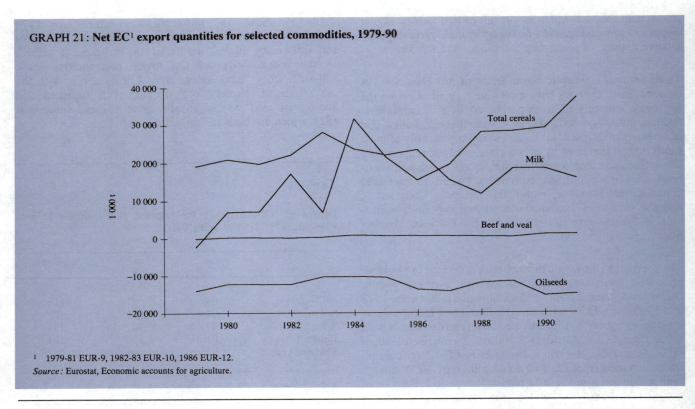

GRAPH 21 : Net EC[1] export quantities for selected commodities, 1979-90

[1] 1979-81 EUR-9, 1982-83 EUR-10, 1986 EUR-12.
Source : Eurostat, Economic accounts for agriculture.

Table 18

Surplus[1] quantities (1 000 tonnes), self-sufficiency indices and annual rate of change 1979-91, for EUR-12[2]

	Surplus quantities			Self-sufficiency indices		
	1979	1991	Growth rate (%)[3]	1979	1991	Growth rate (%)
Total cereals excluding rice	− 2 377	37 117		98.0	127.9	1.7
Wheat	5 091	26 126	9.5	111.7	141.4	1.1
Common wheat	5 518	20 397	7.3	114.1	134.9	0.6
Durum wheat	− 427	5 729		90.6	220.6	5.5
Coarse grains	− 7 468	10 991		89.8	115.7	1.9
Barley	3 861	10 570	8.3	110.7	126.3	1.0
Maize	− 10 984	1 145		62.2	104.6	3.9
Oats	− 345	− 724		95.7	85.5	− 0.4
Rice	− 66	− 56		94.9	97.6	0.6
Oilseeds	− 14 060	− 15 013	(1.2)	9.4	44.8	13.1
Rapeseed	− 612	− 290	(7.9)	66.3	96.2	0.9
Soyabeans	− 12 213	− 14 333	(1.6)	0.2	9.7	
Sunflower	− 1 235	− 390	(− 15.9)	15.4	91.2	14.3
Refined sugar	2 498	2 550	− 0.2	124.8	121.5	− 0.6
Milk	19 064	15 801	− 2.8	122.7	116.2	− 0.7
Beef and veal	− 114	1 010		98.4	113.4	0.8
Pigmeat	− 51	737		99.5	105.5	0.4
Poultry	192	354	0.5	105.2	105.6	− 0.3
Sheepmeat	− 291	− 255	(− 0.5)	69.0	82.4	1.3
Eggs	277	509		105.9	111.3	0.1

[1] Surplus is defined as production minus consumption.
[2] EUR-10 until 1986.
[3] Figures in brackets give the growth rate for the net import quantity.
Source: PSE database, OECD.

Table 19 shows EC 'intervention' stocks for selected commodities over recent years. The figures reveal considerable fluctuation, which can be related to both the variation in EC production over the years, and the state of world markets, which may encourage or discourage storage as against the alternatives of immediate export or internal disposal.

Table 19

EC intervention stocks (1 000 t)[1]

Marketing year	Common wheat	Barley	All cereals	Butter	Skimmed-milk powder
1983/84	3 318	222	4 335		
1984/85	10 256	2 013	13 927		
1985/86	10 312	5 296	18 502	1 122	646
1986/87	7 319	4 235	14 271	1 188	765
1987/88	4 567	3 916	11 748	640	240
1988/89	2 906	3 242	9 146	64	7
1989/90	5 521	3 320	11 795	820	21
1990/91	8 520	5 538	18 729	324	354

[1] At end of marketing year.
Source: EC Commission, *Agricultural situation in the Community,* (various issues).

By the seasonal nature of much agricultural production, considerable storage facilities (including processing facilities such as freezing plants) are necessary to maintain continuous supplies through the year. The uncertain nature of crop harvests also encourages the establishment and management of stocks by both governments and private companies in order to guard against the likelihood of shortage. Well-established financial institutions (advanced contracts, futures markets) have grown up for several products. It was therefore natural for CAP policy-makers to address the problem of surpluses by exploiting the existence of such arrangements.

'Intervention' buying and storage has played a very significant part in CAP activities at certain times. However, the costs involved (including physical depreciation of products, especially livestock products, in store) are substantial. They have, in 1992 values, increased from around ECU 1.5 billion 1973-75 to around ECU 5 billion 1990-92 (Table 20). In order to determine optimal policy, official economic judgments of future domestic and world market conditions must be made in order to decide when, and how long, to store, against other alternatives. When the Community is a major player in world markets, as for milk products, cereals and meats, or when substantial quantities of product are already entering subsidized domestic markets, these judgments (normally made weekly or monthly by management

committees of Commission and Member State representatives) must take into account the effects on prices and costs.

The CAP has therefore entered the storage system as an extra actor, both in the management of 'public' stocks and to subsidize private stockholding. To some extent at least, its activities have substituted for (rather than added to) purely private stockholding; the profit-making attractiveness of private enterprise in this area is reduced when government activity, backed by substantial financial resources and uncertain motives, is increased. To this extent, therefore, as well as in the light of other disposal mechanisms, the size of intervention stocks cannot be taken as an absolute measure of 'surplus' product, although they do indicate potential short-run and long-term inefficiencies in the operation of the CAP.

6.3. Budget expenditures

The evolution of the EC agricultural budget will be considered here. The structure of the budget is discussed in more detail in Chapter B.

Various factors have affected the trend of CAP revenue, including reductions in the volume of imports of the main EC-produced commodities, rising horticultural and other 'special' imports, Community enlargement, and the changing relationship between EC and world prices. In sum, CAP revenue of this kind has grown from levels below 1 billion UA (pre-ecu units of account, each roughly equal to USD 1) in the early 1970s to around ECU 2.5 billion in the late 1980s.

The expenditure side is represented by spending from the European Agricultural Guarantee and Guidance Fund (EAGGF, or FEOGA from the French equivalent). Guarantee Section expenditure — which carries nearly all the non-structural costs — increased tenfold in nominal terms over the 1970s and 1980s, from about 3 billion UA for the EC-9 in 1974 to ECU 30 billion for the EC-12 in 1990. This sum includes expenditure on rural development schemes linked to market operations, stock depreciation and disposal, and set-aside totalling about ECU 1.5 billion, but is net of cereal and milk co-responsibility levy revenue of the same magnitude. An additional ECU 3 billion approximately is expended on Guidance (structural) and other schemes.

In real terms, the rise in Guarantee spending is less marked, but still substantial, from around ECU 12 billion (1992 values) in 1973-75 to nearly ECU 31 billion in 1991, an average rate of 7.6%.

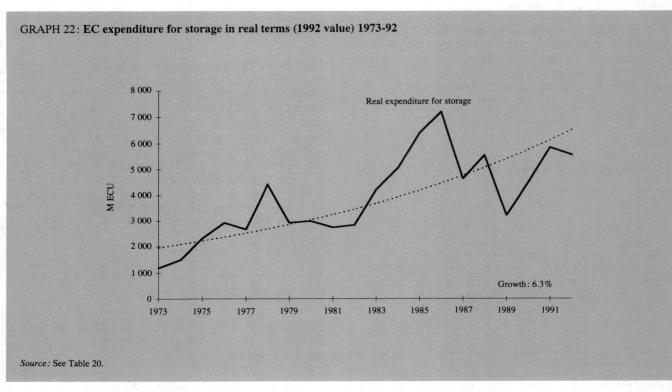

GRAPH 22: **EC expenditure for storage in real terms (1992 value) 1973-92**

Real expenditure for storage

M ECU

Growth: 6.3%

1973 1975 1977 1979 1981 1983 1985 1987 1989 1991

Source: See Table 20.

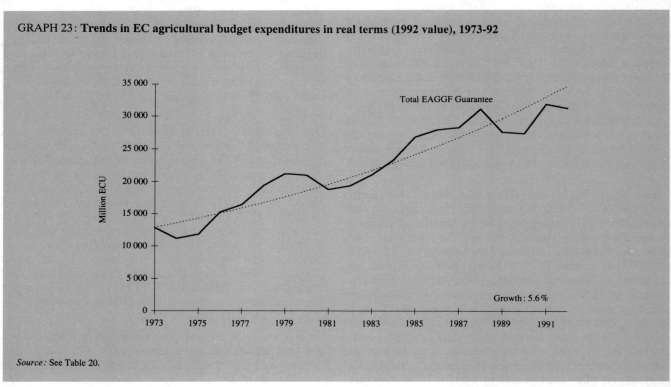

GRAPH 23: **Trends in EC agricultural budget expenditures in real terms (1992 value), 1973-92**

Total EAGGF Guarantee

Million ECU

Growth: 5.6%

1973 1975 1977 1979 1981 1983 1985 1987 1989 1991

Source: See Table 20.

The Guarantee total may be broken down into three components: storage expenditure, export refunds and 'other' — mainly direct price supports such as producer and consumer subsidies (Table 20). Since the mid-1970s, storage and export-refund expenditures taken together have roughly equated with the level of the third category. However, over the 18-year period as a whole, each in real terms has grown at average rates of 5.6, 6.3 and 7.6% per year respectively, and the proportions of these components have altered significantly from time to time, with a clear change in pattern about 1983.

Table 20

CAP budget expenditures, million ECU, 1992 value

	Expenditure for storage	Export refunds	Other EAGGF Guarantee	Total EAGGF Guarantee
1973	1 181	3 839	7 815	12 835
1974	1 503	1 769	7 893	11 164
1975	2 315	2 640	6 860	11 815
1976	2 939	3 922	8 359	15 221
1977	2 668	6 326	7 378	16 372
1978	4 426	7 902	7 040	19 368
1979	2 934	9 654	8 605	21 193
1980	2 994	10 094	7 860	20 948
1981	2 745	8 312	7 694	18 752
1982	2 833	7 425	9 076	19 335
1983	4 215	8 478	8 344	21 037
1984	5 048	9 465	8 796	23 309
1985	6 402	9 160	11 259	26 820
1986	7 189	9 368	11 392	27 949
1987	4 628	11 493	12 174	28 295
1988	5 539	11 836	13 762	31 137
1989	3 211	11 118	13 253	27 581
1990	4 493	8 469	14 385	27 346
1991	5 846	10 519	15 519	31 884
1992[1]	5 554	9 348	16 334	31 236

[1] Figures for 1992 are appropriations.

Source: For the years 1973-85: Koester and Tangermann, 1989. For the years 1986-92: *The agricultural situation in the Community,* various issues.

Up to that time, real spending on storage increased relatively gradually from about ECU 1 to 3 billion, while export refunds grew rapidly from 1974 to reach nearly ECU 8 billion in 1980. 'Other' expenditure fluctuated around ECU 8 billion. After the early 1980s, real storage expenditure increased very rapidly to over 6.4 billion in 1985, before falling erratically back to about 4 billion by 1990. Meanwhile, export expenditure, having dipped in 1981-82, rose again to a peak of ECU 9 billion in 1988, falling thereafter to 1990 as the US drought of that year pushed up world prices. Other forms of price support doubled in size to over ECU 16 billion

in 1992, thus restoring the position of the mid-1970s when this component dominated the other two combined.

The Agricultural Fund is an integral part of the Community budget, and the net cost of the CAP is therefore financed from non-agricultural sources, i.e. import taxes on manufactured products, VAT-based contributions from Member States, and the 'fourth', GNP/GDP-based, financial resource. Since the first of these is relatively small and rather static in amount, and is linked to GATT-agreed tariff rates, it is reasonable to ascribe the net budgetary cost of the CAP to the general tax-raising systems of the Member States, i.e. a mixture of personal and corporate direct income taxes, and indirect taxes such as VAT on goods and services.

7. Evolution of the CAP until 1992

7.1. Introduction

Chapters B and C provide an economic framework for examining the development of the CAP since its introduction in the 1960s. Chapter B explains the transfer and real income effects of various support instruments. Chapter C attempts to explain agricultural policy development, as represented by the types and levels of the various instruments utilized, in terms of attempts by the political system to redistribute income (in this case towards farm producers) while minimizing the economic costs (distortionary and administrative) of doing so. The specific development of agricultural policy in any one country or group of countries is seen as depending ultimately on the evolution of economic fundamentals in the agricultural sector itself and on wider technological, economic and political developments in society as a whole.

Application of this framework to the CAP thus requires recognition and understanding of both these sets of underlying developments. The preceding sections of this chapter have set out the evolution of trends in EC agricultural production, consumption and trade, as well as those in farm prices, incomes and structures. It is clear from the statistics reported in these sections that over the past three decades there has been marked and persistent, if not regular, change in most of the variables studied. In terms of technology, food self-sufficiency and farm labour levels, amongst other measures, the Community in the 1990s finds itself in a very different position than was the case in the late 1950s and early 1960s.

As regards more basic socio-economic developments, the two key economic features are the substantial rise in general living standards in the Community since the 1960s, and the much reduced share of agriculture in EC GDP. Higher real incomes are associated not only with a lower share of consumer expenditure on food (and especially the share paid for raw foodstuff materials), but also with significant changes in the population's way of life. These changes have been partly associated with the demographic drift from the countryside to urban areas, or at least away from land-based occupations, and partly with changing recreational activities and increased environmental concerns. In most EC countries, public expenditure has risen to about 40% of GDP, reflecting increased involvement of government in both economic activity and social welfare. This has altered public perceptions and expectations of policy, as well as developing governmental experience of new policy administration systems.

The internal and external political and institutional structure of the Community has also not been static. The CAP was set up by the Six with the main negotiations being concerned with reconciliation of the levels (rather than types) of existing market price support between France and Germany. Other matters, such as the Community's attitude to external agricultural trade, the ultimate financial responsibility for product surpluses, and the relative importance of market ('Guarantee') and structural ('Guidance') intervention in agriculture were largely ignored, or regarded as irrelevant at the time. By the 1990s, the Community had experienced three enlargements (and the incorporation of East Germany). Amongst the Twelve can now be found a much wider range of agricultural and socio-economic conditions, and the budget situation of the Community has become both more serious and more complex. Decision-making on the CAP has also altered, with a shift away from annual fixings of the common support prices to the formulation and adjustment of longer-term and much more complex policy instruments, now within the single market. Input to this decision-making from the representatives of farm producers and agri-business has become oriented to the Commission and Council of Ministers in Brussels rather than national capitals.

Externally, the post-war background of European reconstruction, the Cold War and decolonization has given way to the rise of the newly-industrialized countries in the Far East, grave crises in much of Africa, and the many ramifications of the break-up of the Soviet Union, including the liberalization of Central Europe. The transformation of the Community from major reliance on the United States for agricultural and other supplies to recurrent tension over export competition, often in the context of depressed world markets, has also altered the economic and political environment within which the development of the CAP must be assessed.

Against this background, the rest of this chapter discusses the developments that have taken place in CAP instruments over the last 30 years or so. The various policy methods utilized — market support, direct income payments, and various additional instruments — are explained in terms of the changing pressures impinging on the policy-makers of the time. The developments are grouped into four phases, although it will be stressed that the various components of the CAP have often co-existed, albeit in different forms and importance. The material also provides a framework for assessing possible future developments in the CAP under current pressures for reform (Chapter D).

7.2. Inception of the CAP

The inception of the CAP by the Community of Six took place during the long post-war recovery in economic prosperity in continental Western Europe. The restoration and renewal of manufacturing industry and the economic infrastructure of communications, energy supplies and housing were matched by equally striking progress in the technology of agriculture, in the form of mechanization and intensification of livestock production, to be shortly followed by advances in crop production and protection. Increased farm output as a consequence of this progress found a ready market in the increasingly affluent urban markets, but only for a few products did this displace imports or result in exports to third countries.

In structural terms, European agriculture remained a problem sector. Low incomes persisted on the numerous small farms, even while the inherent labour surplus gradually dispersed to the towns and cities where employment in the growing manufacturing and service sectors was assured. Many of these farms were substantially self-sufficient as regards such inputs as animal feed and capital works, though the efforts of national extension services, both public and private, was encouraging dependence on external supplies and assistance for such activities as fertilization and insemination.

With the possible exception of the Netherlands, all six countries had traditionally pursued agricultural policies based on market price support. However, early efforts in the Benelux countries, and the failed proposals for a 'Green Pool' High Authority for European agriculture along the lines of the Coal and Steel Community, had shown the problems of agreeing a common framework for agricultural policy. The degree of trade preference to be awarded to partner States and to third countries, the basis for determining the methods and levels of support, and the relative roles of Member-State governments and Community authorities, were all highly contentious issues. Amongst other effects, these considerations isolated the United Kingdom and hence

Denmark and Ireland from the various discussions of the 1950s.

The Spaak Report which preceded the Treaty of Rome left several crucial aspects of agricultural policy unresolved, but it did determine in a forceful way the fundamental question as to whether agriculture should form part of the new Community's arrangements: the Treaty specified that there should be (uniquely) 'a common policy in the sphere of agriculture' (Article 3), and the objectives of the policy were laid out in the well-known paragraph of Article 39. These objectives make no specific reference to the Community's agricultural self-sufficiency or trade policy, although Article 110 aims at '... the harmonious development of world trade'.

The 1958 Stresa Conference, which was convened to draw up proposals for the CAP, recognized the emerging issues of trade and over-production, but this was done with little attention to the international implications. Possible United States objections to the nascent policy were weakened by that country's generally benevolent attitude to the emerging Community on wider political and economic grounds, and by its rejection of the *montant de soutien* proposal that each country should be authorized a given level of support. Instead, the attention of the Commission and the national governments of the Six in 1960-62 focused on the establishment of a system of market price support, the general dismantling of tariffs on intra-EC trade and the introduction of a common external tariff, along with the detail of the initial CAP regulations themselves.

The implementation of the CAP during the mid-1960s established an internal market for agricultural products, with a rather rigid system of market protection for nearly all farm products, based on fixed Community-wide ('common') support 'target prices'. Three basic instruments were introduced in order to maintain CAP market prices. First, import levies, with rates varied daily or weekly according to offer prices for extra-Community supplies, forced external competition to surmount a 'threshold price' set to ensure 'Community preference' on internal markets. Second, should domestic supplies threaten to lower the Community market price below the 'intervention price', agencies were empowered to purchase product for storage or other disposal. Third, export 'refunds', again varying according to world market conditions, were to be made available to enable Community supplies to be sold to third countries.

The explanation for this approach lies primarily in the historical situation of the Six (their pre-existing policies based on administrative and trade considerations), and in the overriding contemporary need to implement a common policy within the framework of the new Community. Other forms of supportive intervention were available, such as the British system of deficiency payments, but these would have involved large payments from the as yet small Community budget, with awkward questions on the method of its financing, whereas market support promised import levy revenue which could be used to offset, and perhaps cover, CAP expenditures. (For durum wheat, olive oil and oilseeds, a 'premium' system much like deficiency payments was in fact introduced — along with problems of fraud — but these were localized products with limited market shares. For sugar, a major product with severe regional imbalances in costs, a special system of production quotas and producer levies, had to be introduced via that product's processing sector.) In addition, the administration necessary to implement direct payments to farmers based on market transactions did not exist in many parts of the continent, in contrast to Britain where detailed regulation of farming and food in a largely urbanized nation had been applied in wartime.

The economic burden of agricultural market support, especially at the relatively high levels eventually agreed, fell on the consumers of the Six, but at retail level they had become accustomed to food being expensive and indeed until lately scarce, and this was not felt as a major impact of the new policy. International trade and technology in highly processed foodstuffs had not yet grown to a level at which major processing companies could object on grounds of unfair competition.

The method of market price support — variable import levies keeping domestic prices steady and effectively insulating the Community from fluctuations in world market prices, rather than fixed levies or tariffs — reflected the widespread view that world markets were unreliable and sometimes artificial, and indeed dominated by the United States against whose hegemony the Community was at least in part a political expression. It was considered that the family farm (written into the final Stresa resolution as 'the essential foundation of agriculture in Western Europe'), required a stable economic environment for its successful transformation into a viable unit. On the other hand, as Tracy (1989, p. 269) has pointed out: 'it was fortunate for world trade that the Commission withdrew its original proposal to regulate imports quantitatively on the basis of annual balance sheets of availabilities', since this would have brought in a much more dirigiste type of policy. Trade disputes with the United States during the 1960s — particularly over poultry and oilseeds — reinforced the feeling that a high degree of Community self-sufficiency in agricultural products was desirable, and that this justified a substantial buffer between internal and external markets.

The effects of this initial phase of the CAP were significant increases in production. Technical advances and structural change in agriculture led to marked increases in farm output, which grew substantially (by about 30% between 1963 and 1973), outstripping slackening demand. Although self-sufficiency grew for most commodities, it fell for some products with income-elastic demand, such as beef and fresh fruit and vegetables. This reduced levy revenue and eventually required substantial expenditures on intervention purchases and exports of cereals, dairy products and sugar. By 1972, Guarantee expenditure absorbed over 2 billion UA (two thirds of the Community's overall budget) compared to agricultural levy revenue of only 800 million UA.

Although farm incomes increased in real terms, incomes in the rest of the economy rose faster, leaving producers with a feeling that they were being maltreated in comparison to the rest of society. The Community's annual price-fixings became steadily more difficult under the budgetary pressure and in the context of still-low inflation, which prevented the politically-easier lowering of real support prices via small nominal rises or freezes.

A further factor hindering the smooth evolution of the CAP was the increasingly difficult political and monetary situation. In 1965-66, French anxiety over the accretion of Commission powers led to the Luxembourg compromise over majority voting, thus making decision-making subject to national veto. The 1969 re-alignments of the franc and the German mark led to the invention of monetary compensatory amounts (MCAs), as devices to avoid cost-push inflation (in France) and negative farm-income effects (in Germany). These MCAs represented a departure from the principle of a common market, and introduced a new element of national flexibility into the CAP.

The budgetary consequences of the growth in market surpluses, and the slow rate of structural adjustment, led to the 1968 Mansholt Plan, which envisaged prices playing a more effective role in ensuring a balance between demand and supply, while the output-increasing effect of creating 'modern production units' was to be offset by the retiral or transfer of five million hectares of land and five million farm people, and the conversion of dairy herds to beef production (then considerably lower than consumption). After considerable debate, the plan was rejected, on the grounds that it threatened the existence of too many family farms, and in all represented too radical a break in policy-making from the short-term adjustment of market price support.

7.3. Enlargement

The consequences of this failure to reform the CAP as soon as its inherent problems became apparent were disguised by a number of events in the 1970s. The 1973 accession of the

United Kingdom, Ireland and Denmark (a net deficit region), and the global economic turmoil successively experienced in the grains, beef, oilseeds, energy and financial markets, did much to hide underlying international and EC trends in agricultural product markets, and allowed ministers to take decisions which were later to have serious long-term consequences. Serious drought in the mid-1970s added to the disruptions. Throughout the mid-1970s, the outlook for world agricultural prices and patterns of farm product trade was exceptionally unclear. This, together with the determination of the Community to establish the CAP as fully recognized in international trade negotiations, meant that the outcome of the GATT Tokyo Round was limited in the agricultural area to concessions on tropical products.

The question of agricultural trade was one of the main factors that led to the United Kingdom staying outside the original Community. Although the UK's domestic agricultural production had risen significantly during the 1950s and 1960s (so much so that the system of deficiency payments had to be modified in the 1960s on account of budgetary cost), the UK remained a leading world food importer, especially from its traditional suppliers in the Commonwealth as well as its two European neighbours. The 1973 enlargement of the Community from the Six to the Nine therefore involved some major adjustments in trade patterns. Several of these adjustments were handled by special arrangements, such as for New Zealand supplies of butter and sheepmeat, and Commonwealth sugar, but the enlargement meant the virtual loss of the UK market to a wide range of non-EC countries.

UK farm production was stimulated by the prospect and then actuality of higher EC support prices (especially as transition to these prices was accelerated by market and monetary developments in the mid-1970s). UK self-sufficiency in temperate food products rose from its mid-1960s level of 65% to over 75% by the beginning of the 1980s, with the growth of substantial British exports of cereals. Thus, the breathing-space afforded to the CAP by UK entry was short-lived. Although intra-EC trade was stimulated, strong productivity growth stimulated by the relatively generous price awards of the 1970s inspired by favourable world market price developments, and sluggish demand growth, led to an increasing degree of Community market imbalance in many agricultural sectors, in particular cereals (where the problem was exacerbated by the low-duty entry of cereal substitutes from third countries) and milk.

Compared to the widespread and substantial intervention on agricultural product markets, structural policy received relatively limited attention during the early years of the CAP, despite the consensus that poor structures were at the root of many of the problems of European agriculture. The original financial plan (Regulation 25/62) for the CAP was to allocate one third of the FEOGA budget to the Guidance Section for 'structural measures', i.e. for assistance towards the modification of farming patterns by (for example) farm consolidation, labour re-training and capital investment. The intention was the joint one of easing the adjustments widely seen as necessary in the small-scale post-war structure of much European farming, and improving the efficiency and viability of the remaining farms. Since 1964, FEOGA grants have been available for a proportion of the costs of approved investments relating to the production or marketing of agricultural commodities. In 1972, just prior to the entry of the United Kingdom, Ireland and Denmark, three 'socio-structural' directives derived from the rejected Mansholt Plan were introduced, dealing respectively with farm moderniza-tion, cessation of farming and land re-allocation, and the provision of guidance and training in new skills.

In 1975, the 'Less Favoured Areas' (LFA) Directive (75/268) introduced the concept of regional discrimination in the application of agricultural policy, permitting Member States to grant annual subsidies ('compensatory allowances', paid on livestock units or crop areas) and enhanced rates of farm improvement grants to producers in certain areas suffering from natural physical handicap, with partial reimbursement from FEOGA. Such discrimination was seen as the only feasible way to approach the desired income redistribution amongst farmers (and, taking budgetary contributions into account, amongst countries) while adhering to the principle of common (single) market price support.

Thus, in practice, this part of the CAP became a mixture of 'adjustment' measures geared to speeding up and compensat-ing for agricultural restructuring on the one hand, and of 'support' measures explicitly or implicitly retarding such adjustment on the other. The application of such measures was also patchy, with a considerable degree of selectivity being exercised, both by Commission officials in the approval of individual projects, and by Member States in the choice of LFA designations and the level of nationally-financed grants. Perhaps because of this, Guidance Section expenditure has approximated only 5% of the total Agricultural Fund instead of the one-third share originally envisaged.

The explanation for this hesitant and limited approach to the structural arm of the CAP lies in a mixture of political, administrative and economic factors. The six original Mem-ber States shared a common problem of non-viable farms and out-of-date infrastructure, but to different degrees and with different ideas as to how these matters might be approached, for example, as between the small and densely populated Netherlands and the extensive regional problems of Southern Italy. The existence of other Community instru-ments in the form of the Regional and Social Funds and the European Investment Bank (and of national and regional

schemes in member countries) created problems of allocating funds and responsibilities. The administrative burden of individual farm projects (until 1977, without even a pro-gramme framework) contrasted with the relative simplicity of a common price and market policy for standard agricultural commodities.

The policies also reflected a trade-off between improving the efficiency and competitiveness of Community production on the one hand, and reducing regional disparities on the other. Indeed, it has been argued (Fennell, 1987, p. 178) that the structural legislation is concerned at least partly to counteract adverse distributional effects of the market support policy, by modifying the operation of the laws of comparative regional competitiveness, by assisting those with limited means to overcome entry barriers to new levels of pro-ductivity, or by easing the adjustment path for those unable to compete within changing market circumstances (all examples of correction of perceived market failure). The greater use of the much more flexible directive instrument rather than the universally applicable regulation, the variety of rates of support between different regions, countries and schemes, and the complex nature of the FEOGA Guidance accounts, all reflect these considerations.

7.4. Surplus disposal and containment

The situation of the CAP as it approached its third decade indicated that substantial adjustments to its methods, if not in its objectives, would be needed to avoid complete breakdown. Declines in world prices after the short-lived 'world food crisis' of the end of the 1970s added to costs. Commodity surpluses emerged, for which the intervention authorities of the Community were buyers of last resort, or which could only be exported with the assistance of subsidy payments. As a result of these changing fundamentals, budgetary expenditure on the CAP doubled between the mid-1970s and 1980.

The policy developments during the 1980s may be seen as an attempt to deal with the surplus situation without fundamentally changing the market support system.

At the same time, real agricultural incomes (net value-added at factor cost per agricultural work unit) fell by 10% between 1978 and 1980. Structural change, though proceeding apace (the total number of EC-9 farms, and the numbers of those engaged in agriculture, both fell at about 3% per year between 1975 and 1980), was not sufficient to reduce the underlying problems (average farm size in the EC-10 increased only from 15.5 to 17.3 ha over the period 1977-87), and rising EC employment generally made unattractive schemes which encouraged the out-migration of farming people. International monetary disorder led to substantial expenditure on monetary compensatory amounts. These problems were recognized in the Commission 'Reflections' and 'Guidelines' documents of 1980 and 1981.

In the milk sector, deliveries to EC-10 dairies began to rise strongly above consumption levels after 1976, reaching a surplus of about 12 million tonnes (14% of consumption — some of which was subsidized) by 1981. Co-responsibility levies or producer marketing taxes (see below) that had been introduced for milk in 1977, and varied in rate between 0.5 and 2.5% of the target price, but Commission efforts ('Guidelines' report, 1981) to add a 'super' or supplementary levy on supplies over a reference quantity and to impose a tax on milk from 'intensive' farms were resisted by the Council, in favour of a 'prudent' support price policy. Investment aids for the dairy sector were limited but not eliminated, and a number of conversion schemes designed to encourage dairy farmers to convert to beef or sheep production or to go out of production had limited success.

In cereals, the EC's degree of overall self-sufficiency had risen from about 85% before the first enlargement to 100% by the start of the 1980s, thus converting the Community from its traditional role as a major world importer towards that of an exporter with the implication that the disposal prices fall from the cif price to the lower fob price. For wheat and barley, the Community was already exporting substantial tonnages by 1980, while remaining an important buyer of maize. The growth in EC usage of the so-called cereal substitutes (manioc, cereal residues, maize gluten feed, fruit pulp, etc.) on which import duties and tariffs were bound under the GATT, aggravated the problem of surplus soft wheat and barley. 'Voluntary' import quotas on manioc were eventually negotiated with Thailand and other EC suppliers, but equivalent efforts on maize gluten feed with the United States failed. At home, no major changes in policy were effected, other than the weak 'guarantee threshold' regime for determining support price changes.

The greater complexity of the meat sector and its products made the development of the CAP in this area more varied. Following the 'beef crisis' of the early 1970s, production fell below consumption throughout the second half of the 1970s, but self-sufficiency rose above 100% by 1981. In addition to intervention buying and export subsidies, expenditure on which had become less onerous, a number of 'premium' or direct-payment schemes were applied under the CAP after 1975. A slaughter premium was operated in the United Kingdom as a successor to that country's pre-CAP deficiency payments system, while Italy, Ireland and later Greece operated a calf premium scheme in support of their producer groups. For sheepmeat, a common market organization was introduced only in 1980, after the accession of the United Kingdom, but before that of Greece, both countries with important sheep and goat sectors. As with beef, a slaughter premium was applied in the UK, but an annual ewe premium was payable elsewhere. For both beef and sheepmeat, a number of concessionary import schemes were in operation, as a result of historical trade links and previous GATT agreements.

Aware of the sensitivity of beef consumption to price, and the costs of freezing and storage of this product, the Commission attempted to limit market intervention in price and quantity, e.g. via quality, sex and carcass-portion criteria, to utilize private storage aids and consumer subsidy schemes, and to design further direct aids. In 1980, it introduced a suckler (beef) cow premium, and in 1987 a 'special' beef premium was paid on male animals. Together with the side-effects of the imposition of milk quotas after 1984 (which triggered a large supply of cow beef), these factors pushed the EC from a net-import position in the 1970s to becoming a major world exporter in the 1980s. These developments required large export-subsidy expenditure and created considerable international friction.

The variety of these developments, arising from the different situations on the various commodity markets, and the different technical alternatives open to the Commission, make it difficult to summarize their economic rationale and effects, except to characterize them as disparate and uncoordinated efforts to contain the rise in surpluses and the consequent growth in CAP budgetary expenditure. The size of the transfers from consumers to agricultural producers appears to have played a much less significant role in policy decision-making.

It is clear that straightforward reduction in the level of market price support, which would have diminished the economic inefficiencies inherent in the basic shape of the CAP, was deeply unpopular. The Agricultural Council regularly undermined Commission efforts to lower support prices at a faster rate during the 1980s. The strong lobbying powers of the farmer interests in Community Member States undoubtedly played a large part in this, coupled with the reduced incentives attaching to the collective financial and decision-making mechanisms of the EC. Thus, despite various weakenings of the intervention-purchasing system, the level of producer income support and of the consumer/taxpayer costs of the CAP remained high as world market disposal prices fall at an increasing rate. Complaints grew in intensity from third countries, particularly Australia, New Zealand and the United States, which was especially angered by the trade-diversion threat of the Iberian enlargement and by the effects of the CAP's highly supportive oilseeds regime.

Given a fixed target or other 'official' price, a co-responsibility or producer tax has the effect of lowering returns to producers (usually on marketings rather than gross production, so that commodities produced and consumed or utilized on the same farm are exempt), while leaving consumers (who would include livestock producers in the case of feed cereal production) unaffected. The attraction of this instrument in the context of the CAP has lain in the discouragement to production while maintaining the transfer from consumers. Over 1989-91, about 20% of the gross financial cost of the CAP cereal regime was offset in this way, and about half the gross cost of the much older sugar regime, in which the levies are attached to quotas. In terms of economic efficiency, co-responsibility levies (as negative output subsidies) bring some reduction in resource-use distortion due to lower than otherwise levels of domestic production, and perhaps slightly higher world price levels due to the parallel fall in exportable surpluses, while, as the name implies, part of the financial burden is switched from taxpayers to producers.

Despite these attractions, wider and more intensive use of the co-responsibility levy approach in the EC has probably been discouraged by the potential for administrative difficulties and costs. Levy payment could be (fraudulently) evaded via such methods as unrecorded farm-to-farm sales and merchant under-recording, and (legally) avoided through changes in affected production systems and markets, for example on-farm feed-mixing and milk-processing and artificial ownership arrangements. There has also been a political tendency to reduce the coverage of the tax by exempting certain categories of producers (e.g. small producers, or those in less favoured areas) from part or all of its impact, in order to introduce the levy more easily in the first place, and to satisfy particular interest groups with fewer complications than would arise with a separate targeted scheme.

Given starting values of support price, domestic supply and demand, and supply/demand parameters (including the rate of shift in supply), the economic effects of the quantum systems of guarantee thresholds and budgetary stabilizers turn on the settings of the maximum quantities eligible for full support, and the degree of reduction in support price for 'excess' output. Compared to the co-responsibility levy, the system has the financial advantage of limiting (and perhaps reducing) taxpayer exposure to the cost of surplus disposal, while from the viewpoint of economic efficiency it offers a gradual lowering of resource-use and consumer-choice distortions. The system also requires policy implementation only at the level of the Council of Ministers and their advisors, avoiding the need to monitor and administer at farmer or trader level. In practice, these attractions were offset by somewhat generous settings of the maximum quantities, uncertainty and controversy over actual pro-

duction levels, and the tendency towards increasing EC agricultural protection arising from declining world prices and the 'green money' system.

For several commodities, efforts were made to stimulate domestic consumption, either directly, by offering cheaper supplies to the market by means of consumer subsidies, or by marketing campaigns financed by Community funds such as co-responsibility levy revenue. The efficiency of these schemes has been criticized, since it is necessary to try and ensure that subsidized demand does not simply replace normal market consumption of the same or other products. Attempts to do this have often led to high administrative costs and fraud levels.

Direct supply control was attempted only for milk during the 1980s, in addition to the original regime for sugar. The explanation of these actions lie in a combination of technical feasibility (most milk and sugarbeet has to pass through central processing facilities where output can be monitored and punitive levies for excess production applied), and urgent financial significance (both commodities, especially milk, involve substantial budgetary expenditures, and the pace of crisis in the dairy sector was alarming). The economic effects of this instrument are to limit resource distortion (in that the marginal production is eliminated) and some financial burden, but as applied the milk quotas did not reduce consumer costs, and the aggregate quota level was set (and kept, despite adjustment) some 15% above unsubsidized consumption levels of dairy products, so that considerable taxpayer burdens persisted. In addition, individual quotas attracted a market value through their transferability with or without the land to which they were initially allocated (with a windfall gain to those land-holders). In turn, these values created several major administrative problems, in disputes over the initial allocations (the SLOM cases), in landlord-tenant relationships (farm workers were not generally considered), and in territorial and other questions of transferability. Finally, there were important downstream effects arising from the limitation on (heretofore rising) milk output, primarily in the closure of milk-processing plants, many in rural settlements. As had happened with the national sugar quotas, the milk quotas became embedded into the policy and capital-asset systems, and resistance to them slowly evaporated.

Various other problems and attempted solutions during this period may be mentioned. The search for alternative farm enterprises was one, with various schemes to diversify farm production. The strong support given to oilseeds — a major source of protein for animal feed, in which the Community was in substantial deficit — resulted in a rapid growth of arable area that might otherwise have been devoted to cereal production, via a processor/producer subsidy (normal market support being prevented by GATT bindings on import tariffs). Though successful in these terms, the regime became increasingly expensive during the 1980s, and created major tensions with the United States. Agri-environmental schemes and set-aside schemes were experimented with in attempts to restrict the amount of land being devoted to commodities in surplus. The production of several 'southern' products, such as wine, olive oil and tobacco, was stimulated by CAP support (and the entry of new Mediterranean Member States), and emerging surpluses were first tackled by a variety of consumption and 'withdrawal' (i.e. destruction) subsidies and schemes, and then by increasingly severe controls on areas and subsidies to encourage a switch to higher-quality and more popular varieties.

As the 1980s progressed, the Community's budgetary crisis deepened as a result of accumulating surpluses and a strong downward trend in world prices despite a rise in the dollar until 1984. Initially, efforts were directed towards modifications to the support-price mechanisms. Smaller and smaller nominal rises in support price rises were implemented over the years, intensifying the cost-price squeeze. Intervention rules were tightened, thus weakening the market-support role of this instrument. However, it was clear that this 'rigorous' price policy was not sufficient to solve the crisis, and that some form of production controls would be necessary. A preliminary form of such controls were the 'guarantee thresholds' introduced for several products, including cereals, milk, some oilseeds and certain fruits. Under this system (a version of the French 'quantum' approach), support prices for the forthcoming market year were to be reduced automatically if aggregate production exceeded a pre-set level, but the starting-point for such reduction (i.e. the intervention price) was still left to annual negotiation. Against the rapid rise in yields after 1981, and sluggish internal demand, none of these measures were adequate in preventing the remorseless rise in budget cost.

In 1984, the first major step towards CAP reform was taken when marketing quotas for milk were imposed, virtually overnight, on individual farms (or cooperatives). For other products, no such radical measures were put in place. Indeed, the invention of the 'green ecu' in 1984, after which CAP common prices were linked to rises in the strongest Community currency, raised the average level of support price by about 15% above what it might otherwise have been by the end of the decade — although it can be argued that ministers would have negotiated higher 'real ecu' prices otherwise. In 1988, the guarantee threshold scheme was resurrected in the form of the 'budget stabilizer' mechanisms for several commodities. These mechanisms combined additional co-responsibility levies with subsequent price reductions should production exceed pre-defined 'maximum

guarantee quantities', and thus added a degree of less-than-perfect elasticity to support demand.

Budget estimates for 1990 and 1991 showed a sharp rise in expected CAP Guarantee spending, from about ECU 26 billion in 1989 (a slight drop on 1988) to ECU 28 billion in 1990 and ECU 31 billion in 1991, with further rises beyond. Experience with the voluntary set-aside scheme was proving disappointing, with limited take-up in most countries (only 2.5% of the total EC cereal area by mid-1991) and much less impact on production due to 'slippage' problems of resource re-allocation by farmers. In the livestock sector, serious problems were apparent, especially for beef and sheepmeat. Some of the reductions in support prices were offset by agri-monetary adjustments resulting from the joint operation of the 'green ecu' system and the move towards eliminating MCAs en route to the single European market by end-1992.

Another group of external factors also intensified the pressures on the CAP. Predictions of world balances of the main traded commodities, and thus world market prices with which CAP subsidies would have to contend, implied rising EC expenditures. The GATT Uruguay Round was confronting the Community with strong demands for reform of the CAP, and the breakdown at Brussels in 1990 brought much closer the threat of international trade turmoil as a result of agricultural intransigence. Events in Central and Eastern Europe presented the Community with opportunities to affect developments in that area, but at a cost in terms of adjustments to its agricultural policies.

The Commission's reflections and proposals (CEC, 1991a and 1991b) recognized the non-sustainability of current CAP methods and initiated the current set of reforms, which are described in some detail in Section 8.1. This section takes a broader look at the rationale and nature of these reforms which are based on lower market prices, a much higher degree of direct payments to farmers and a range of other structural and other agri-environmental measures.

Analysis of the unreformed CAP had showed that many of its provisions were working with limited and distorted effect. Although food self-sufficiency had been largely attained, and markets considerably stabilized, farmer incomes were falling (after a rise to 1989) despite a 30% rise in CAP expenditure, and large numbers of farmers were leaving the land, or were expected to do so as age and retirement took their toll, or general economic conditions outside improved. There were very large and costly accumulations of surplus products (at end-1990, public stores held 14.4 million tonnes of cereals, 600 000 tonnes of dairy products, 530 000 tonnes of beef), and these were continuing to grow. There were also persistent and increasing complaints of fraud and inefficiency in some of the CAP commodity regimes.

From an economic point of view, these developments can be viewed in a number of ways. First, the 'transfer efficiency' of the CAP, in terms of the benefits received by the intended recipients compared to the burdens borne by consumers and taxpayers, was low and deteriorating. At the simplest level, welfare benefits to producers were being eroded by higher land and other input prices, while increasing surpluses involved ever-higher taxpayer costs which at least partly went simply to depress world market prices still further. Certain sections of the agricultural population (e.g. hired workers) were virtually ignored. If costs and benefits were taken to include the rural environment, enjoyment of countryside externalities was being reduced and offset by landscape deterioration through land 'improvements' for crop-growing and over-stocking of animals, and by water and air pollution by agri-chemicals and animal waste.

Second, a large number of farm households were threatened with inadequate income levels (particularly anticipated incomes, relative to alternative opportunities for earnings and life-styles outside agriculture, as expected by potential entrants to farming, mainly in family succession to ageing current farmers). For these people, there was little realistic expectation that cost efficiencies, farm-level structural adjustments, or diversification to alternative farm or non-farming enterprises would be sufficient to permit economic survival. Although some farm costs, such as feed and fertilizer, had fallen or risen relatively slowly in recent years, this was not expected to continue, and other costs, such as those for land (largely dependent on interest rates), labour and marketing, were high and rising.

Third, the Community's fundamental competitiveness on world agricultural markets was clearly low. In the face of industrial competition from the Far East and the United States, the Commission and Community had become increasingly aware of this aspect of its general economic performance and were concerned to avoid deterioration in the farm trade sector, partly for straightforward budgetary and balance-of-payments reasons, and partly to avoid discouragement to the establishment in the Community of new crop-based industries such as bio-energy and materials manufacture.

Fourth, the distribution of CAP support amongst farmers was clearly unsatisfactory. It had been estimated that 80% of CAP expenditure, largely tied to volume of production and somewhat weighted towards 'northern products', was directed at only about 20% of its farmers. 'Modulation' of CAP price support in order to discriminate amongst different groups of farmers had proved difficult and where agreed

expensive, and new ways of protecting the family-farm structure of EC agriculture were urgently needed.

Fifth, the administration of the CAP was becoming increasingly complex with the numerous modifications to the originally fairly simple price supports and a number of experimental and *ad hoc* schemes. The application of framework directives within Member States usually resulted in slow and acrimonious negotiations after the original decision, while individual 'registration' of producers was necessary for milk quotas, set-aside, etc. On the other hand, these developments demonstrated that a different, more direct, form of policy would be possible.

Sixth, the supply control mechanisms of the 'old' CAP were insufficient to avoid the appearance of surpluses under the joint stimulation of high support prices and technological progress. Farmers were proving highly capable of switching resources to avoid the restrictions being imposed, and in any case the measures applied tended to be insufficiently restrictive. While adjustments in these measures (e.g. reduction in quotas, higher diversification subsidies) were possible in principle, negotiating these amongst farmers and Member States proved difficult, slow and expensive. A more effective (in terms of supply control) and more flexible (in terms of annual adjustment) approach was needed.

Finally, the environmental aspects of the CAP could never be satisfactorily addressed either by simple market support or by a set of individual voluntary schemes: a universal ('horizontal') mechanism was needed, however hard this might be to agree amongst Member States with a wide variety of environmental concerns and problems. In most cases, this would point towards incentives for extensification (lower levels of other inputs applied to land), or at least disincentives or outright bans on intensification.

A further aspect of CAP policy-making into the 1990s was the increasing attention being paid to regional problems. While in a sense inevitable if the basic economic philosophy of comparative advantage in farm production was to apply, the adjustment problems faced by regions with poor and outdated agricultural structures and technologies were considered by many so severe as to deserve special consideration under the 'cohesion' principle enshrined in the Single European Act.

A number of possible approaches were (and are) open to the Commission in addressing these issues. Basic was a lowering of market price levels in the Community, since all other measures had in a sense to 'compete' against the artificially high market value of mainstream farm production. Taxation or limitation of variable inputs (e.g. fertilizer)was possible, but the effectiveness of this in terms of supply control had been long placed in doubt by a number of modelling analyses, while the farm-income impacts would have been severe, especially for some groups. Extension to further commodities of farm-level production (or marketing) quotas were another possibility, but the experience of milk quotas did not much encourage this. Faster and more severe application of the stabilizer-type measures would combine the two approaches, while retaining the freedom of individual producers to adjust or not as each saw fit, but again did not guarantee quick reductions in protection levels, surpluses and budget costs.

A 'social' approach, dominated by outgoer and farmer-retirement schemes (alongside price reductions and/or land retirement), was advocated by some, notably in the form of the 'bond scheme' suggested by Tangermann (Marsh *et al.*, 1991) to the European Parliament. This promised the gradual and permanent elimination of the 'problem groups' of farmers by means of generous financial incentives, but did not address some of the regional and environmental concerns.

In the event, the 1992 reforms put in hand by the Commission and Council contain aspects of several of these approaches. The numerous (and perhaps increasing) objectives of the CAP, and the structure of the Community, are no doubt responsible: a single-minded approach would not have addressed satisfactorily the various problems of farm incomes, budget cost, environmental and regional concerns, etc., and the interests of 12 Member States are almost bound to lead to a compromise position. The new ability of more sophisticated administration and information systems to register land uses and other activities by a much smaller population of full-time farmers is being exploited in this effort.

However, given the restrictions on storage and internal disposal outlets, the major outcome of increasing imbalance in supply and demand is evidenced in changes in the EC's net trade position, as outlined above. The Community's share of world exports (and imports) of feed grains (barley, maize, etc.) is still under 10%. However, it is responsible for over 15% of world exports of wheat and sugar, 20% for beef and veal, pigmeat, poultrymeat and eggs, and 50% for butter, milk powder and wine, while approximating 45% for oilseed imports. Thus changes in EC trade balances can have a substantial effect on several world market prices.

8. Reform of the CAP

8.1. The May 1992 CAP reform package

On 21 May 1992, the Council of Ministers reached agreement on far-reaching changes to the CAP, on the basis of proposals put forward by the Agricultural Commissioner, Mr Mac Sharry, and the Commission itself, in 1991 (CEC, 1991b). Since that date, a number of regulations have been brought forward and approved, and at time of writing (June 1993) EC agriculture is operating under the conditions of the first transitional year, while the Council has just agreed support prices and other measures for the year 1993/94. Further proposals and changes are likely during the transitional period to 1996, but the details of the 'reformed' CAP are now clear. For a precise specification of the reforms, official texts from the Commission and national governments must be consulted, but the following are the main features:

Crop Products

The target, intervention and threshold prices for cereals are being reduced by about 30% from their 1992 levels, with a per-hectare compensatory payment (subject to set-aside, see below) to offset the income effects of these price reductions. The basic rates are as outlined in Table 21 below.

Table 21

Target, intervention and threshold prices for cereals, 1992-96

Marketing year	Target price	Intervention price	Threshold price	Compensation rate per tonne[2]
		ecu per tonne		
1992/93[1]	206.16	155.33	201.37	
1993/94	130	117	175	25
1994/95	120	108	165	35
1995/96	110	100	155	45

[1] Barley, rye and meslin. Support prices for common wheat in 1992/93 were some 5 to 10% higher.
[2] For calendar years 1993, 1994, 1995.
Source: EC-Commission.

The compensatory payment per hectare is calculated on a regional basis (regions being parts or the whole of a Member State, as chosen by that State) by multiplying the typical historical (1986/87-90/91) regional yield by the rate in the above table. There is a supplement of ECU 297 per hectare for durum wheat grown in traditional areas. Where the sum of individual claims for compensatory payments exceeds the regional base area (the average of arable cropped land, including set-aside, in 1989, 1990 and 1991), individual claims are reduced proportionately and, in the following year, an extra set-aside percentage will be required.

For oilseeds, new market arrangements were made in December 1991 (CEC, 1991c), with aid payable to growers at the rate of ECU 359 per hectare, adjustable should world market prices for rape, sunflower and soya move by more than 8% from the reference level of ECU 163 per hectare. In the May 1992 reforms, Member States were allowed to regionalize this aid along the lines for cereals. For protein crops (peas, field beans, sweet lupins), compensatory payments of ECU 65 per hectare multiplied by the regional cereal yield replaced previous minimum price arrangements. Arrangements for dried fodder and tobacco were also modified, but there were no changes (other than extensions in time) to the common market organizations for sugar, fruit and vegetables, fibre plants (e.g. cotton) and wine.

For all but 'small' producers of cereals, oilseeds and protein crops (COPs), i.e. those with an area less than that needed to grow 92 tonnes of cereals (about 20 ha, depending on region), receipt of compensatory payments is dependent on the setting aside, in rotation, of 15% of the 'reference' COPs area, calculated for each producer or on a regionalized basis. The set-aside applies to the whole COPs area and not to each crop individually. Compensation payments on set-aside land were initially based on ECU 45 per tonne (see above table) for 1993, 1994 and 1995, later raised to ECU 57 per tonne for 1994 as part of the 1993/94 price package. The package also defined a non-rotational (permanent) set-aside rate of 20% (18% in areas already subject to environmental restrictions or in regions where over 13% of the land is already set-aside in aggregate).

Livestock products

The intervention prices for beef are being reduced in three stages, by 15% over three years (to 291.55 per 100 kg carcass weight by 1 July 1995), and normal intervention ceilings scaled down from 750 000 tonnes in 1993 to 350 000 in 1997. Four premiums will be payable: (a) a special premium on a male animal, payable twice in its life at 10 and 23 months, with no individual quotas (the previous special premium was limited to 90 head per farm) but with a regional reference herd limit which, if exceeded by the number of claims, will reduce the number of eligible animals per claimant; (b) a suckler cow premium payable on a 'quota' equal to such premiums paid in 1990, 1991 or 1992; (c) a processing premium payable in Member States where and when autumn slaughterings exceed 40% of the annual total; and (d) an extensification premium payable in addition to the

special and suckler cow premiums where the stocking rate is less than 1.4 livestock units (LUs) per forage hectare. Member States were allowed to introduce a dairy calf slaughtering premium or an intervention scheme for light animals.

For sheepmeat, the existing system of premiums (payable at full rate up to 1 000 head in less favoured areas, and 500 head elsewhere, with half-rate premiums for additional animals), but a premium 'quota' is now based on premiums paid in 1991.

Payment of the special beef and suckler cow premiums is dependent on keeping the stocking rate, defined in terms of premium-eligible animals (i.e. male cattle, cows and ewes), for each holding below two LUs per forage hectare. For both beef and sheep, the rights to premium payments ('quotas') will be transferable between producers under regulations to be determined by each Member State, with the purpose of preventing transfer out of sensitive areas or regions. National reserves of premium 'quotas', for allocation to new entrants or exceptional cases, are created both by initial reduction in individual quotas and by 'taxation' of these transfers.

There are no changes to market rules for pigmeat and poultry products, although the reduction in cereal prices is expected to have a significant impact on production costs, and this will be taken into account in the trade mechanisms. Minor changes to the dairy regime were decided upon in May 1992 (later modified in May 1993), involving a reduction in general EC quotas (but increases in Spain, Greece and Italy), and a reduction of 3% in the intervention price for butter by 1994/95.

Accompanying measures

Three further types of measures were introduced alongside the above commodity measures, to be financed partly by the Community (50% in general, 75% in Objective 1 regions). An early retirement scheme, not compulsory for Member States, could offer retirement grants or annual compensation payments (ECU 4 000 plus ECU 250 per hectare up to a maximum of ECU 10 000 per holding, payable for not more than 10 years), releasing land to improve the economic viability of new owners or for non-farming purposes, compatible with environmental requirements.

Afforestation aid will be available, with FEOGA contributions of up to ECU 3 000 per hectare for softwoods and ECU 4 000 per hectare for broadleaves, and ECU 600 per hectare per year for five years to offset loss of farming income.

Several types of agri-environmental measures will be payable for such activities as: protection of water resources, conversion of arable land to extensive pasture, organic farming, extensification of animal stocking, maintenance of environmentally friendly farming practices, public access and forestry training.

Economic commentary

The reforms represent a significant adjustment in the CAP although they do not amend its objectives and principles, and seem unlikely to resolve some of the problems associated with the policy over the last few decades. Greater market orientation has been achieved through the price reductions, which will reduce distortions in consumer and user choice, and lower the cost of export subsidies. The reforms do not represent a major step in the direction of quotas or direct input controls (e.g. on fertilizer use), but rather rely on economic mechanisms and a mixture of indirect disincentives. The income objective of the CAP is re-addressed via the compensation payments, which have been at least partly modulated by region and farm-size to reflect better the large implicit redistributional aims of the Community's policy-makers, and are no longer directly linked to individual marketed quantities. The payments represent a significant additional budgetary commitment by the EC's taxpayers, but the size of this burden is contained by the conditions for regional areas and herd sizes, which limit the financial outlay for several sectors. Naturally, the outcome will depend on future decision-making by the Council, particularly in terms of adjusting rates of compensation in the light of yield increases and inflation.

In addition to the disincentive effect of lower product prices, several features of the reforms limit or discourage the use of factors of production, particularly set-aside and the stocking-rate conditions for animal premiums. However, these are not always individual and/or absolute limits: for example, the area sown to COP crops can expand (subject to increased proportional set-aside), and animals not eligible for premium payments can be stocked above the defined limits.

Including pig and poultry products, whose prices are dependent on feed-ingredient prices, the reforms cover about 50% of EC agricultural production, and the reductions in support prices therefore represent a significant fall in protection for the sector as a whole even though some important regimes have been left largely or wholly unchanged so far. The ultimate intervention price for cereals of ECU 100 per tonne represents the Commission's expectations for the world market price under stabilized conditions, i.e. with equivalent policy reforms in other major trading countries. However,

substantial EC protection (55%) remains via the threshold price.

Before and after the May 1992 agreement, the proposals of the Commission have often been weakened by the Council, for example in lowering the target cereal price to ECU 110 per tonne instead of ECU 100 as proposed, and in removing the 90-head limit on suckler-cow premium payments. Proposals for larger reductions in milk quotas and dairy intervention prices, with a compensatory dairy cow premium, and for an upper limit of premium payments on sheep, were defeated or delayed. There have also been relaxations in the set-aside rules (e.g. for maize forage), and an increase in the set-aside payment rates.

The environmental aspects of the reforms fall into two categories: the 'cross-compliance' aspects of the arable and livestock schemes, and the direct agri-environmental measures. The former include the conditions under which set-aside must be managed and the stocking-rate conditions for livestock premiums. Neither can be regarded as very powerful or effective: the environmental benefits of rotational set-aside are strictly limited due to the short time-period involved, and the stocking rates have been set at a rate and defined in such a way as to affect only the more intensive grazing enterprises. (There are however other measures such as the nitrate-sensitive areas which address some of these problems.) The impact of the accompanying measures will depend very much on the willingness and ability of national governments to implement (where non-mandatory) and to administer and finance (where mandatory) the various schemes involved.

8.2. The Uruguay Round agreement

The traditional treatment of agriculture in the GATT has been characterized as 'a combination of special exemptions, vague rules, neglect of important policies, and tolerance of continuous infringement' (Tangermann, 1991). Many countries contributed to this situation, including the drafters of the original agreement, which permits export subsidies for agricultural products (and other primary commodities) subject to an 'equitable share in world export trade' and omits mention of measures such as minimum import prices and variable import levies. The United States obtained its 1955 waiver allowing quantitative import restrictions without restricting domestic production. The European Community, through its common agricultural policy, transformed its trading stance in farm products through a mixture of direct and indirect challenges to GATT rules and procedures, notably 'voluntary' import agreements with several trading partners, and refusal to convert its variable levies into fixed tariffs.

History of GATT agricultural negotiations

The CAP was first considered within the GATT context in the 1960-61 Dillon Round, with the outcome that the alterations to internal and external EC trade patterns caused by the creation of the CAP, as well as its instruments of variable levies and export subsidies, were (tacitly) tolerated by the United States, in exchange for zero or low bindings of EC tariffs on oilseeds and non-grain feeds. Standstill agreements on grains and poultry products were tested during the 1962 EC-US 'chicken war'.

In the 1963-67 Kennedy Round, US proposals to convert variable levies into bound tariffs were rejected by the EC, as were subsequent proposals for a guaranteed US share of the EC cereals market and a maximum EC self-sufficiency rate in cereals of 90%. On its side, the US rejected as insufficiently liberalizing the EC's *montant de soutien* proposal to limit the gap between domestic and world prices (thus dealing, *de facto*, with non-tariff barriers). Agreement was reached on some reductions in bound tariffs, such as corn gluten feed, and on a new International Grains Arrangement, but the latter did not survive the stress of historically low world wheat prices in 1968.

The 1973-79 Tokyo Round again concluded somewhat unsatisfactorily, with further cuts in bound tariffs, two international commodity agreements — for bovine meat (with no economic provisions) and dairy products — and a subsidies code which has not in practice reduced tensions in agricultural trade. As soon as 1982, OECD Ministers felt it necessary to issue a declaration aimed at agricultural policy reform, and authorized monitoring and outlook work which has resulted in an annual series of PSE/CSE estimates and associated commentary since 1987.

The Uruguay Round, initiated in 1986, specifically addressed the difficulties of international agricultural trade. An opening declaration referred to improving market access and increasing discipline on the use of all direct and indirect subsidies affecting agricultural trade directly and indirectly, the latter a significant widening of the scope for analysis and negotiation, since it opened up domestic agricultural policies (including the CAP) for debate. At the mid-term review in December 1988, there was no agreement between the various proposals made by different participants, such as the US 'zero' option for complete elimination of farm programmes by the year 2000, and the EC's proposal for short-term stabilization and re-balancing measures, to be followed by longer-term reductions of an aggregate measure of support (AMS). The

Cairns Group of agricultural exporters supported the US approach, while willing to accept greater flexibility in its application, while Japan and the Nordic countries refused to accept the dismantlement of their strongly protectionist policies. However, in April 1989, further proposals were promised by end-1990, resulting in a US call for a 90% reduction in export subsidies and a 75% reduction in internal support over a 10-year period, while the EC proposed a 30% reduction in the AMS and conversion of its border measures (i.e. variable import levies) into tariffs, contingent on safeguards against large world-price fluctuations and acceptance of re-balancing EC protection for grains, oilseeds and non-grain feeds. The gap between these revised US and EC proposals again proved too wide to be bridged by the Hellström compromise paper at the 'final' meeting at Brussels in December 1990. Complete breakdown was avoided by the offer of the GATT Director-General, Artur Dunkel, to prepare a further compromise paper (the Draft Final Act), which by the end of 1991 was accepted as the basis for further negotiations. At the same time, the EC began serious internal discussions on reform of the CAP (see above). Eventually, in late November 1992 (i.e. six months after the adoption of internal CAP reforms by the EC), the EC Commission and the US administration announced the Blair House 'pre-accord' on a GATT settlement in the area of agriculture. With some adjustment for 'front-loading' of subsidized exports to enable existing EC stocks to be reduced in the earlier years of the 1995-99 adjustment period, this formed the basis for agricultural aspects of the final and overall Uruguay Round agreement of 15 December 1993.

The Blair House/Uruguay Round agreement on agriculture

The agreement contains six sets of provisions, as follows:

1. *Market access:* With 1986-88 as a basis, border protection measures are to be converted into tariffs, whose simple mathematical average over all commodities is to be reduced by 36% over six years, with a minimum reduction of 15% for each tariff. For the EC, the tariff will be the difference between the world fob market price and the intervention price plus 10% and any monthly increments. However, if the EC import price falls by more than 10% of the 1986-88 import price (defined in ecu), a variable element may be added to the tariff, thus providing a 'special safeguard' for the Community markets. Tariff quotas, with tariffs equal to 32% of the basic tariff, will be opened to permit minimum market access of 3% at the start and 5% at the end of six years; the quantities thus involved are wheat (281 000 tonnes), meat (78 000 tonnes), skimmed-milk powder (69 000 tonnes), butter (10 000 tonnes), cheese (104 000 tonnes) and eggs (208 000 tonnes). Existing EC import arrangements such

as those for New Zealand butter and sheepmeat (but not those for bananas) are to be 'tariffied', but will not affect their quantitative outcomes.

2. *Internal support:* With 1986-88 as a basis, global internal support (i.e. the AMS) is to be reduced by 20%, with credit given for reductions since 1986. Direct CAP aids such as the compensatory payments of the May 1992 reforms are excluded from this commitment, as being based on fixed areas, animal numbers and yields, as are aids exempted as non-trade-distorting in the Dunkel text 'green box'.

3. *Export subsidies:* With 1986-90 as a base, direct export subsidy expenditures are to be reduced, product by product, by 36% over six years, and volumes of subsidized exports by 21% over the same period. These commitments exclude unsubsidized exports, food aid and (as regards volumes) processed products, and may involve unequal annual instalments.

4. *Rebalancing:* If EC imports on non-grain feed ingredients increase to a level which threatens CAP reform, the EC and US will consult each other over a solution.

5. *Peace clause:* Internal support measures and export subsidies are to be considered exempt from actions and claims under GATT Article 16 (on export subsidies and equitable trade shares).

6. *Oilseeds:* As a follow-up to the GATT oilseeds panel, the EC agrees to create a separate base area for subsidized oilseed production, equal to 5 128 000 hectares from 1995/96, i.e. the 1989-91 average used for the CAP arable reforms. Each year, this area will be reduced by a set-aside rate not less than 10% (currently 15%), with penalties similar to current arrangements if the area so calculated (and excluding oilseeds grown for industrial purposes, up to 1 million tonnes soyameal equivalent) is exceeded. A tariff quota of 500 000 tonnes of corn imports into Portugal will be opened, and the base area will be adapted if the Community is enlarged. The US gives up any claims for compensation in this field.

Constraints on EC agricultural policy

From the details given above, it is possible to assess the extent to which the EC's agricultural policy may be affected by the Uruguay Round agreement, Future enlargement of the EC, and/or developments in association agreements with Central and East European countries, as well as the pace of general economic development in the Community itself, may well affect the situation. Nevertheless, the EC Commission (1992, 1993), as well as others, have provided commentary on how the Blair House agreement might affect future CAP development.

In general, the choice of 1986-88 and 1986-90 as base periods, and the ability to claim 'credit' for reductions in support since 1986, coupled with the use of the ecu rather than the dollar as a currency unit, mean that the commitments on subsidy and therefore price levels are unlikely to prove constraining to the Community, which has already reduced many support prices in nominal terms, and is about to go much further with cereals and beef under the CAP reforms. The exclusion of direct aids unlinked to production (as can now be claimed for most such payments in the CAP) further reduces the likelihood of difficulties in meeting the AMS and expenditure commitments. However, unless world prices fall drastically, so that the special safeguard operates to re-install a variable levy regime, the tariffication of border measures will mean that EC market prices from now on fluctuate in parallel with world market developments, albeit at considerably higher levels.

Specific problems may be encountered with the quantitative restrictions. For cereals, the tariff quota merely permits total wheat imports to return to mid-1980s levels of about 500 000 tonnes. The EC's exportable surplus of wheat and coarse grains depends much more critically on (a) yield trends on the planted area, and (b) the amount of grains used for animal feed. Although the historic rate of increase in cereal yields may be expected to slow from its recent pace of 1.8 % per year, and might even fall as a result of lower market prices (and other factors, such as greater market uncertainty and perhaps technological deceleration), they may not stabilize completely. Also, the set-aside provisions are more flexible than planting-area quotas, and permit changes in area between crops, and indeed higher total (cropped and set-aside) area. The use of grains for feed depends on the substitution effect of increased competitiveness of cereals as against other feedstuffs (e.g. soya meal and manioc), and the growth effect of higher pig and poultry production (but lower beef production).

The Commission has estimated the combined influence of the two consumption effects as an additional 12 million tonnes of grains (soft wheat). With this estimate, the balance of the yield and consumption factors has been calculated by the Commission (1993) as leading to exportable surpluses of wheat and coarse grains quite close to, or above, those allowable under the GATT pre-accord, depending on either of two yield trends.

References

Arkleton Trust, *Rural change in Europe structural policies and multiple job holding in the rural development process,* report of second review meeting, Waldkirchen, Institut für Landliche Strukturforschung, Frankfurt, 1988.

Behrens, R. and de Haen, H., 'Aggregate factor input and productivity in agriculture: a comparison for the EC member countries', 1963-76, *European Review of Agricultural Economics,* 7-2, pp. 109-46, 1980.

Bowler, I., *Agriculture under the common agricultural policy,* Manchester University Press, 1985.

Commission of the European Community (CEC, various years), *Agricultural situation in the Community,* Brussels.

Commission of the EC CAP reform and GATT compatibility, DG-VI paper, April, Brussels, 1992.

Commission of the EC, Communication on agriculture in the GATT negotiations and the reform of the CAP, SEC(92) 2267, 25 November, Brussels, 1992.

Eurostat, *Basic statistics of the Community* (24th edition), Luxembourg, 1987.

Frohberg, K., *Assessment of the effects on labour income and outflow of labour of lower support prices,* 1992.

Gardner, B. L., 'Changing economic perspectives on the farm problem', *Journal of Economic Literature,* 30, pp. 62-101, 1992.

Henrichsmeyer, W. and Ostermeyer-Schloder, A., 'Productivity growth and factor adjustment in EC agriculture', *European Review of Agricultural Economics,* 15-2/3, pp. 137-54, 1988.

Hill, B., *Total income of agricultural household 1992 Report,* Paper to Eurostat (May), Luxembourg, 1992.

Kislev, Y. and Peterson, W., 'Prices, technology and farm size', *J. Econ.,* 90, pp. 578-95, 1982.

Koester, U. and Tangermann, S., 'The European Community', in Sanderson, F., (ed.) *Agricultural protectionism in the industrialized world,* 1989.

Larsen, A. and Hansen, J., *Agricultural support and structural development,* 1992.

Neville Rolfe, E., *The politics of agriculture in the European Community,* London, Policy Studies Institute, 1984.

Sanderson, F. H. (ed.), 'Agricultural protectionism — the industrialized world', *Resources for the future,* Washington DC, 1990.

Tangermann, S., 'Agriculture in international trade negotiations', in *Agricultural economics and policy: international challenges for the nineties,* ed. Berger, K., de Groot, M., Post, J. and Zachariasse, V., Elsevier, 1991.

Tracy, M., *Agriculture in Western Europe: challenge and response 1880-1980,* 2nd ed., Granada, 1982.

Whitby, M. C., 'The CAP and the countryside', Chapter 8 in *The common agricultural policy and the world economy,* ed. Ritson, C. and Harvey, D., CAB International, 1991.

Chapter B: The economic costs of agricultural policy[1]

---

[1] This chapter was prepared by Knud J. Munk and Ken Thomson.

Chapter B

The economic costs of agricultural policy

1. Introduction

Based on a conceptual framework representing the various instruments of agricultural support, this chapter considers how to measure the economic costs of the common agricultural policy. The chapter also provides a basis for appreciation of the modelling results reported in Chapter D with respect to budget and real income effects.

Section 2 defines the concepts of transfers, distortionary costs, transaction costs and the real income effects due to government intervention in agricultural markets. It also considers the effects of market price support and other support instruments and the trade-off between various type of costs within this framework. Section 3 analyses the EC agricultural budget which is often considered to provide the main indicator of 'the costs of the CAP'. In the spirit of the conceptual framework, however, it is pointed out that the total budgetary cost is a partial and in itself misleading indicator of economic costs. Section 4 considers the methodology issues involved in measuring the economic costs of the CAP and reviews some of the empirical evidence.

2. The effect of different support instruments

Support instruments have two main effects: they create transfers which reflect changes in the distribution of income and they impose economic costs for the economy.

2.1. Transfers

'Transfers' are defined as payments from one agent in the economy to another, for which there is no corresponding flow of goods and services. Transfers contrast with 'non-transfer spending' where the flow of payments has a counterpart in the value of the flow of goods and services going in the opposite direction.

The 'transfers' created by agricultural support instruments can be calculated without the use of model assumptions, based on accounting data and price information.

Transfers may be either non-distortionary or distortionary. 'Non-distortionary transfers' or 'lump-sum payments' are payments where the receiving agent cannot influence the size of the payment and where the marginal rates of transformation are therefore not distorted.

'Distortionary transfers' are transfers which create distortions in the sense of preventing the marginal rate of transformation being the same for all agents in the economy.

Since transfers are always from one agent to another agent, the sum of transfers between producers, consumers and taxpayers due to agricultural policy instruments is, by definition, zero .

Transfers due to support policies generally differ from the real income effects. The transfers would be equal to the real income effects only if the support instruments creating the transfers did not effect the behaviour of the agents (consumers, producers and taxpayers) in the economy and if they were not associated with transaction costs.

2.2. Economic costs for the economy

Government support instruments which create distortionary transfers always reduce aggregate real income in a situation without initial government intervention. In an economy which is already distorted, such instruments may, however, increase aggregate real income. This may, for example, be the case for consumer subsidies in a situation where consumer prices are increased by market price support measures, or where tariff revenue replaces other taxes with even higher distortionary costs.

The 'economic costs for the economy' may be defined as the sum of the real income effects for farmers, consumers and taxpayers created by the government intervention. These real income effects and hence the economic costs cannot be directly observed. They can be calculated only with the help of models representing economic behaviour. Such models are not always available, and, when available, are often based on controversial assumptions.

The 'economic costs for the economy' of support instruments may be divided into distortionary costs and transaction costs.

'Distortionary costs' are created when support instruments create a (price) wedge between the marginal rate of transformation of different agents in the economy (in this context the foreign sector is also considered an agent). With an efficient allocation of resources, the marginal rates of transformation between commodities and factors are the same for all agents. For example, market price support for agricultural products creates a price wedge between both producer and consumer prices on the one hand and world market prices on the other hand. This changes the consumption and production decisions compared with a situation where producers and consumers face world market prices, and thus creates distortionary costs.

'Transaction costs' are the costs other than distortionary costs of the government and other agents associated with government intervention. These costs include the costs of rule implementation, the costs of producing, collecting and processing information, and the costs of control and enforcement. The cost of rent-seeking behaviour may also be considered as part of the transaction costs.

The economic costs of government intervention may also be divided into direct and indirect costs.

The 'direct costs' of a given support instrument are the distortionary and transaction costs directly associated with the use of the instruments.

The 'indirect costs' are the distortionary and transaction costs associated with financing the budget expenditures which, in general, are associated with government intervention. The indirect costs may however be negative when, for example, in the case of a tariff, support to agricultural income generates revenue to the government which may be used to decrease other distortionary taxes. In calculating the budget costs, one must also take the spillover effects on other taxed or subsidized commodities and factors of production into account.

Taking account of this two-way classification, we define 'direct distortionary costs' as distortionary costs which are directly associated with the use of the instrument in question, and 'other costs' (see Table 22) as the sum of the 'direct transaction costs', 'indirect transaction costs' and 'indirect distortionary costs'.

Table 22

Classification of economic costs of support instruments

	Direct costs	Indirect costs
Distortionary costs	Direct distortionary costs	Indirect distortionary costs
Transaction costs (administrative costs), etc.	Direct transaction costs	Indirect transaction costs

2.3. Transfer instruments and the trade-off between different types of costs

Disregarding transaction costs, theoretical considerations suggest the following ranking of support instruments in terms of increasing 'direct distortionary costs':

1. Targeted lump-sum transfers;
2. Proportional primary factor subsidies;
3. Output subsidies, or subsidies for the use of intermediate inputs;
4. Market price support.

Whatever policy instrument is used to transfer income to farmers will be associated with economic cost, i.e. imply a decrease in aggregate real income. Different instruments are, however, characterized by a different combination of 'direct distortionary costs' and 'other costs', as defined above.

There seems to be a tendency for instruments which have relatively high 'direct distortionary costs' to be associated with relatively low 'other costs' and vice versa. There seems therefore (see Table 23) to be a trade-off between, on the one hand, 'direct distortionary costs' and, on the other, 'other costs'.

Table 23

The economic costs associated with different types of support instruments

Instruments	Direct cost		Indirect cost
	Distortion	Transaction	
Targeted lump-sum transfers	0	very high	very high
Proportional primary factor subsidies	low	high	high
Output/input subsidies	high	low	high
Market price support			
(i) exporter	very high	low	low
(ii) importer	very high	very low	negative
Output quotas in a situation with market price support	potential decrease	increase	potential decrease
Set-aside in a situation with market price support	potential decrease	increase	potential decrease

'Targeted lump-sum transfers' have, by definition, no 'direct distortionary costs', but significant 'other costs'. Targeted lump-sum transfers are associated with high 'transaction costs' because, in order to achieve their objectives, i.e. to increase the income of those with low income or those who deserve compensation, such transfers need to be based on detailed information about individual households. They also have high 'indirect costs' because they need to be financed by distortionary taxation. The budget costs may be particularly high when seen in a time perspective. In the case of other types of support, after a certain time, a number of farmers would have left the agricultural sector and hence decrease the budget costs. But as lump-sum transfers cannot be made contingent on such a decision, they will also have to be paid to farmers who, at the initial prices, would have left the agricultural sector anyway and, therefore, do not need compensation. The problem for the government is that the farmers' intention to leave the agricultural sector cannot be observed directly and that the individual farmer has no incentive to reveal this information.

'Proportional primary factor subsidies' require information to distinguish between factors used for agricultural and non-agricultural purposes. This may also imply high transaction costs. Primary factor subsidies distort the household's supply of labour to different purposes, but if applied at the same level to all factors, i.e. when they are proportional, do not distort production decisions in the agricultural sector.

'Output subsidies' require that a price wedge within the economy can be policed. This is relatively easy if it can be done at the level of processing firms, but very costly if it has to be done at the level of each farmer. The indirect costs are as high as or even higher than in the case of primary factor subsidies. The distortionary costs are, however, higher because the production decision in the agricultural sector is also distorted. The case of 'intermediate input subsidies' is, with respect to the distortionary cost, equivalent to output subsidies; the transaction costs are also similar. Output subsidies leave the government free to fix consumer subsidies according to fiscal and distributional considerations. 'Co-responsibility levies' may be seen as a combination of a consumption tax and a producer subsidy where the producer price is lower than the consumer price. The assessment of the costs associated with using a co-responsibility levy is therefore similar to that of an output subsidy.

'Market price support' in the case of an importer has the lowest transaction cost. Only a price wedge at the external border has to be policed. The distortionary costs are, however, the highest of all the four types of support instruments because both production and consumption decisions are distorted.

Agricultural policy instruments which impose 'quantitative restrictions', such as output quotas and set-aside, find their rationale in the fact that they reduce the use of inputs, and hence the distortionary effects of other support instruments, without significantly reducing the transfers to producers. For a given transfer, however, they may achieve a reduction in distortionary costs, but at the expense of increasing transaction costs. They in themselves also create other distortionary costs which may be higher than the reduction in distortionary costs due to reduced input use.

The trade-off between 'direct distortionary costs' and 'other costs' depends on the efficiency of public administration (see also Chapter B).

One would expect countries with less efficient public administrations to be more likely to adopt market price support systems than countries with more efficient administrations. Since the efficiency of public administration increases more than for other economic activities with increasing level of economic development, one would expect countries at a higher level of economic development to adopt less distortionary support instruments, other things being equal, for example to move away from market price support towards direct income support.

For market price support, the trade-off between direct distortionary costs and other costs depends crucially on the trade position. In the case of a product for which the country is an importer, this generates government revenue, whereas, if the country is an exporter, it is associated with budget costs. The economic costs of providing a given level of support are therefore higher for a net import sector than for a net export sector. This tendency is reinforced when terms of trade effects, which for big countries may be significant, are taken into account.

3. The EC agricultural budget

The representation of the CAP as essentially a price support policy comprising: (a) import taxes (variable levies) to provide protection against external supplies, and (b) government purchases (intervention buying), and (c) export subsidies (refunds) to dispose of 'surplus' domestic production, is a simplification which, however, captures the essence of the CAP. These instruments involve budgetary expenditures and revenues between the taxpayers, producers and consumers of the Community, via the

81

budgets of the EC and its Member States. In practice, the CAP also includes a large number of supplementary instruments which over time have increased in importance. Certain commodity regimes involve direct payments to farmers, output subsidies, subsidies to processors and consumers to compensate for the high domestic prices, and quantitative restrictions to reduce the budget costs of export subsidies. Storage of intervention purchases, via public stocks and subsidized private storage, has been an important instrument to stabilise (rather than support) the domestic prices of agricultural commodities. Finally, there are groups of 'structural' instruments aimed at improving the efficiency of agricultural production and marketing, at encouraging rural development, and at maintaining the countryside environment, often through investment grants and interest subsidies. Most of these additional instruments also involve costs (and occasionally revenue to the budget).

The common agricultural policy is almost entirely financed through the European Agricultural Guidance and Guarantee Fund (EAGGF, or FEOGA from the French title), which in recent years has represented the expenditure of around ECU 30 000 million (1988 ECU 27 297 million; 1992 ECU 36 128 million), accounting for about 60% of all EC budget expenditures, or around 0.6% of EC GNP. As its name implies, the EAGGF consists of two components: the Guarantee Section which covers the costs of income and price support to the agricultural sector, and the Guidance Section which concerns the structure of the agricultural and agricultural processing sectors. Partly because most Guidance Section expenditure is largely cofinancing (with Member States), the Guarantee Section is by far the most costly to the EC budget, with net expenditures of around ECU 26 000 million (1988) to ECU 33 000 million (1992). Since the Brussels Agreement of 1988 on budgetary discipline, the bulk of total Guarantee expenditure, calculated on a reference basis of ECU 27 500 million for 1987, and including appropriations for the depreciation of new agricultural stocks, must not exceed a 'guideline' ceiling which grows at a rate of 74% of EC GNP; the 1992 ceiling was ECU 35 029 million, which was fully taken up in the initial EC budget.

The bulk of EAGGF expenditure is funded from general taxation, via its claims on the EC Common Customs Tariff and on the VAT-based and other national contributions to the EC budget. However, the CAP generates revenue to the EC budget via its variable import tariffs and from producer levies associated with the sugar policy, in total roughly ECU 2 500 million. There have also been contributions, treated for historical reasons as negative expenditures, within the EAGGF Guarantee Section, from the co-responsibility levies on milk and cereals, amounting to about ECU 1 000-1 500 million. Thus a distinction should be drawn between the

published FEOGA total expenditure figure and the gross or net figures arrived at by adding in, or subtracting, these components.

Following the analysis in Section 2, budget costs arising from the CAP can, at least in principle, be divided into those costs which are transfers and those which are non-transfer expenditures (i.e. expenditures which imply government purchases of goods and services). The transfer expenditures may further be devided into those to agricultural producers on the one hand and those to consumers and processors on the other.

Transfer expenditures to agricultural producers provide income support to farmers; nearly all of this is related to (and thus normally influences) their levels of output (usually marketed production). On the other hand, budgetary costs do not correspond to the total economic transfer to producers as a result of the CAP, since they exclude transfers from consumers via higher food prices, assuming that farm gate prices are transmitted to retail level via a processing and distribution system whose margins in absolute terms are not significantly affected by the general level and variability of raw material prices.

Transfer expenditures to consumers and processors provide partial compensation for the fact that domestic purchaser prices for agricultural products under the CAP are often higher than world market levels. These measures can take several forms: for example semi-permanent subsidies exist for the use of farm commodities in processing and animal feed, and for the supply of foodstuffs to certain social groups such as institutional communities, and for special disposal schemes, e.g. for 'Christmas butter'.

The non-transfer expenditures represent the purchase of goods and services by the EC authorities as part of its own activities, mainly storage of agricultural products for the purpose of stabilising (rather than supporting) domestic market prices. Such costs might in principle be incurred without providing income support to farmers, but with the objective of stabilising agricultural prices. Some of the non-transfer budget expenditure, such as Guidance spending on rural development, represents public-good expenditure which may in fact improve resource allocation by correcting for market failure.

Table 24 shows the main EAGGF Guarantee budget (including negative items) for the period 1989-92, divided into:

(i) transfers to agricultural producers via:

    (a) border measures (export refunds net of import

levies but including the costs of depreciating new stock in advance of disposal),

(b) domestic production subsidies (output subsidies, net of producer levies),

(c) other payments and receipts (accessionary and monetary compensatory amounts);

(ii) transfers to consumers and processors via user subsidies;

(iii) non-transfer expenditures on storage and other agricultural policy activities.

From Table 24 it can be seen that total net budget expenditure rose in current ecu by about a third from under ECU 22 000 million in 1989 to over ECU 29 000 million in 1992. Transfers from taxpayers to producers and consumers increased by about 20% from ECU 18 000 million in 1989 to ECU 22 000 million in 1992, whereas the non-transfer budget costs doubled from ECU 3 750 to 7 600 million over the same period. Of the transfer expenditure, about ECU 15 000 million was directed to producers, while between ECU 3 500 and 5 000 million is classified as transfers to consumers and processors. Thus about half the net budget cost of the CAP in recent years has been production-related transfers to agricultural producers, while about a sixth is directed to consumers and processors, and the remaining third is devoted to, stabilization, and other 'public-good' activities under the policy.

The budget cost of export subsidies net of tariff revenue were around ECU 9 000 million, i.e. less than a third of the total.

It must be emphasized that transfers from taxpayers do not correspond to the real-income costs of the CAP. First, they do not take into account the costs directly imposed on the EC economy by the policy through distortion in the choices of producers (in terms of their allocations of farm resources), consumers (in terms of their food expenditure patterns) or taxpayers (in terms of their work-leisure behaviour). Second, not all non-transfer costs of agricultural and tax-raising policy measures are included in the agricultural budget: some EC Commission costs are included elsewhere in the overall EC budget, and the bulk of the administrative costs are borne by Member States, with some recompense in the form of a 10% share of tariff revenue.

4. Transfer and real income effects of the CAP

4.1. Introduction

From both a theoretical and an empirical point of view, estimating the 'economic costs of the CAP' is a complex task: most of the estimates reported in the literature are calculated using static partial equilibrium models based on first-best assumptions (see Chapter C). Such estimates do not provide a fully reliable guide to the real income gains of removing the CAP. This section considers the theoretical issues involved in calculating the economic costs of market price support and other CAP support instruments, and reviews the OECD transfer measures and an estimate of the real income effect of the CAP at Member State and Community level.

4.2. The real income effects of market price support

In a market price support system — the most widely used method of agricultural support — the government fixes prices to both consumers and producers at a level higher than would be the case under free market conditions. For a traded commodity, market price support requires the use of border measures. These usually take the form of import quotas or variable import levies to prevent or restrict imports, and export subsidies in order to dispose of production in excess of domestic consumption requirements.

The introduction of market price support generates transfers, which may be measured directly, and changes in real income of consumers, producers and taxpayers, which may be estimated on the basis of theoretical assumptions.

Market price support implies a transfer from consumers to producers. In the case of a product which is exported it also involves a transfer from the government budget. If a commodity is imported, government revenue is generated through the accrual of receipts from tariffs or levies, or through the sale of import quotas if the quota rent is not captured by importers or exporters.

The transfers from consumers are calculated as the difference between the domestic price and the world market price, times the quantity consumed. The transfer to producers is the same price gap multiplied by production. The price gap multiplied by the import or export quantity represents, respectively, the transfer to or from the government budget. Assuming that domestic policies do not affect world market prices, the sum of the transfers to or from consumers, producers and taxpayers is, by definition, zero (see Table 25).

Table 24

CAP budget, 1989-92, million ECU[1]

	1989	1990	1991	1992
A. Budget transfers to producers				
Export refunds	9 708	7 722	10 080	9 487
Import levies	−1 283	1 173	−1 261	1 353
Depreciation of extra stocks to world prices[2]	—	—	—	—
(Net export subsidies)	(8 425)	(6 549)	(8 819)	(8 134)
Output subsidies[3]	7 784	8 908	10 216	10 885
Withdrawal	785	640	634	642
Co-responsibility levies	−1 579	−938	−1 238	−1 467
Sugar levies	−1 382	−911	−1 288	−1 236
(Net domestic output subsidies)	(5 608)	(7 699)	(8 324)	(8 824)
ACAs, MCAs	364	307	159	25
Total transfers to producers	**14 397**	**14 555**	**17 302**	**16 983**
B. Budget transfers to users				
Subsidies to consumers and processors	3 591	3 808	4 801	4 759
Total budget transfers (A + B)	**17 988**	**18 363**	**22 103**	**21 742**
C. Non-transfer expenditures				
Storage (public and private)	1 563	1 328	1 842	1 098
Depreciation from price changes and deterioration[2]	1 235	1 630	3 819	4 969
Guidance premiums	974	712	1 103	939
Other costs	−21	−171	535	606
Total non-transfers	**3 751**	**3 499**	**7 299**	**7 612**
Total net budget expenditure (A + B + C)	**21 739**	**21 862**	**29 402**	**29 354**
EAGGF Guarantee Section expenditures[4]				
Total	25 873	26 453	32 386	31 277
Subject to guideline	24 406	25 069	30 961	
Guideline	28 624	30 630	31 197	35 039
Margin	4 219	5 561	236	

Source: Court of Auditors Reports, CEC (1993), *Agricultural situation in the Community: 1992 Report,* and own estimates.

[1] This table shows nearly all expenditures reported under the EAGGF Guarantee Fund commitments, with some minor exceptions in all or some years, e.g. costs of disposing of old (pre-1989) stocks, fisheries and set-aside expenditures.

[2] Reported depreciation totals have been divided into two components. 'Depreciation of extra stocks to world prices' represents the writing-down of the value of EC stock changes from domestic to world market levels, in order to account for the accumulation of intervention stocks in the year of purchase rather than the year of disposal; stock increases normally represent a cost, stock decreases a credit, to the EAGGF budget. Changes in the value of EC stocks due to world market price variations and physical deterioration are reported as 'depreciation from price changes and deterioration'.

[3] 'Output subsidies' are normally reported in official publications as 'price compensation aids' to 'production'. For 1992, the following items were classified on the basis of previous years as 'subsidies to consumers and processors', and subtracted for total reported as 'price compensation aids' to give 'output subsidies': ECU 397 million (cereals); ECU 800 million (olive oil); ECU 800 million (fruit and vegetables); ECU 134 million (wine); ECU 1 896 million (milk and milk products); ECU 532 million (beef and veal); ECU 200 million (sheepmeat and goatmeat).

[4] Reported (CEC, *Agricultural situation in the Community: 1992 Report,* p. 112) expenditures, including milk and cereals co-responsibility levy revenue as negative expenditure. 1992 expenditure from Court of Auditors Report (1993).

Table 25

Transfers (directly observable)

	Exporter	Importer
Transfer to producers	A + B + C + D + E + F + G + H + I + J	A + B + E + F + G
Transfer from consumers	A + E	A + B + C + E + F + G + H
Transfer		
to taxpayers		C + H
from taxpayers	B + C + D + F + G + H + I + J	
Net transfer	0	0

Table 26

Real income effects in a partial equilibrium analysis (require estimation)

	Exporter	Importer
Disregarding world market effect		
Producer gain	A + B + C + E + F + G + H	A + E
Consumer gain	A + B + E + F + G	A + B + C + D + E + F + G + H + I + J
Taxpayer gain		C + H
loss	B + C + D + F + G + H + I + J	
Net 'dead weight' loss	B + D + F + G + I + J	B + D + F + G + I + J
Change in world market price	Increases net loss: + H	Decreases net loss: − H

The real income gain to producers resulting from the price increase is less than the transfer to producers. This occurs because production is expanded at increasing marginal cost. The greater the slope of the supply curve, the lower the real income gains to producers relative to the size of the transfer. The real income loss to consumers is on the other hand greater than the transfer from consumers because the consumers also have the benefit of purchasing at a lower price the extra amount they would consume at that lower price. In the case of an exported commodity, the effect on the joint budget is negative because of export subsidies and, in the case of an imported commodity, it is positive as a result of tariff revenue.

The real income loss to taxpayers is equal to the effect on the government budget if government revenue can be raised without economic costs. Market price support imposes a cost on the economy, as indicated in Table 26 and illustrated in Graph 24. This loss is often referred to as the 'dead weight loss' and always occurs in a market price support system under the usual partial equilibrium assumptions where all other distortions in the economy and the effect in world market prices are neglected.

The calculation of the real income effects of market price support based on a model framework depends critically on the assumptions made (explicitly or implicitly, as when a partial equilibrium approach is used). Assuming fixed world market prices, the real income effects may be calculated in a partial equilibrium model using domestic agricultural supply and demand elasticities. It is easy under these assumptions to illustrate that the aggregate real income loss to consumers and taxpayers due to the introduction of market price support is greater than the resulting increase in the income of farmers. The 'transfer efficiency', defined as the increase in farmers income per unit decrease in the real income to the rest of society, is therefore less than 1.

In general, market price support has the effect of decreasing world market prices for the product which is supported. Reductions in consumption and increases in production combine to increase net exports which in turn depress world market prices. The effect may be significant for a large country but may be ignored for small countries trading in homogeneous agricultural products. Estimating the real income effects of existing market support prices on the basis of the observed world market prices will therefore exaggerate the real income loss for consumers and taxpayers and the real income gain for producers. The aggregate loss in real income will for an importing country be overestimated but it will be underestimated in the case of an exporter (see Table 27). In other words, the transfer efficiency for importing countries will increase, whereas for exporting countries it will decrease when the effect on world market prices is taken into account.

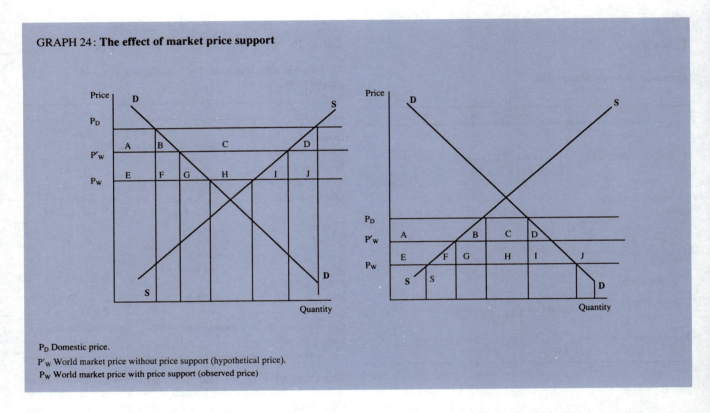

GRAPH 24: **The effect of market price support**

P_D Domestic price.
P'_W World market price without price support (hypothetical price).
P_W World market price with price support (observed price)

Table 27

Modification of partial equilibrium estimates of the real income effect of market price support

	Exporter	Importer
Transaction costs of market price support	Increases net loss	Increases net loss
Transaction costs and distortion costs of general tax collection	Increases net loss	Decreases net loss
Transaction and distortion costs of alternative means to achieve the redistributional objectives	Decreases net loss	Decreases net loss
Spill-over effects to other subsidized sectors	Decreases net loss	Decreases net loss
Spill-over effects in other taxed sectors	Increases net loss	Increases net loss
Longer time horizon	Increases net loss	Increases net loss
Macroeconomic considerations	?	?
Income stabilization	?	?

The effect on aggregate real income also depends on a number of other factors which need to be taken into account, but which are left out in the partial equilibrium analysis.

(i)   Transaction costs associated with market price support

Market price support in its simplest form is likely to be associated with relatively low direct transaction costs as the only control required is at the border. None the less, if market price support schemes are subsequently amended to include intervention purchasing and restrictions on production in various forms, the associated transaction costs may become significant.

(ii)   Transaction and distortionary costs associated with tax collection

In the case of an importing country, a market price support system will generate tariff revenue and hence reduce the need to raise government revenue by other means. The resulting saving in transaction and distortionary costs associated with raising government revenue should be set against the sum of the transaction costs associated with the market price support and the aggregate loss, as calculated in

Table 26. In the case of an exporter, however, government expenditures are increased due to export subsidies. Taking the transaction and distortionary costs of tax-raising measures into account therefore increases the economic costs.

(iii) Costs associated with alternative instruments to achieve the redistributional objectives

When calculating the total real income loss associated with price support, it is important to be specific concerning the basis of comparison. So far, the discussion has implicitly assumed a benchmark of no government intervention. This is not likely to be a realistic assumption. Market price support has often been instituted or increased in response to decline in agricultural terms of trade which would otherwise result in falling incomes and therefore has a redistributive objective which in the absence of market price support will therefore be pursued by other means. In assessing the economic costs of market price support, the transaction and distortionary costs of the alternative redistribution mechanism should be taken into account. In a comparison of instruments, all of which are associated with transaction costs and all of which distort the resource allocation, the net gain from removing market price support will be relatively lower than when the point of comparison is a situation without redistributional measures.

In relation to consumers, a market price support measure operates as an indirect regressive tax. Measures may therefore be undertaken to compensate for this, e.g. in the form of welfare food programmes. The costs of these corrective measures, to mitigate the distribution impact on consumers of market price support, should also be taken into account.

(iv) Spill-over effects to other distorted markets

Market price support may transfer resources from other highly protected sectors rather than to unprotected ones. Taking this into account may reduce the estimate of the real income loss. This point is of particular importance when the costs of market price support for one agricultural product is considered.

(v) The time horizon

The length of the time period in which market price support is kept in place is also very important in assessing the real income effect. The extent to which the real income gain to producers falls short of the transfer depends on the slope of the supply curve. In general, the shorter the time horizon the lower the supply response, as only intermediate inputs can respond to the higher prices in the short term. In the longer

term, both labour and capital are able to adapt, and producers can expand production by transferring resources from other sectors at increasing marginal costs. As a result, the difference between the actual real income gain and the transfer (which represents the upper limit for the real income gain) to producers, calculated on an annual basis, increases over time. The budget situation also changes as production increases and a country forfeits tariff revenue or finances export subsidies through increased taxation. The annual real income losses associated with a given level of market price support therefore increase over time.

The time horizon is also important for the assessment of the costs, compared with market price support, of alternative redistributional schemes. Direct income support schemes may have significant set-up costs (e.g. because they require individual registration of each recipient) but rather small annual running costs. Overall, therefore, the aggregate real income loss generated by a market price support scheme may, relative to an alternative redistributional scheme, increase the longer the time horizon. This suggests that the real income costs of market price support compared to alternative instruments may be more favourable when used in response to temporary decreases in world market prices than if made in response to a long-term problem.

(vi) Macroeconomic considerations

The above arguments have assumed that the general economy is in a state of equilibrium. If this is not the case, the assessment of real income loss from market price support needs to take at least two effects into consideration. Firstly, the resources released from the agricultural sector may not find employment in other sectors. Secondly, there is the more complicated argument based on the assumption that industrial workers have a reservation wage in real terms below which they will not accept work. Industrial workers will be unemployed if their reservation wage is higher than the value of their marginal product. A reduction in food prices will reduce their reservation wage in nominal terms and hence increase employment. Neither of these effects may be very important in the long run, but may be significant in the short term.

(vii) Income stabilization

Market price support can, in principle, be achieved by a system of fixed tariffs and export subsidies. Alternatively, it may be achieved by administratively determined domestic prices combined with variable tariffs (levies) and variable export subsidies. In the first case, domestic prices fluctuate in line with world market prices whereas, in the second, prices are in principle fixed. However, it is difficult in practice to maintain fixed domestic prices without direct intervention in the market by government or its agencies. Such buying and selling operations and the associated storage may involve substantial costs.

Domestic price stabilization tends to stabilise farmers' incomes in the case of traded commodities because it isolates domestic producers from fluctuations in (world market) prices. This is not necessarily the case for commodities which are not traded internationally because fluctuation in production in this case is negatively correlated with price movements. Moreover, stabilising domestic prices tends to destabilise world market prices. It therefore imposes a negative externality on other trading nations which may provoke reactions on their side.

An income stream received with certainty is valued more highly than an uncertain prospect with the same expected income. Stabilizing income in itself therefore represents a gain in real income. Price stabilisation may also have other beneficial effects. Stable prices may stimulate investments and growth through the positive externalities associated with investments. However, it is an open question to what extent stabilising domestic agricultural prices will result in stabilizing agricultural income and to what extent this will result in a net gain, when the administration and storage costs are taken into account.

The administrative determination of prices may also prevent non-competitive behaviour, for example the exploitation of farmers by a processing firm with a dominating position.

4.3. The economic effects of policy instruments which supplement market price support

Market price support may be combined with supplementary instruments which either reduce consumption or reduce production distortions. 'Consumer and processors' subsidies' belong to the first category. These schemes compensate processors or consumers, partly or fully, for the fact that market price support increases prices compared to world market prices. Such schemes may decrease the distortionary costs of market price support, but will in general increase 'other costs'.

In 'producer levy' (such as the co-responsibility levies of the EC) and 'market board' schemes, the revenue from market segments with low price elasticity, such as domestic consumer markets, is used to subsidize market segments with high price elasticity, such as export markets. Such schemes have the effect, compared with market price support, of reducing producer prices without eliminating the transfer from consumers. Compared with market price support at the same level as the consumer prices, this reduces budget costs and direct distortionary costs, but increases transaction costs because such measures introduce a price wedge between producer and consumer prices. This price wedge must be controlled. Market board schemes require that producers' associations have the sole right to sell a given product, which may also lead to inefficiencies.

'Quota restrictions on output' encourage the transfer of resources to other uses. This shift is likely to result in an improved allocation of resources if resources are moved out of agriculture, but not necessarily if they are shifted to other protected commodities within agriculture. If the country is an exporter, quota restrictions reduce budget costs. The introduction of fully transferable quotas corresponds in principle to a decrease in the farm price, to the level of the opportunity cost value of the resources used to produce the agricultural product in question, combined with a lump sum transfer, and the introduction of a consumer tax leaving the consumer price unchanged. They therefore reduce the direct distortionary costs of market price support. Quota schemes may, however, be associated with considerable transaction costs because they require control at the level of the individual farmers. These costs may be reduced if quotas are not transferable, but then the distortionary costs rise over time as production is not carried out by the most efficient producers.

'Set-aside', whereby arable land is taken out of production, implies a waste of land resources, but may increase real income if the opportunity value of the reduction in other inputs (fertilizer, capital, etc.) is higher than the opportunity value of the reduction in output (i.e. output evaluated at world market prices). Transaction costs are incurred, as in quota schemes, as it is necessary to check compliance with the terms of the programme. Set-aside increases the rent for land remaining in production and hence creates a transfer from land users to land owners. At unchanged producer prices, the land remaining in production will be farmed more intensively, which may have adverse consequences for the environment, whereas the idle land may represent a positive or negative aspect in terms of environmental and landscape values.

4.4. Measures of the transfer to the agricultural sector due to the CAP

Apart from public-expenditure budgetary figures such as those discussed above, perhaps the best-known measures of agricultural policy support are the producer and consumer subsidy equivalents (PSEs/CSEs) estimated for member countries by the OECD as part of that institution's 1987 ministerial mandate to monitor and report regularly on developments in agricultural policy in the light of reform principles established at that time. For a given set of agricultural policies in a given year, the PSE 'measures the value of the monetary transfers to producers from consumers of agricultural products and from taxpayers', while the CSE 'measures the value of monetary transfers from domestic consumers to producers and taxpayers' (OECD, 1993, pp. 231-2). These concepts therefore relate to economic flows between identified groups in (domestic, not foreign) society. They are calculated on the basis of the policy-induced differences in observed domestic and world market values established between producers and consumers of agricultural commodities, as well as budgetary (taxpayer) flows to the targeted group.

The PSE calculations include all transfers that specifically result from agricultural policy measures, grouped in five categories: market price support, direct payments to farmers, input subsidies, general services and other indirect support (such as tax concessions). However, they do not include measures specific to the food distribution and processing sectors, outlays for stockholding, environmental payments, rural social security (welfare) expenditure, and budgetary payments for permanent withdrawal of resources from agriculture. There are therefore substantial differences between the published budgets of the EC and the transfer from taxpayers included in the PSE/CSE calculations. In terms of the transfer/non-transfer classification described in the previous section, the OECD PSEs/CSEs emphasize transfers, since the major CAP expenditures on holding stocks of surplus products are excluded.

Furthermore, the OECD PSEs and CSEs are calculated on the basis of official data supplied for 12 major commodity groups (wheat, coarse grains, rice, oilseeds, sugar, milk, beef and veal, pigmeat, poultrymeat, sheepmeat, wool and eggs). They therefore cover only a proportion of the total (farm gate) value of agricultural production. In the case of the European Community in 1992, this proportion was 74%, the main omissions being fruit and vegetables, wine, tobacco, seeds and textile fibres. Many of these products are the focus of considerable intervention and budget expenditures within the CAP.

Despite these limitations, the OECD estimates are of considerable interest and influence. Having now been calculated for a number of years on a consistent basis for all major OECD Member States, and disseminated in a widely available annual report, they have been used extensively in the Uruguay Round of GATT negotiations. They also form the basis for more widely based 'total transfer' estimates, to be discussed below.

Table 28 shows the OECD PSE and CSE estimates for the EC in recent years. As can be seen, total PSE has been running at about ECU 65 000 million since 1990. Expressed as a share of the total value of production (of the commodities included, valued at domestic prices), and adjusted for direct payments and levies, the 'percentage PSE', at 41-49%, is at or slightly above the OECD average of 44% for the period 1987-92. This indicates that the transfers from consumers and taxpayers to EC agriculture defined in this way are of the same order of magnitude as the total remuneration to the primary factors, land, labour and capital, employed in agriculture.

The CSE figures (negative because the CAP represents an implicit tax on consumers) fluctuate around ECU 50 000 million, or about 40% of total (farm gate) value, again slightly above the OECD average.

Table 28

OECD PSE and CSE estimates for the European Community

	Av. 1979-86	1987	1988	1989	1990	1991	1992
PSEs							
Total (billion ECU)	39.2	62.2	58.6	54.2	64.8	68.3	66,0
As % of:							
total value of production	37	49	46	41	46	49	47
CSEs							
Total (billion ECU)	− 29.8	− 53.5	− 47.8	− 42.9	− 48.9	− 52.9	− 51.3
As % of:							
total value of production	− 30	− 46	− 40	− 34	− 40	− 42	− 40

Source: OECD (1993, pp. 262-265) (R-12).

As recognized by the OECD itself, PSEs and CSEs do not include all transfers to agriculture from domestic consumers and taxpayers resulting from a given set of policies, since there are a number of important expenditure categories such as other commodity regimes, tax concessions to farmers, and schemes which may not benefit farming alone or very directly. In the case of the EC, several national (EC Member State) measures fall into these categories.

Table 29 shows the OECD 'total transfer' estimates, defined as 'the sum of all transfers from taxpayers, plus all transfers from consumers, less estimated budgetary receipts from tariffs on agricultural imports' (OECD, 1993, p. 158). Transfers from taxpayers include all budgetary outlays that are included in the PSEs and CSEs, plus those excluded from the PSEs including some which in the terminology adopted here are non-transfer expenditures. Transfers from consumers correspond to the total (all-commodity) market price support element of the CSE, net of consumer subsidies borne by taxpayers. The 'total transfer' to the EC agriculture amounted in 1992 to ECU 120 000 million.

Table 29

Total EC agricultural policy transfers

	1988	1989	1990	1991	1992
Total transfers (ECU 1 000 million)					
from taxpayers	38.7	37.0	39.3	47.5	51.8
less budget revenues	− 0.9	− 0.8	− 0.7	− 0.5	− 0.6
from consumers	64.6	58.0	66.1	71.4	69.3
Total	102.4	94.2	104.8	118.4	120.5
Total transfers (ECU)					
per head of population	320	289	300	340	350
per full-time farmer	11 600	10 700	11 900	13 400	13 700
per hectare of farmland	730	670	750	850	870

Note: EC includes GDR in 1990, 1991 and 1992.
Source: OECD (1992, pp. 348-9 and 1993, pp. 159-63).

4.5. Real income effects

Neither of the two OECD concepts — 'total PSEs' and 'total transfers' — should be interpreted as the aggregate real income loss to the economy due to the CAP or as an indication of the real income gain to the farmers.

The information on which these measures are based may, however, be used to calculate model-based estimates of the 'economic costs' of the CAP. In order to do this, a reference situation has to be determined as the basis for comparison, i.e. a set of 'counterfactual hypotheses' about what policy, if any, would have been applied instead of that actually operated, must be made. Assumptions have to be made in particular concerning the behaviour of other countries and about how the income distributional issue due to the structural adjustment problems in agriculture would have been addressed in the absence of the CAP.

The removal of all border and domestic instruments related to EC farming may provoke changes in world market prices, especially if the behaviour of the EC's agricultural trading partners is affected by CAP 'abolition'. Thus some analyses, through global trade modelling, or by simpler methods, have attempted to take account of world-market reactions. For many products (but not necessarily livestock feed ingredients, for some of which international demand might fall in the case of reduced protection for animal products), this involves higher world prices, reducing the losses to producers and gains to consumers of removing the CAP. An example of such an exercise is reported below.

The perceived political need for income redistribution may, if not achieved via the CAP, have to be addressed by other methods which will also involve economic costs. Thus the 'economic costs of the CAP' should involve comparison with the budgetary and other costs of some alternative policy, such as a set of national agricultural policies, or an extended social-welfare system at national and/or Community levels. Such comparisons, which should cover also administrative and tax-related economic costs, have not been made. However, because of differences in the severity of the structural adjustment problems and in social institutions and preferences, the first step in such an assessment is the calculation of the real income effects at the Member State level.

The analysis of the real income effect of removing the CAP, as reported in Table 30, has been based on the following elements in addition to the partial equilibrium methodology explained above:

1. Countries both (a) contribute to the EC budget, according to a somewhat complex system taking into account their agricultural and non-agricultural imports from outside the EC, and a number of special provisions modifying the VAT-based and other national payments for particular Member States, and (b) receive CAP transfer expenditures, including export subsidies from that budget. With assumptions about the proportion of the total budget contribution allocated to the Agricultural Fund, these opposing flows give rise to a 'net budget transfer' for each Member State.

2. Trade in agricultural products with Member States is encouraged by Community 'preference' arising from the structure of the CAP's internal and border support prices. Such trade is conducted at prices which are subject to the distortions imposed on the internal EC markets by the CAP, so that, in general, imports cost more and exports earn more than the equivalent flows would do at world market prices. This gives rise to a 'preferential trade effect' for each country, positive in the case of net intra-EC exporters, and negative for net intra-EC importers, with the algebraic total summing to zero.

Table 30

Transfers, gains and losses arising from the CAP Guarantee Section (million ECU)

	BLEU	DK	D	GR	E	F	IRL	I	NL	P	UK	EUR-12
Transfers												
Transfers from EC[1] budget	500	1 003	3 642	1 403	961	4 899	1 040	3 390	2 842	90	1 460	21 230
Transfer to EC[2] budget	758	478	5 635	284	1 653	5 018	185	3 430	1 170	200	2 439	21 230
Net budget transfer	−258	525	− 1 993	1 119	− 692	− 119	875	− 40	1 672	− 110	− 979	0
Preferential trade effect[3]	− 15	527	− 598	− 73	182	1 360	746	− 1 998	258	− 81	− 328	0
Net transfer	− 273	1 052	− 2 591	1 046	− 510	1 241	1 621	− 2 038	1 930	− 171	− 1 307	0
Real income effects												
Producer gains	859	1 072	4 704	1 108	2 895	7 150	936	3 917	1 758	400	3 820	28 619
Consumer losses	824	423	4 858	756	2 513	5 129	330	4 150	1 172	516	4 313	24 984
Budget costs[4]	797	416	4 540	329	1 213	3 587	173	2 461	1 161	140	2 513	17 330
Net gains	− 762	233	− 4 694	23	− 831	− 1 566	433	− 2 694	− 575	− 256	− 3 006	− 13 695

[1] Adjusted for import levies and levies on sugar and isoglucose.
[2] The budget transfers to the EC are distributed between Member States according to their VAT contribution.
[3] Net transfers arising from internal trade taking place at EC prices rather than at world market prices.
[4] The total budget transfer to the EC of ECU 21 230 million has been reduced by the budget transfer adjusted for the estimated producer surplus for products which are not included in the analysis of gains and losses, consumer gains arising from internal market support for, in particular, dairy products, development support, etc. (total ECU 3 900 million). These budget costs are distributed between Member States according to their VAT contributions.
Source: Institute of Agricultural Economics, Copenhagen.

During the period analysed, the average budget costs of CAP transfer expenditures amounted to just over ECU 21 300 million. As has been well recognized, 'net budget transfers' have favoured certain 'agricultural' Member States such as Denmark, Ireland and Greece (especially on a per capita basis, not shown here), while representing a public-expenditure cost to others, notably Germany and the United Kingdom.

The addition of 'preferential trade effects' to the net budget transfers, to give 'net transfers', does not greatly alter this pattern. The sizes of gains and losses are in most cases enlarged (Belgium and Luxembourg, Denmark, Germany, Ireland, the Netherlands, Portugal, the United Kingdom and very significantly for Italy), in some diminished (Greece, Spain) and in one case (France) reversed. These transfer balances may be compared with estimates of real income gains and losses, which, as explained above, do not sum to zero across the Community. The decrease in aggregate real income for the Community as a whole is estimated to be ECU 13 700 million. This is, in other words, the estimate of the 'direct distortionary costs' of the CAP.

However, once again, the cost-benefit calculations for the different Member States cannot be made solely, on the basis of the net economic costs calculated in this way. Neither the substantial non-transfer expenditures related to the CAP nor the costs of redressing the negative effects on farmers' income of removing the CAP have been taken into account. The differences between Member States with respect to needs and social preferences may significantly influence the results. In other words, the different components of the aggregate real income effects on consumers, taxpayers and farmers and the effect on the environmental and rural conditions may be valued differently by the Member States. This theme is further developed in Chapter C.

Chapter C: Explaining agricultural policy[1]

---

[1] This chapter was prepared by Knud J. Munk. David Blandford, Carmel Cahil, Ulrich Koester and Ken Thomson provided helpful comments. Søren Nielsen provided helpful technical assistance.

Chapter C

Explaining agricultural policy

1. Introduction

This chapter sets out to explain why market price support policy has been the core element of EC agricultural policy, and why there has been increasing pressure over time to reform this policy. The analysis, in establishing a theoretical basis for understanding EC agricultural policy, focuses on how changes in the pressure on farm income and in the efficiency of various policy instruments in support of farm incomes explains changes in agricultural policy. Agricultural policies are also motivated by other objectives than farm income. The provision of research and development of agricultural products and processes and the dissemination of information about efficient production methods is an important government concern in many countries. Food security has historically been an important issue, and remains so in many developing countries. The environment has become a major concern in recent years. However, among developed countries, support of farm incomes has been the dominating issue in agricultural policy formulation.

The approach adopted here uses three central assumptions to explain the development of EC agricultural policies in the past and their likely evolution in the future. The first is that the behaviour of political systems, which are not marred by sharp ethnic or religious divisions reducing social cohesion, may as a first approximation be represented as the outcome of the maximization of a social welfare function exhibiting egalitarian value judgments. This implies that governments will redistribute income from the better off to the less well off.

The second central assumption is that such redistribution will involve economic costs whatever instruments are used. Government behaviour may therefore be seen as a compromise between achieving distributional objectives and limiting the economic costs of redistribution.

The third is that the preferences inherent in the political system are relatively stable, but that the costs associated with different instruments may differ according to circumstances. Government policies may therefore evolve as a consequence of changes in economic fundamentals affecting the trade-off between these two basic objectives, without any change in government preferences.

It is important to emphasize that although this approach implies that EC agricultural policies are explained as the outcome of the maximization of a social welfare function, this does not imply in itself a justification of these policies from a normative point of view.[1] If the value judgments underlying the social welfare function are not considered attractive from a normative point of view, then neither will the outcomes. It may be argued, for example, that an inherent characteristic of the political system in Western democracies is a heavy discounting of costs and benefits which will materialize only after the next election. The pain of adjustment is felt primarily in the short term, whereas the benefits in terms of a better allocation of resources are only realized in the long term. In the case of agriculture, the long term could cover the length of several electoral cycles. Agricultural policies which are rational, based on the time preferences implicit in the political system, may therefore appear not to be so if their assessment is based on time preferences involving a lower discount factor.

The chapter starts by providing a general theoretical framework for sectoral support policies. This framework is used to identify two basic trade-offs which are important in order to understand agricultural policies: the trade-off between redistributional objectives and economic efficiency and the trade-off between direct distortionary costs (often called dead weight loss) and other costs due to government support policies.

The third section, based on this theoretical framework, identifies those characteristics of the agricultural sector and the politico-economic system as a whole which make the adoption of market price support attractive and which, when adopted, make a high level of support more likely.

The fourth section reviews the empirical evidence. First, evidence is reviewed why farmers' incomes, in the process of economic development, come under pressure. Then new but compelling evidence indicates (as implied by the theoretical assumptions) that government support of farmers' incomes takes the economic costs of doing so into account. Results of an econometric analysis is presented which indicates that the differences in level of support among OECD countries may, to a large extent, be explained by

---

[1] To describe behaviour as the outcome of an optimization process does not necessarily imply justification of that behaviour, but can be considered merely as an explanation. Behaviour which is explained as the outcome of an optimization process can only be considered as justified if the underlying preference function (or the value judgments which this preference function expresses) is considered appealing and if the decisions are based on a correct perception of reality. It is possible, for example, to explain a consumer's behaviour implying the purchase of drugs or some other unhealthy consumption as the outcome of an optimization process, without justifying that behaviour.

differences in relative income positions of farmers and differences in the share of agricultural exports in agricultural production.[1]

The fifth section, based on the theoretical analysis of the previous sections, provides an explanation of why market price support became a key element of the Community agricultural policy, and why it has subsequently come under pressure.

A concluding section summarizes the main results of the analysis and raises the question of the role of the economist in providing an input to the process of improving agricultural policies.

2. The general theoretical framework

2.1. The preference function underlying the behaviour of the political system

The basic assumption adopted here, which allows the analysis to exploit the well-established body of welfare economic and public finance theory, is that the behaviour of a political system — government behaviour for short — can be explained as the outcome of maximizing a social welfare function which is degressively increasing in the real income of each member of society, i.e. which exhibits egalitarian value judgments.

Consistent preferences

The assumption that political decisions can be explained as if they were the outcome of the maximization of a preference function subject to constraints, reflecting what is feasible, has been unfashionable since Arrow's famous impossibility theorem. This implies that there is no guarantee that the decisions of a democratically-elected government are rational in the sense that they provide a consistent social ranking, even if the preferences of the individual voters are consistent. To try to avoid misunderstandings, the nature of this assumption is therefore considered in some detail.

First, the assumption that the outcome of the political process can be explained as the result of the maximization of a social welfare function does not imply that any person or institution consciously undertakes such an optimization. Rather, to

move from less desirable to more desirable outcomes only represents the ability of the social systems under normal conditions to change behaviour in response to changing circumstances. The approach adopted here is in fact based on a similar rationale as that used to justify the use of utility theory to explain household behaviour in response to income and price changes. From a psychological point of view, the assumption that households maximize utility is clearly not a reasonable theory of human decision-making. In both cases we have a limited understanding of the underlying dynamic process and must content ourselves with the optimization assumption as a helpful construction for the purpose of comparative static analysis.

Secondly, to explain the behaviour of a system from the micro level, if possible, in general provides valuable insight, but attempts to do so may often be an unpromising research strategy. Attempts based on public choice theory to explain the behaviour of political systems based on the behaviour of voters, interest organizations, parties, etc. have, for example, often been disappointing.

Egalitarian value judgments

The basic value judgment in welfare economics, which here is transformed into a behavioural assumption about the political system as a whole, is that the social welfare of society, represented by a social welfare function defined on the real income of each member of society, should be maximized. Pareto-efficient allocations are defined as those feasible allocations where no one can be made better off without someone else being made worse off. The allocation which maximizes the social welfare function is called the social optimum or the socially optimal allocation. The social welfare function is defined according to the Pareto value judgments which essentially imply the acceptance of the individual as the best judge of his own welfare and a set of supplementary value judgments which make it possible to compare the marginal welfare of income between households, i.e. the value of extra income, allocated to different households. We assume here that the supplementary value judgments defining the social welfare function, i.e. the preference function underlying government behaviour, are egalitarian. This means that the marginal welfare of income to each member of society falls as income increases.

The basic justification for this assumption is the consistent pattern across modern societies, in relation to a large range of policy areas including tax policies, education, health and social insurance and various sectoral policies that governments redistribute income from the relatively well off to the less well off.

---

[1] Swinnen, based on a somewhat different approach, reaches very similar conclusions (see Swinnen 1992, 1993, de Groter and Swinnen 1993, Swinnen and de Groter 1993 and Swinnen and Van der Zee 1994).

The obvious explanation, which may be justified based on ample anthropological evidence, why redistributional policies in support of social cohesion have broad support in society, is that man, being a social animal, has inherently altruistic preferences which are reflected at the social level through the political process. However, altruistic preferences may only develop in relatively small groups and may therefore be of less relevance for the behaviour of large social systems.

An alternative explanation is that altruism is an emerging property, i.e. a property which exists at the macro level although it does not exist at the micro level. Two related reasons may be given as to why the political system reveals a preference for more equal distribution of income although individual society members do not have altruistic preferences. The first is simply that the political élite realizes that it has more to lose than to gain from a more equal income distribution because of the risk of social unrest or lack of support for the political system. Another explanation may be the existence of an implicit social contract for the political system to provide an insurance to groups which, through no fault of their own, experience adverse conditions. There seems to be a willingness to accept that government provides support at a higher level to people who experience an unexpected decrease in income than to people who have never been able or willing to earn a living (unless this is due to a physical handicap). For example, in many countries unemployment benefits, funded via the general tax system, are provided at a higher level than are welfare payments. This may reflect this attitude. Industries with structural adjustment problems such as coal, steel and textiles have, as has agriculture, a high level of protection. The perception of policy-makers that there exists a 'farm income problem', namely that farmers, due to factors beyond their own control, have low and fluctuating incomes, may therefore provide an alternative explanation for the high level of support to the agricultural sector in most developed countries. Lindert (1991), for example, finds that a fast rate of decline in agricultural employment is the econometrically most significant factor in explaining high levels of agricultural support.

2.2. The trade-off between efficiency and equity

The purpose of this section is to explain why traditional welfare economics based on first-best assumptions ignore the trade-off between efficiency and equity, which under more realistic second-best assumptions becomes very important in understanding any government intervention in the economy and in particular in agricultural markets.

First-best welfare economics

Under first-best assumptions, it is assumed that in a market economy the government can, without cost, change the income distribution which would be the outcome of unfettered market forces based on the initial distribution of ownership rights to the means of production. The socially optimal allocation is therefore characterized by all individuals having the same marginal welfare of income. If the relation between income and welfare is the same for all, this implies that in the social optimum all will have the same level of income.

The two basic theorems of classical welfare economics suggest that, on the one hand, a market economy will generate an allocation of resources which is Pareto-efficient, and on the other, that any Pareto-efficient allocation, including the socially optimal allocation, can be achieved in a market economy by appropriate lump-sum transfers and taxes, i.e. transfers which the individual is not able to affect. These results are subject to a number of conditions, notably that all have perfect information, that markets for all commodities exist and that lump-sum redistribution is cost-free.

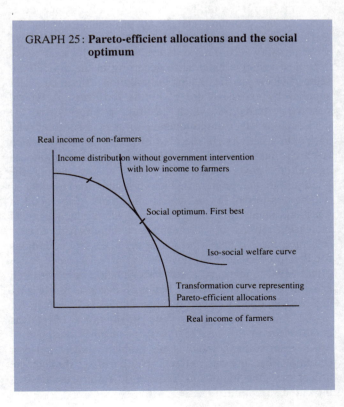

GRAPH 25: **Pareto-efficient allocations and the social optimum**

Real income of non-farmers

Income distribution without government intervention with low income to farmers

Social optimum. First best

Iso-social welfare curve

Transformation curve representing Pareto-efficient allocations

Real income of farmers

A necessary condition for a market economy to be Pareto-efficient under first-best conditions is that the marginal rate of transformation between any pair of factors and goods must be the same for all agents in the economy. Intervention by governments to fix prices at levels other than market-clearing levels involves a breach of these conditions. Hence, the general prescription in favour of non-intervention by government in the agricultural sector, and the more specific recommendation in favour of free trade in agricultural products (as the foreign sector is considered as just another production sector) is derived from the fact that competitive markets will satisfy the conditions required to achieve Pareto-efficiency and that any adverse income distributional outcome can be corrected at no cost.

As mentioned above, for a market economy to achieve Pareto-efficiency requires that competitive markets for all goods, including goods delivered in the future (perfect capital markets) and under different states of nature (contingent commodities) exist. When these conditions are not satisfied there is market failure. The most commonly recognized instances of market failure involve externalities, public goods and increasing returns to scale. In the case of an externality, where the economic activity of one agent alters the profit or utility function of at least one other agent in the economy and is not accounted for by the market, government should intervene to tax or subsidize the externality according to its evaluation by those affected. A typical negative externality occurring in the agricultural sector, which justifies a tax, is pollution caused to water supplies by excessive use of nitrate fertilizers. A typical positive externality, which justifies a subsidy, is the landscape or other environmental services associated with agricultural activity. In the case of public goods, of which research and extension activities are typical examples in agriculture, government should intervene to supply the good up to the point at which the sum of individuals' willingness to pay for an increase in supply of the good in question equals the marginal cost of producing it. If increasing returns to scale result in a monopolistic market structure, there is also a breach of the necessary conditions for Pareto-efficiency and government may intervene to set prices equal to marginal costs. This situation does not often arise in primary agriculture but may occur in processing and distribution. Finally, if interventions to correct for market failure create undesirable distributional effects (as could occur in the case of taxes or subsidies designed to offset externalities), there is no problem under first-best conditions because such effects may be offset through the use of cost-free lump-sum transfers to restore the desired income distribution.

Second-best welfare economics

The modern public finance theory as developed during the 1970s and 1980s by Atkinson, Mirrlees, Stiglitz and others adds further constraints to the government's maximization problem by recognizing that perfect information is never available, neither to the government nor to other agents in the economy and that obtaining or using information involves costs. One important implication of this is that cost-free lump-sum taxes and transfers are not available as instruments to the government. The characteristics on which a government would like to base differential lump-sum taxes and subsidies are not observable, or are observable only at great cost, and individuals have incentives not to reveal them (Atkinson and Stiglitz, 1980 p. 356 et seq.). In practice, taxation and income transfers must therefore be based on criteria such as income, which households are usually able to influence. Taxation and transferring income is therefore associated with costs in terms of distortions of the resource allocation. There are also transaction costs associated with the implementation and enforcement of government schemes to tax and redistribute income. Policy recommendations may, for these reasons, differ from those based on first-best welfare economics.

Not only instruments to redistribute income, but also instruments used to correct market failures are associated with transaction costs. A solution which satisfies the conditions for Pareto-efficiency may be associated with high transaction costs and may, therefore, be less desirable than a solution which does not. For example, it may not be worthwhile to correct for certain positive and negative externalities associated with agricultural production because the transaction costs outweigh the gains from an improved resource allocation.

The distortionary and transaction costs of raising government revenue imply that the opportunity cost of increasing government expenditure by one ecu is likely to be higher than that of reducing consumer income by the same amount. Import tariffs and export taxes on agricultural commodities — as used seen in many developing countries — may therefore be justified on purely efficiency grounds if the distortionary and transaction cost of generating government revenue using border measures is lower than the cost of using alternative tax instruments.

Due to the cost of redistributing income, allocations which are Pareto-efficient under second-best assumptions differ from those which are Pareto-efficient under first-best as-

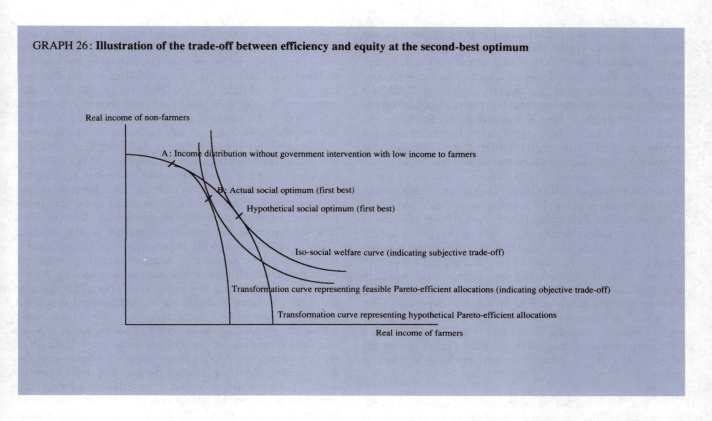

GRAPH 26: **Illustration of the trade-off between efficiency and equity at the second-best optimum**

Real income of non-farmers

A: Income distribution without government intervention with low income to farmers

B: Actual social optimum (first best)

Hypothetical social optimum (first best)

Iso-social welfare curve (indicating subjective trade-off)

Transformation curve representing feasible Pareto-efficient allocations (indicating objective trade-off)

Transformation curve representing hypothetical Pareto-efficient allocations

Real income of farmers

sumptions. To avoid confusion they are therefore sometimes called 'restricted Pareto-efficient allocations'.[1]

Thus there exists a trade-off between equity and efficiency (see Graph 26). A solution which involves a more equal income distribution may be associated with high transaction and distortionary costs and may therefore be less desirable than a solution with a less equal income distribution but lower transaction and distortionary costs. This implies that even when an unrestricted Pareto-efficient allocation is feasible (A), the social optimal allocation (B) will in general be a restricted Pareto-efficient allocation. The social optimal allocation therefore need not be characterized by government non-intervention in agricultural markets. From a second-best perspective, there is no *a priori* reason why governments, in countries where the transaction costs of less distorting transfer instruments like income tax and means-tested social benefit schemes are very high, should not intervene in agricultural markets to bias prices in favour of either the urban or the rural poor (Newbery, 1987).

The trade-off between equity and efficiency implies that the rules for dealing with externalities and public goods in agriculture become more complex than under first-best assumptions. The polluter-pays principle, for example, may not be optimal when the distributional consequences of identifying and taxing the polluter are taken into account. On the other hand, the revenue generated by environmental taxes has a high opportunity value due to the cost of raising government revenue. Under first-best conditions, correction of market failures due to externalities and public goods can ignore the effect on other markets. This is not the case under second-best conditions. For example, the optimal level of a fertilizer tax needs to take into account the effect the tax has on subsidized production, and hence, on the government budget. The optimal level of agricultural research must, on the one hand, take into account that increased production should only be valued at opportunity cost prices (world market prices), and on the other, that increased income to farm households having, on average, a low level of income, represents a relatively high social value.

The second-best framework also provides a justification for government intervention to stabilize farmers' income. Incomplete contingent markets and imperfect capital markets due to lack of perfect information constitute market failures which may justify government intervention (Newbery and Stiglitz, 1981). Because of asymmetric information and high transaction costs, capital markets may not absorb the risk due

---

[1] It is important, however, to emphasize that the restrictions are not political ones, but due to limited information. They are as 'real' as any other technical constraints.

to price and quantity fluctuations sufficiently. A moral hazard problem arises in capital markets because the borrower can make decisions which effect the chance of bankruptcy without the credit-provider being able to observe behaviour and, on this basis, adjust the interest rate charged. Adverse selection arises because individuals at high risk of bankruptcy are more likely than those at low risk to ask for loans and thus push up interest rates. Asymmetric information and high transaction costs also create moral hazard and adverse selection problems in insurance and futures markets.

In the case of small, risk-adverse family farms, capital and insurance markets cannot be relied upon to re-allocate risk in an optimal way. Few small farmers use futures markets to cover price risk. Farmers may feel at an informational disadvantage compared to large traders and may fear manipulation (Stiglitz, 1987). This will be detrimental to welfare for two reasons. Firstly, because consumption of farm households will not be distributed optimally over time. There may be periods when a fall in income depresses farm household consumption more than if farmers had access to perfect capital markets. Secondly, it reduces production efficiency because farmers will not fully exploit economies of scale, but, rather, produce several products in order to reduce risk.

With respect to direct stabilization of farmers' income, governments face the same moral hazard problems as private agents even if they avoid the adverse selection problems by making schemes compulsory. Price stabilization schemes may not, or only to a limited extent, stabilize farm income. Furthermore, such schemes are susceptible to speculative attacks (Knudsen and Nash, 1990; Anderson, 1992). In any case, instability cannot be avoided. Successful price stabilization will destabilize either government credit or budget requirements which may in themselves be undesirable.

On the basis of static analysis, it has been argued that the welfare gain due to price stabilization is likely to be limited (Newbery and Stiglitz, 1981). On the other hand, it has also been argued that high risk is likely to discourage investment, in particular in new technology, and that loss due to these dynamic effects could be significant (Stiglitz, 1987; Crawford, 1988; Timmer, 1989).

To summarize, in the first-best framework it is possible to separate the issues of allocational efficiency and distributive equity entirely. The main policy recommendations when applied to the agricultural sector are that government should not intervene to set prices and should not adopt protective measures which impede free trade. Government should intervene in the sector only to the extent required to correct for market failures due to positive externalities (landscape value, etc.), negative externalities (pollution), public goods (agricultural research) and monopolistic practices in upstream and downstream sectors. The answer to the question of how to provide support is, in this framework, that low farm income should, on the basis of egalitarian value judgments, be corrected using lump-sum transfers, i.e. transfers, the size of which neither the households being taxed nor the recipient households are able to influence. The first-best welfare economics is unrealistic in its assumptions, cost-free lump-sum transfers are clearly not feasible, and fail spectacularly, interpreted as a positive theory, to explain agricultural policies and other sectoral policies. The modern public finance theory recognizes that government and other agents in the economy have limited information and that cost-free lump-sum income redistribution therefore is not feasible. There is a basic trade-off between equity and efficiency which has to be taken into account in any government intervention which may affect income distribution. Where agriculture is concerned, this implies that policies to redistribute income to farmers should not be pursued until they have the same income as non-farmers, but only to the point where the marginal gains in terms of an improved income distribution correspond to the marginal losses due to a less efficient resource allocation and other economic costs. Furthermore, imperfect information is an additional cause of market failure which may justify government intervention, particularly in capital and insurance markets. The basic insight is that equity and efficiency considerations cannot generally be separated in the context of government intervention.

2.3. The trade-off between direct distortionary costs and other costs

The general framework presented above suggests that the government will support low-income groups the stronger its redistributional preferences and the smaller the economic costs associated with income redistribution.

The economic costs of redistribution may be divided into 'direct distortionary costs' — corresponding to the dead weight losses which may be illustrated, as in Chapter B, in traditional partial equilibrium supply-demand diagrams — and 'other costs' covering the transaction costs directly associated with the managing of the policy instrument and the excess costs of financing the budget expenditure to provide the income transfer.

Redistributional objectives can, however, be achieved by different instruments. Therefore, in achieving the right balance between efficiency and equity considerations the government not only has to decide on the level of support but also on which instrument to use, taking into account the economic costs associated with the use of various instruments.

In order to gain more insight into the government's decision-making problem in providing sectoral support to achieve income distributional objectives, a simplified model is formulated. The model, which for the sake of expositional simplicity, is based on a partial equilibrium approach, disregards public goods, externalities and increasing returns to scale and other reasons for market failure which provide additional justifications for government intervention in the economy. The model also takes the price at which the product in question is traded as given, disregarding the terms of trade effects of domestic support policy.

The model represents the government choice of sectoral support policies in terms of the producer price p, the consumer price q, a sector specific primary factor subsidy t_z, and a lump-sum transfer scheme where the level of transfer is indicated by ζ. The level of general taxation, which when other instruments are changed, in general, needs to be adjusted to maintain balance on the government budget, is denoted by τ. The details of the model are set out in the appendix.

The government's maximization problem may, within the framework of the model, be formulated as follows:

(1) $\text{Max NB} = B(q,p,t_z,\zeta) - C(\tau)$ subject to $T(\tau) - G(q,p,t_z,\zeta) = 0$

q,p,t_z,ζ,τ

where:

(i) $B(q,p,t_z,\zeta) = \Sigma \beta^h S^h(q) + \Sigma \beta^h \pi^h(p,t_z) + \Sigma \beta^h L^h(\zeta)$ is the net social benefit, where $S^h(q)$ is the consumers' surplus function, $\pi^h(p,t_z)$ the sectoral producers' surplus function, $L^h(\zeta)$ the lump-sum subsidy function and β^h the marginal social welfare of household h;

(ii) $C(\tau) = \Sigma \beta^h k_1 \theta(Y^h,\tau)$ is the social costs, and (k_1-1) the distortionary costs of raising extra general tax revenue and $\theta(Y^h,\tau)$ a tax function indicating the general tax payment for a household with an income Y when the level of taxation is τ;

(iii) $G(q,p,t_z,\zeta) = k_2[E^i - (q - pW)X(q) + (p - p^W)Y(p) + t_z Q(w) + \underset{h}{\Sigma} L^h(\zeta)]$ is the government's revenue requirement to finance its sectoral policy assuming that other government expenditures are kept fixed, and k_2 the transaction costs of raising general tax revenue. X(q) is the aggregate demand function, Y(p) the aggregate supply function and Q(w) the aggregate supply functions for primary factors employed in the sector.

The model allows different support instruments and the different combinations of 'distortionary costs' and 'other costs', to be represented. The model allow the representation of lump-sum transfers, primary factor subsidies, output subsidies, co-responsibility levies, market price support and quantitative restrictions such as output quotas.

In the model, the direct distortionary costs of the government's sectoral support policy are represented by the elasticities implicit in the consumers' surplus function (the supply elasticity, E^D) and the producers' surplus function (the supply elasticity, E^S). The direct administrative costs and other transaction costs are represented by E^i which are supposed to differ between support regimes (the index i indicates the support regime). The indirect distortionary costs are represented by k_1 and the indirect transaction costs by k_2 (see Table 31).

Table 31

Model parameters and types of economic costs associated with sectoral support

	Direct distortionary costs	Direct administrative costs	Indirect distortionary costs	Indirect administrative costs
E^S	x			
E^D	x			
E^i		x		
k_1			x	
k_2				x
$Z=Y-X$		(x)	x	x
$(p-pW)/p$	x	(x)	x	x

NB: E^i is partially a function of $Z=Y-X$ and $(p - pW)/p$. The model does not take into account marginal changes in E^i due to these variables.

There seems, as argued in Chapter B, to be a trade-off between 'direct distortionary costs' and 'other costs'. There seems to be a tendency for instruments which have relatively high 'direct distortionary costs' to be associated with relatively low 'other costs' and vice versa. Furthermore, there seems to be a tendency for this trade-off to depend on the level of economic development (see Graph 27).

The trade-off between direct distortionary costs and other costs also depends crucially on the trade position. Market price support, in the case of a product for which the country is an importer, generates government revenue, whereas, if the country is an exporter, it is associated with budget costs. This tendency is reinforced when terms-of-trade effects —

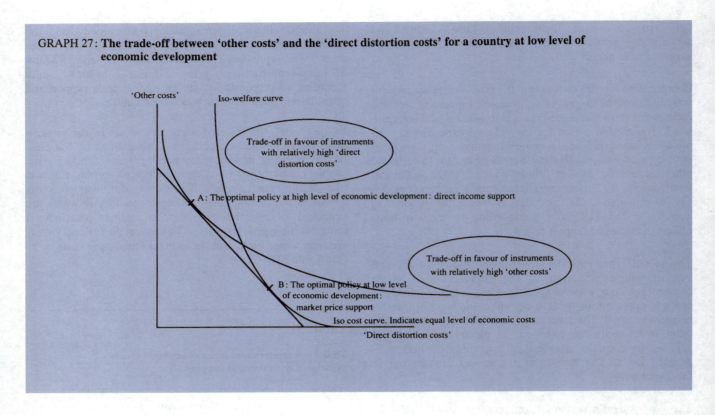

GRAPH 27: **The trade-off between 'other costs' and the 'direct distortion costs' for a country at low level of economic development**

which for big countries may be significant — are taken into account. Also, the direct administrative costs are likely to be higher for an exporter than for an importer. The economic costs of providing a given level of support is therefore higher for an import sector than for an export sector.

Another important point is that the trade-off depends on the length of the time-period that the structural adjustment pressure in the sector in question is expected to persist. Systems to provide support have significant set-up costs. These, by definition, are of relatively greater importance for instruments where the transaction costs constitute the bigger share of the costs. Furthermore, the distortionary costs increase with time because the supply response is usually significantly greater in the long run than in the short run. A tariff may therefore be the most cost-efficient instrument to deal with the income distributional problems associated with short-term income problems, for example, due to temporarily low world market prices, while a direct income support scheme may be more cost-efficient in the case of a permanent decline in world market prices. In the model used here, the time horizon for a change in a policy instrument is reflected in the size of the elasticities implicit in the producers' surplus functions and the consumers' surplus functions. If a tariff is to be in place only for a short period, relatively low elasticities should be used to assess its impact.

The factor by which future costs and benefits are discounted also plays an import role for the trade-off. A high discount factor will make instruments with relatively high distortionary costs, such as market price support, more attractive because over time distortionary costs increase and redistributional benefits decrease. Distortionary support increases the income of factor owners today, but will also increase the structural adjustment problem tomorrow because the transfer of resources to other sectors which would otherwise have taken place is delayed (see Graph 28). To justify such support the welfare gains in terms of avoiding low levels of income must outweigh the losses in economic efficiency due to the delay of the adjustment of the resource allocation. Since the welfare gains in terms of a more equal income distribution materialize mainly in the short term, whereas the efficiency losses are incurred mainly in the longer term, it is obvious that the form and level of support provided to an industry depends crucially on the implicit discount factor adopted. In the comparative static framework used here a high discount factor is represented by small supply elasticities generating smaller direct distortionary costs.

2.4. Market price support

When a market price support regime has been chosen to support sectoral income, government still needs to decide on the level of support. In the model this involves choosing that

GRAPH 28: **Evolution of relative income and farm employment**

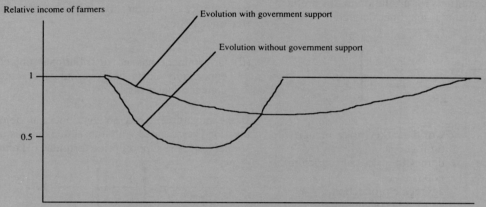

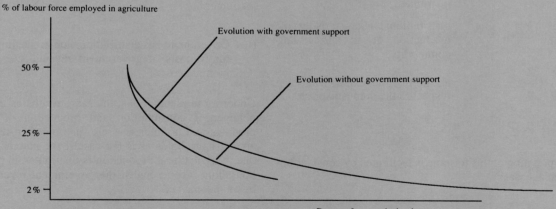

level of p, in the case of a market price support regime representing both the producer price and the consumer price, which maximize the net benefit, i.e. which solves

(2) $\max_{p} NB = B(p,p) - C(\tau(p,p)) = \Sigma \beta^h S^h(p) + \Sigma \beta^h \pi^h(p)$
$- \Sigma \beta^h k_1 \theta(Y^h, \tau(p,p))$

From the first-order conditions for a solution to this problem the following price formula may be derived (see the appendix for details)

(3) $\dfrac{p^* - p^W}{p^*} = \left[\dfrac{\dfrac{Y}{Z} R_Y - \dfrac{X}{Z} R_X}{k R_\tau} - 1 \right] \dfrac{1}{-E_Z}$

where

p^W:	world market price of agricultural goods,
p:	domestic price of agricultural goods,
Y:	aggregate production,
X:	aggregate consumption,
$Z = Y - X$:	net export of agricultural goods,
$k = k_1 k_2$:	opportunity cost of government funds,
$R_X = \Sigma \beta^h x^h / X$:	distributional characteristics of consumption of an agricultural commodity,
$R_\tau = \Sigma \beta^h x^h \dfrac{\partial \theta^h / \partial \tau}{\partial T^h / \partial \tau}$:	distributional characteristics of increase in the alternative tax instrument,
$R_Y = \Sigma \beta^h y^h / Y$:	distributional characteristics of production of an agricultural commodity,
$E^Z = \dfrac{\partial Z}{\partial p} / \dfrac{Z}{p}$:	elasticity of net export with respect to the domestic price.
$= \dfrac{Y}{Z} E^s - \dfrac{X}{Z} E^D$	

The interpretation of this formula is facilitated by considering three special cases:

(i) Government has no distributional objectives and the opportunity costs of government revenue are equal to nominal costs

We first notice that if the government has no distributional objectives (i.e. if the marginal social welfare of income is the same for all households) so that $R_X/R_\tau = 1$ and $R_Y/R_\tau = 1$, and if taxation is not associated with transaction and distortionary costs so that $k = 1$, then the support price formula (Equation (3)) reduces to

(4) $p^* = p^W$

This means that the domestic price will be equal to the world market price or, in other words, the government will adopt a free trade policy.

(ii) Government has no distributional objectives, but the opportunity costs of government revenue are greater than nominal costs

If the government has no distributional objectives, but if taxation is associated with transaction and distortionary costs so that $k > 1$, the support price formulae (3) reduces to

(5) $\dfrac{p^* - p^W}{p^*} = \left[\dfrac{1}{k} - 1 \right] \dfrac{1}{-E^Z}$

The net export supply elasticity, E^Z, is positive if the net export is positive, and negative if there are net imports. The support price, therefore, in the absence of distributional considerations, is below the world market price in the case of exports and above the world market price in the case of imports. In both cases, the difference between the support price and the world market price is greater the smaller the net export supply elasticity and the bigger the transaction and distortionary costs associated with the alternative tax instrument.

(iii) Government has distributional objectives and the opportunity costs of government revenue are greater than nominal costs

Under these assumptions, the same results as under (ii) are obtained if consumption and production of agricultural products and tax increases are distributed in the same way among households as is the case if the income elasticity is one, if agricultural production is distributed in proportion to household income and if the government revenue is raised by an income tax.

Therefore as seen from Equation (3), taking distributional aspects into consideration will lead to higher prices than when this is not the case if farmers have a small income compared with other households, if poor farmers have a relatively big share of production and if according to the value judgments of the government the social welfare of income is increasing strongly with decreasing income i.e. if

R_Y is high; and if the consumers are relatively rich compared to the farmers and if the relative rich consumers have a relatively big share of the consumption of agricultural products i.e. if R_X is small.

For an importing country distributional considerations will lead to a price even further above the world market price than if distributional considerations are not taken into account. For an exporting country, however, R_Y needs to be very large for a price above world market price to be chosen as without the distributional aspects being taken into consideration the price will be below the world market price.

The model framework and the price formulae make it possible to identify the factors which determine when market price support is chosen as an instrument to support sectoral income and, when chosen, the level of support.[1]

Generally speaking, market price support is chosen to redistribute income when real income transfer achieved using this instrument is well targeted and when the economic costs are perceived to be smaller than if the same effect on real income had been achieved using alternative instruments.

Market price support is likely to be chosen to support sectoral income:

(a) when it increases the income of factor owners with relatively low income;

(b) when it decreases the real income of consumers and taxpayers with relatively high income;

(c) when governments have relatively strong redistributional preferences;

(d) when 'the distortionary costs' of market price are (perceived to be) relatively low. This will be the case if supply and demand elasticities are small, if the support is only provided for a short period and if political decision-making processes imply a high discount factor;

(e) when direct administrative costs are low, which will be the case if the country is an importer and already has an administrative system for collecting border taxes;

(f) when the budget costs and hence the 'indirect costs' are low or even negative, i.e. when the country is an importer;

(g) when for an importer (exporter) the administrative and distortionary costs of raising government revenue using general tax instruments are high (low);

(h) when the 'other costs' of less distortionary support instruments are high and difficult to target to low income factor owners, as will be the case in countries with a weak administrative infrastructure.

The same factors which make it more likely that market price support is chosen as a support instrument also explain why, when market price support is used, a relatively high level of support is provided.

The theoretical analysis suggests that a large number of factors, some which are difficult to measure, determine when market price support is chosen and, when chosen, at what level support is provided. Two factors which are however both crucial and relatively easy to observe are the relative level of income of the factor owners in the industry in question relative to that in the economy as a whole and the share of net trade relative to domestic production for the commodities produced in the industry (see Section 4).

2.5. International spill-over effects

Sectoral support policies have important spill-over effects on international markets due to their effect on world prices. Support instruments with high direct distortionary costs will normally tend also to have a strong effect on world market prices. Price support policies increase production and decrease consumption and hence increase net exports if surpluses are not disposed of by other means. This in turn depresses world market prices. The effect on world market prices under first-best assumptions represents a gain to importing countries and a loss to exporting countries. Under second-best assumptions the analysis becomes more complicated. The decrease in world market prices not only has terms-of-trade effects but also creates supplementary structural adjustment pressure and may therefore — even for importing countries — have negative effects. The interaction between different countries may have the structure of a prisoner's dilemma where each player disregards the negative spill-over effects of his own action leading to a non-optimal outcome. A situation where decisions on the form and level of sectoral support are taken by different governments individually without regard to the spill-over effects may, by coordinated action, be changed to provide benefits (as defined by the different political preference functions) to all countries involved. Such action, however, requires that an operational basis for making a commitment to reduce trade-distorting support can be established and that the players have sufficient trust in each other to be satisfied that neither will cheat on commitments made to reduce support. It may also require side payments to be made to those

---

[1] The framework may also be used to explain why governments in developing exporting countries may choose a negative level of market price support. However, since the focus here is on sectoral policies in developed countries, this avenue is not pursued.

(importing countries) which may be negatively affected by reduction in sectoral support.

Creating the level of trust necessary for international coordination is always difficult. If the desired form and level of support were the same for all countries this would facilitate the process, but the analysis presented here suggests that countries, depending on their export position, the severity of their structural adjustment problem, their level of development and other factors, will prefer different levels of protection even when they take into account the coordination gains which can be achieved by mutual reduction of the level of protection.

International coordination may not only affect the level of support provided but also the form of support. One would, for example, expect international coordination among exporting countries to shift support from market price support to direct income support since the latter allows the distributional objectives to be achieved at a lower cost in terms of negative international spill-over effects than does the former.

Price support policies isolate domestic prices from international price fluctuations and therefore 'export' the price effect of domestic supply-and-demand shocks which in general increase price fluctuations in international markets. This constitutes a negative spill-over effect on all trading nations, in particular on developing countries which lack the financial and social institutions to deal with fluctuating prices.

3. Explaining agricultural policy

3.1. The public finance approach

All developed countries provide financial support for their farmers. Although the form and level of support differs between countries and changes over time, market price support is clearly the core instrument in agricultural policies worldwide.

Given a public finance approach, the first problem is to explain why farm incomes tend to be lower (in particular without support) than those of other social groups, and the second to explain why the factors which make market price support attractive according to this approach are likely to be found in agriculture.

The theoretical explanation for the low agricultural incomes in industrialized countries is based on assumptions concerning the demand for agricultural products, the effect of productivity increases on income and on agricultural production and concerning the mobility of agricultural factors of production. Demand for agricultural products is assumed to be income-inelastic. Increases in productivity, even if they affect agriculture and non-agriculture to the same extent, will tend to increase the demand for agricultural products more slowly than they increase the supply of agricultural products. This would not put pressure on farm incomes if the resources employed in agriculture were easily transferred to sectors where they could gain a normal return, since this would restore the income level for the remaining factors of production. However, due to low mobility, agricultural labour does not leave the sector sufficiently rapidly to prevent falling real prices of agricultural products, and falling remuneration of labour relative to other sectors where the remuneration of labour is increasing over time.

In most developed countries, market price support to farmers is introduced at the time of the industrial take-off where the share of the agricultural labour force is still more than 25%.

At this level of economic development the mobility of labour is relatively limited, production highly intensive in land, labour and other semi-fixed primary factors. This makes the supply elasticities low, which implies low direct distortionary costs.

Farmers at this level of development often constitute a relatively homogenous group with the occurrence of part-time employment in high-income industries due to a less developed transport infrastructure being rare. Under these circumstances, market price support is a relatively well-targeted support instrument.

International trade is often small relative to domestic production due to high transaction costs. Border taxes are used to raise government revenue due to high costs of administratively more-demanding tax instruments. The additional direct administrative costs to use market price support to increase farmers' income are therefore relatively small, especially if the country is an importer.

The opportunity costs of government revenue are in general high due to a primitive administrative infrastructure. This implies that market price support for imported agricultural products will have significant indirect benefits by generating government revenue.

The income elasticity of food is relatively high, implying that the welfare costs of higher food prices are relatively low.

At this level of development, the cost of support instruments with less direct distortionary costs tends to be relatively high due to the large number of (often illiterate) farmers and to the weak administrative infrastructure which makes it difficult to ensure that direct income transfers will reach those for whom they are intended. Direct income support is extremely costly both in terms of the costs of making individual payments to a sizeable part of the population and in terms of the excess costs of raising government revenue to cover the budget costs. Most countries at this level of development have no social security net covering farmers, whereas schemes may be in place to support industrial workers in case of unemployment.

Financial markets might also be primitive and associated with high transaction costs and high profit margins. Without government intervention, price instability may therefore lead to high concentrations of land ownership, which, for efficiency and social reasons, are undesirable.

Rural communities based on agriculture at this level of development often constitute a cohesive force which by a rapid transfer of employment to urban centres may be eroded, leading to increased crime and social unrest. Market price support may be an effective force in halting the exodus from rural areas.

3.2. The public choice approach

Public choice theory, often based on anecdotal rather than solid empirical evidence, constitutes an alternative approach to explaining agricultural policy (Gardner 1992). The fact that agriculture in developed countries has been able to obtain a high level of support, but not in developing countries, is in this approach explained by the observation that the articulation of group interest constitutes a public good in relation to the members of the group and, as such, is associated with a free-rider problem. The seemingly disproportionate influence of farmers on agricultural policies in developed countries is explained by the fact that they constitute a relatively homogeneous group with strong interests in higher agricultural prices, whereas consumers, who have an opposite interest in lower agricultural prices constitute a non-homogeneous group with many members and a much lower intensity of interest (see, for example, Olson, 1965).[1] An interest group is more likely to overcome the

---

[1] This point may be illustrated by an example. At a low level of economic development where, say, farmers constitute half the population, where average income is ECU 1 000 per year and the share of food in the consumers' budget is 50%, and where world market prices are 20% below domestic prices (creating a gross transfer to farmers of ECU 200) the net income gain of farm households is only ECU 100 (because farmers are also consumers) compared with an income loss of ECU 100 for non-farm households. Compare this with a situation where 10% of the population are farmers, where average income is ECU 1 000 and where the share of food in the consumer budget is 20%. In this case, world market prices of 20% below domestic prices will provide a transfer to the average farm household of ECU 3 600 at the cost of only ECU 400 to the average non-farm household.

free-rider problem the more important the common interest of the members of the group (the price of food is more important for farmers than for consumers), the more homogeneous the group with respect to the type of interest of its members (the interests of farmers are more homogeneous than are those of small shopkeepers), but not necessarily with respect to the intensity of their interests (it may be easier for a group of farmers with some big farmers to overcome the free-rider problem than for a group where all are of the same size). Empirical evidence suggests that the farm sector gets most protection when it employs 3 to 4% of the employed labour force (Honma and Hayami, 1986; Lindert, 1991).

3.3 Combining the two approaches

That social groups articulate their interests and that bureaucrats and politicians pursue their own interests does not necessarily contradict the public finance representation of the behaviour of the political system as the outcome of the maximization of a social welfare function. Firstly, the public choice approach may, based on theoretical explanations of the behaviour of the component parts of the political system, potentially provide a deeper insight into why and under what circumstances the political system behaves as if it were the outcome of the maximization of a social welfare function based on egalitarian value judgments. Secondly, it may draw attention to some of the limitations of basic assumptions of the public finance approach, that the government's preference function can be defined on the real income of the social groups in society as given independently of the choice of policy instruments. The possibilities for interest groups to overcome the free-rider problem of collective action may depend on the instruments used and the power of the government apparatus (political parties, bureaucracy, ministers, etc.) may also depend on the instruments used. Bureaucrats and politicians may not be able to capture directly any of the rents associated with agricultural policies. They may however be able to increase their own power by influencing agricultural policies in directions which are not in the interest of either producers, consumers or taxpayers. This may translate into attempts to expand administrative expenditures associated with agricultural polices and to adopt policies like import quotas, which give bureaucrats more discretionary power than do tariffs, which would provide farmers with the same level of support. Similarly, in pursuit of maximization of their own power and influence, bureaucrats may seek to prevent the contraction of the industry for which they are responsible. Politicians, in order to secure support from special interest groups without alienating bigger groups of voters, may choose less transparent instruments with complex operational rules rather than direct transfers, the direction and magnitude of which are difficult to identify.

To summarize, agricultural policy may, following a public finance approach, as a first approximation be explained as if it were the outcome of the maximization of a social welfare function defined on the real income of each member of society and reflecting egalitarian value judgements. The interest of the political élite to maintain the social peace and implicit social contract to provide 'insurance' against adverse circumstances may be the motivation behind redistributional policies. The length of the electoral cycle and the need of politicians to be elected may explain why the economic costs of trade-distorting support instruments, when assessed on the basis of the time preference revealed in the market place, tend to be underestimated in the political process. Public choice arguments may supplement the public finance approach to gain insight in agricultural policy formulation. It may also highlight cases where the basic public finance assumption is particularly unrealistic.

4. Empirical evidence

4.1. Introduction

The purpose of this section is to provide empirical evidence for the public finance explanation of agricultural policy presented above. The same empirical evidence may be exploited to support different theoretical explanations. It is therefore of particular interest to focus on evidence which supports the public finance explanation while being inconsistent with that provided by alternative approaches. The theoretical analysis presented here suggests that net agricultural exports relative to agricultural production and the income per person employed in agriculture relative to that in the economy as a whole are both crucial variables in explaining differences across countries and over time in the use of and in the level of market price support. The first variable is closely related to the budget cost of providing support and may, both from the point of view of a public finance approach and a public choice approach, be expected to be a significant variable. However, only the public finance approach suggests that the relative income variable should be negatively correlated with the level of support.

The section first considers the empirical evidence for the farm income problem. It then reviews the use of market price support worldwide and finally reports results of an econometric, combined cross-sector time series analysis for the OECD countries.

4.2. The farm income problem

Empirical evidence seems to support the various elements of the theoretical explanation that farmers' incomes tend to fall behind in the course of economic development. Price elasticities of demand for agricultural products are typically found to be low, as are income elasticities. That consumers spend a declining share of household budgets on food is a global phenomenon observed as economies grow and make the transition from developing to developed status. Moreover, most econometric estimates of the elasticity of demand for exports, which can be an important component of total demand in an open agricultural economy, confirm rather than reject the low-elasticity hypothesis. That total demand for food grows only slowly is also readily verifiable, the rate of growth in many developed economies closely approximating the rate of population growth. Technological progress even seems to increase agricultural production capacity faster than in other sectors and to be labour-saving in character. There is also clear evidence that established farmers, even under pressure of incomes significantly lower than those in other sectors, have a high degree of immobility. This may be attributed to non-wage preferences because adjustment entails wholesale changes in lifestyle, social networks and location. Also the limited relevance in other sectors of a training in agriculture implies that labour leaving agriculture has difficulty in securing employment at the level of remuneration prevailing outside the sector.

In all OECD countries, the value-added per person employed in agriculture is in fact lower than in other sectors, significantly so in the countries with a long history of agricultural production and therefore, in general, more severe structural adjustment problems (see Table 32 , column 2).

The evolution of world market prices for agricultural products in real terms has, since the war, shown a downward trend of 2% p.a. The trend can be traced further back (see Tracy, 1989). This suggests that productivity growth in agriculture has been higher than in other sectors. The downward trend during the 1980s of more than 6% has been even steeper. The downward trend of almost 4% in real domestic EC prices for traded agricultural commodities is less than that on world markets, but is still very significant. Due to high productivity growth, value-added per person employed in EC agriculture has remained constant although at a very low level (see Graph 29). This reflects a considerable outflow of agricultural labour of around 3% per year. The steep decline in agricultural employment is also a common feature in all developed economies. In some of the wealthiest economies the proportion of the labour force engaged in agriculture is now as low as 2%. Agricultural employment has adapted to the lower-than-normal remuneration, but the speed of adaptation seems not to have been fast enough to equalize the return to labour in the agricultural sector with that in other sectors.

Recent empirical work (Gardner, 1992; Hill, 1992), however, places a question mark over whether in the most developed economies the income of farm households (including the

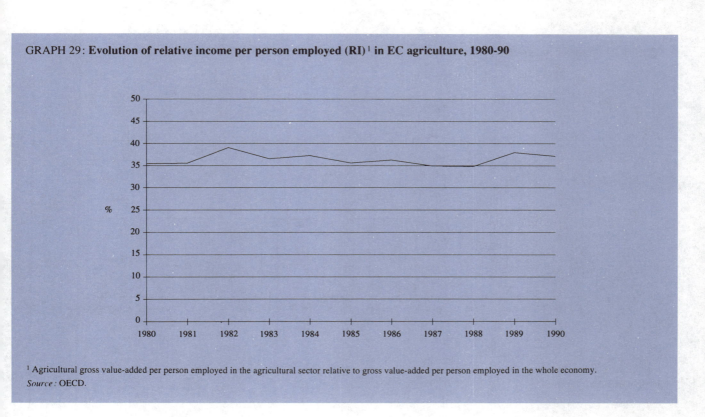

GRAPH 29: **Evolution of relative income per person employed (RI)** [1] **in EC agriculture, 1980-90**

[1] Agricultural gross value-added per person employed in the agricultural sector relative to gross value-added per person employed in the whole economy.

Source: OECD.

income due to government support) — as opposed to the income from agriculture per person employed in agriculture — is really low relative to that of non-farm households. A feature of agriculture which has become more pronounced in the most highly-developed economies is the prevalence of part-time farming where the farm household has a source of income other than farming. In these countries, transport infrastructure and communications generally have become so developed that part-time farming combined with non-agricultural employment becomes an economically viable alternative to leaving agriculture altogether. The painful implications in terms of change of lifestyle, location and social network can therefore be avoided. In many farm households another family member, typically a spouse, also has off-farm employment. The inter-sectoral mobility of agricultural labour may for this reason have increased. This may not only in itself have decreased the disparity in full-time income in the agricultural sector and outside agriculture, but, to an even greater extent, have increased the income of farm households by adding income obtained outside agriculture to that obtained from agricultural activities.

4.3. The policy response: the pattern of agricultural support worldwide

All OECD countries have provided significant support to their agricultural sectors during the 1980s. The most com-

monly used method to support farm income has been a system of market price support. Throughout the OECD countries in 1990, support of this type accounted for 80% of all assistance granted to the sector as measured by the PSE (producer subsidy equivalent). Domestic prices are in excess of market-clearing levels for imported commodities through border measures such as tariffs, and by export subsidies for exported commodities. Excess supplies which are not exported are disposed of in various ways — by destruction, as food aid to developing countries, as subsidized input to industry or as subsidized food for certain consumer groups. Public storage also plays an important role. Direct subsidies to agricultural producers and subsidies for the use of inter-mediate inputs in the agricultural sector are much less used. Subsidies linked to primary factors are more common, especially in the form of special tax provisions.

There are striking differences in the level of support and how it is provided. Graph 30 shows that for 1980-90, the average level of total assistance as measured by the percentage producer subsidy equivalent, i.e. the transfer to producers relative to the farm gate value of agricultural production, varies from around 70% of output value in Switzerland to only 12% in Australia, with the Community in a middle position at around 40%.

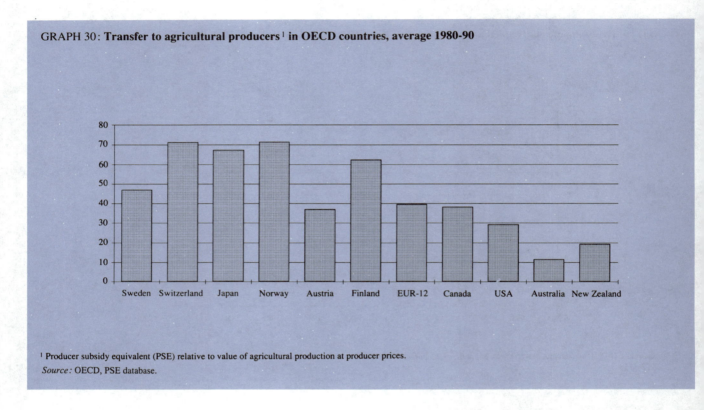

GRAPH 30: **Transfer to agricultural producers** [1] **in OECD countries, average 1980-90**

[1] Producer subsidy equivalent (PSE) relative to value of agricultural production at producer prices.

Source: OECD, PSE database.

The share of support provided by market price support also varies greatly, from 20% in New Zealand to over 100% in Austria, as shown in Graph 31.

The level of agricultural support, on the other hand, shows a very distinct pattern among developed countries, as revealed in Table 32.

Countries with the greatest disparities between agricultural incomes and non-agricultural incomes tend to provide the highest levels of assistance (see Graph 32). This may be illustrated by the cases of New Zealand and Australia, on the one hand, and by Japan on the other. During the period 1980-90, the gross value-added (GVA) per person employed was close to 60% in the non-agricultural sector in New Zealand and Australia. In Norway and Japan, however, where GVA per person employed in agriculture was only about 25% of that in the rest of the economy, the level of assistance was very high. Sweden and Austria, both with relatively low incomes in agriculture, recorded PSEs in the range of 40-60%.

Furthermore, the level of agricultural support tends to decrease with the size of net exports by the agricultural sector

Table 32

Average PSE, relative income, net export relative to agricultural production and share of market price support in PSE for OECD countries based on the period 1980-90

	Rate of transfer PSE[1]	Relative income[2] RI	Export share[3] EXP	Share of price support[4] SMPS
	%	%	%	
Canada	36.3	39.8	17.4	58.5
United States	30.3	64.0	9.8	55.0
Japan	67.3	25.5	−29.5	81.9
Australia	12.0	62.9	54.9	30.2
New Zealand	18.8	61.8	89.7	20.1
Austria	37.8	39.1	−20.1	104.9
Finland	62.5	30.4	− 7.4	88.1
Norway	71.8	26.7	−29.6	43.9
Sweden	48.1	26.7	−38.8	100.4
Switzerland	71.5	41.7	−42.6	88.0
EUR-12	39.9	36.4	− 8.7	90.9
OECD	45.1	41.4	− 0.5	69.3

[1] PSE may be defined as the $(P-P^W)/P$, when P is the producer price and P^W is the world market price.
[2] Relative income, RI, is defined as the income per person employed in agriculture relative to the income per person employed in the economy as a whole.
[3] Export share, EXP, is defined as agricultural net exports divided by agricultral production.
[4] Share of price support, SMPS, is defined as the share of transfer due to market price support relative to PSE.

GRAPH 31: **Share of transfers due to market price support, average 1980-90**

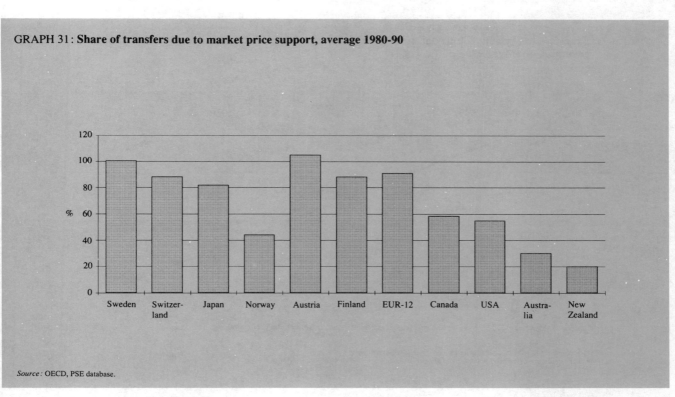

Source: OECD, PSE database.

GRAPH 32: **Transfer to agricultural producers[1] and relative value-added[2] in OECD countries, average 1980-90**

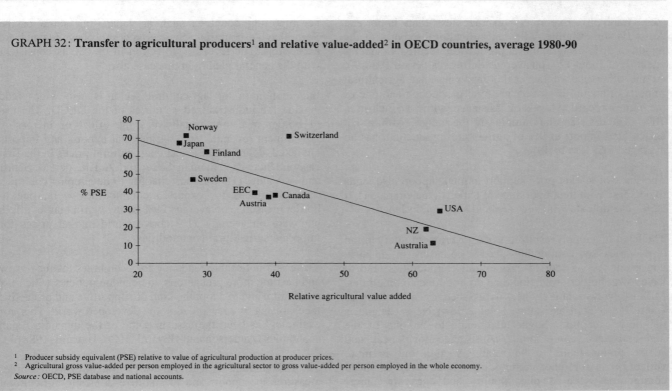

[1] Producer subsidy equivalent (PSE) relative to value of agricultural production at producer prices.
[2] Agricultural gross value-added per person employed in the agricultural sector to gross value-added per person employed in the whole economy.
Source: OECD, PSE database and national accounts.

GRAPH 33: **Transfers to agricultural producers[1] and share of net agricultural export in agricultural production in OECD countries,[2] average 1980-90**

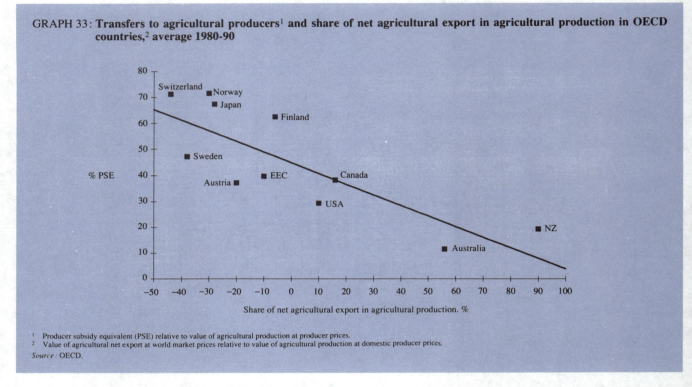

Share of net agricultural export in agricultural production. %

[1] Producer subsidy equivalent (PSE) relative to value of agricultural production at producer prices.
[2] Value of agricultural net export at world market prices relative to value of agricultural production at domestic producer prices.
Source: OECD.

(see Graph 33). Exporters subsidize less than importers. Australia for example, with net agricultural exports in the region of 55% of agricultural production, records a percentage PSE of about 12% on average during the period 1980-90. At the other end of the scale, Japan has net agricultural imports of about 30% of agricultural production and one of the highest recorded levels of assistance, with a PSE close to 70%. The EC, in the middle of the range, with a net agricultural import of 9% of agricultural production, has an average PSE close to 40%.

The share of market price support in total support also tends to decrease with the importance of exports (see Graph 34). It is, for example, low in New Zealand and high in Japan.

The level of support resulting from government intervention also varies by commodity across countries in a fairly consistent way. Exported agricultural commodities tend to have lower border protection than do imported commodities. Milk is always relatively heavily assisted, even in countries where the overall assistance level is low; New Zealand is the only exception. Sugar also tends to be one of the high-assistance commodities. Assistance for wheat and coarse grains tends to be relatively high but is more variable than for other commodities. Intensively-produced commodities such as pigs, poultry and eggs are almost always the least heavily assisted, even in high-assistance,

net-importing countries such as Japan, but some of the Scandinavian countries, Switzerland and New Zealand are exceptions. The level of protection in the EC is consistent with the general pattern in this case also.

Intervention in the agricultural sector is also widespread outside the industrialized countries of the OECD. The use of border measures usually has the effect of increasing government revenue. Both agricultural exports and imports are taxed, depressing domestic agricultural prices in the first case and increasing them in the second. A. Krueger, M. Schiff and A. Valdes (1988) report that for 19 developing countries domestic prices for exported commodities were, due to border measures, on average 29% below world market prices but were on average 21% above world market prices for imported agricultural commodities.

There is a noticeable tendency for economies, as they grow and become more prosperous, to abandon policies which tax agriculture and to adopt the kind of supportive and protective mechanisms so widespread in the developed world. This, for example, has been the case in some of the dynamic Asian economies (Anderson and Hayami, 1986; Hayami, 1988).

The EC common agricultural policy system of using border measures to support and to stabilize domestic agricultural prices at levels different to those on the world market is

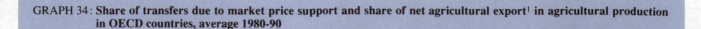

GRAPH 34: **Share of transfers due to market price support and share of net agricultural export[1] in agricultural production in OECD countries, average 1980-90**

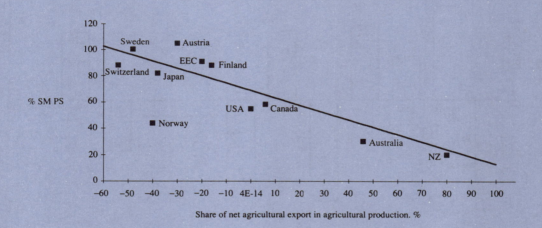

Share of net agricultural export in agricultural production. %

[1] Value of agricultural net export at world market prices relative to value of agricultural production at domestic producer prices.
Source: OECD.

therefore by no means unique. It is consistent with a pattern of protection which can be seen worldwide. Price support systems were used by most European countries well before the creation of the EC (Tracy, 1989) and in this sense the CAP represents a consolidation of national policies in the original six Member States. Given its trade position, level of development and level of agricultural income relative to income in other sectors, and given its position historically as a net importer of most agricultural products, the EC's policy response to the farm problem is seen to conform to a general pattern which has existed over time and space.

4.4. Econometric analysis

The impression obtained based on a purely descriptive basis is confirmed by econometric analysis. As mentioned above, it is not possible to obtain data and estimates for all the variables and parameters which, according to the simplified model presented above, are important for explaining variations in the use and level of market price support. In order to obtain a functional relationship which can be subjected to econometric estimation, a number of simplifying assumptions have to be made.

Equation (3) may be rewritten as

$$(6)\ \frac{p^* - p^W}{p^*} = -\left[(1 - \frac{R_Y}{kR_\tau})\,Y - (1 - \frac{R_X}{kR_\tau})\,X\right]\ /\ \frac{\partial Z}{\partial p}$$

Disregarding differences in k, R_τ, R_X and $\dfrac{\partial Z}{\partial p}$, assuming that the distribution of agricultural production is constant, such that R_Y can be expressed as a function of the average income, we obtain

$$(7)\ PSE = PSE(EXP, RI)\ \text{where}\ \frac{\partial PSE}{\partial RI}, \frac{\partial PSE}{\partial EXP} < 0$$

where:

$PSE = \dfrac{p^* - p^W}{p^*}$ is percentage producer subsidy equivalent,

$EXP = (Y - X)/Y$ is the net export intensity, and

RI = the average income of farmers relative to the average income of non-farmers.

Combined cross-section time series analysis based on data from 11 OECD countries (treating the EC as one country) covering the period 1979-90 shows that relative income, RI,

113

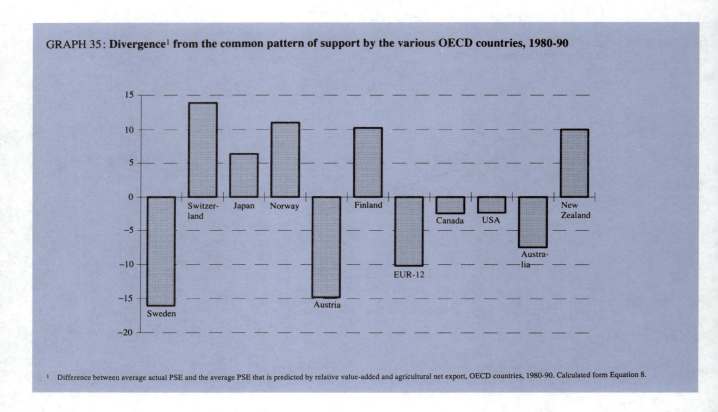

GRAPH 35: **Divergence[1] from the common pattern of support by the various OECD countries, 1980-90**

[1] Difference between average actual PSE and the average PSE that is predicted by relative value-added and agricultural net export, OECD countries, 1980-90. Calculated form Equation 8.

and net export intensity, EXP, are very significant in explaining the variation in the level of support over time and space. The estimations has been made using the GAUSS software.[1] In the case of the second equation, an iterative procedure was used in order to establish convergence with respect to the estimate of the equilibrium level of support.

$$(8) \quad PSE_f^c = a_1 + b_1 RI_f^c + c_1 EXP_f^c + E^c + E_t$$
$$= 93.4 - 46.3 RI_f^c - 29.3 EXP_f^c + E^c + E_t$$
$$(10.5) \quad (-4.1) \quad (-3.8)$$

The parameter estimates are, as indicated by the t statistics provided in parenthesis, significant at the 1 % level.

Graph 35 and Table 33 show the differences between the actual level of support and those predicted by Equation 8 for the various OECD countries. The differences are clearly much smaller than the difference in PSEs across countries. Furthermore, the levels of support in the EC during the 1980s were lower than in many other OECD countries when the

difference in levels of support due to differences in relative levels of income per person employed and when the agricultural trade positions are taken into account.

Table 33

Difference between predicted and actual PSE, 1980-90 average

	Difference	Actual PSE	Predicted PSE
		Average 1980-90	
Canada	− 2.4	38.2	40.6
United States	− 2.4	29.3	31.7
Japan	6.4	67.4	61.0
Australia	− 7.4	11.5	18.9
New Zealand	10.0	19.3	9.3
Austria	−14.8	37.1	51.9
Finland	10.3	62.5	52.2
Norway	11.0	71.5	60.5
Sweden	−16.0	47.1	63.1
Switzerland	13.9	71.2	57.3
EUR-12	−10.2	39.6	49.8
OECD	− 0.1	45.0	45.1

Source: OECD, own calculations.

---

[1] Equation (8) has also been estimated using AREMOS with an auto-correlation term to eliminate the auto-correlation, but without country-specific error terms. This successfully eliminated the auto-correlation. The regression results were consistent with the results obtained estimating Equation (9) in GAUSS but suppressing the country-specific error terms.

GRAPH 36: **Real ECU-USD exchange rate, 1980-90**[1]

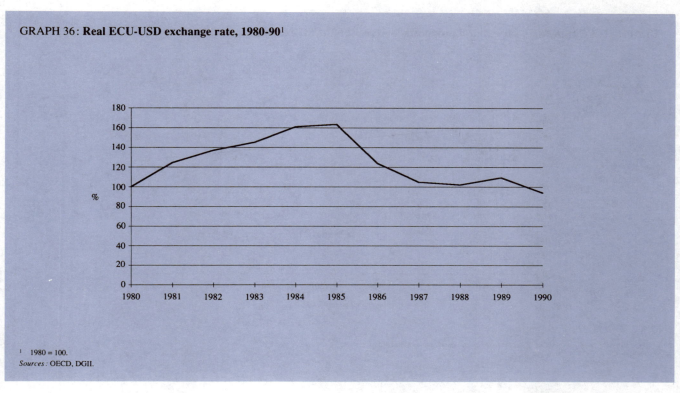

[1] 1980 = 100.
Sources: OECD, DGII.

The estimated equation naturally refers to the equilibrium relation between endogenous variables which are determined simultaneously. It is therefore not surprising that the regression results show strong auto-correlation and a less than satisfactory statistical fit. It is reasonable to assume that the level of support does not adjust instantaneously to changes in world market prices, in particular when these are due to US exchange-rate fluctuations.

During the estimation period, the real US exchange rate has fluctuated strongly in relation to most other OECD currencies. The real US dollar exchange rate is indeed a significant explanatory variable in explaining the level of support in OECD countries.

To take the gradual adaptation of the level of support into account, the difference between the long-term equilibrium level of support, PSE_t^{c*}, and the level of support during the preceding period, PSE_{t-1}, has been included in the estimation equation. The co-integrated relationship, however, remains unchanged from the initial specification.

(9) $PSE_t^c = a_1 + b_1 RI_t^c + c_1 EXP_t^c + d_2 (PSE_t^{c*} - PSE_{t-1}^c)$
        $+ E^c + E_t$

$= 92.1 - 55.6RI_t^c - 22.5EXP_t^c$
  (14.6) (−6.6)   (−4.0)
  $- .76 (PSE_t^{c*} - PSE_{t-1}^c) + E^c + E_t$
  (−9.9)

This improves the statistical significance of the parameter estimates, and the overall statistical fit significantly and almost removes the auto-correlation.

Equation (9) explains 95 % of the total variation in the PSE over time and countries. A significant part of this variation is, however, due to the country-specific term, E^c, which captures differences between the countries other than the difference in export intensity and relative income.[1] Of particular significance is that 74 % of the variation in PSE across countries is explained by variations in EXP and RI.

---

[1] This may, however, be due to differences which are captured by the theoretical model, but which have been assumed away in the specified model represented with Equation (7) which forms the basis for the estimation. One such variable is R_Y, which is more likely to be greater if agricultural production is distributed evenly among farmers than if some farmers with a relatively high income also have a disproportionate share of the production. This may, for example, explain the difference in the level of PSE between Norway and Sweden. In Sweden, the differences between income and production are, due to the fertile south, much more pronounced than in Norway.

115

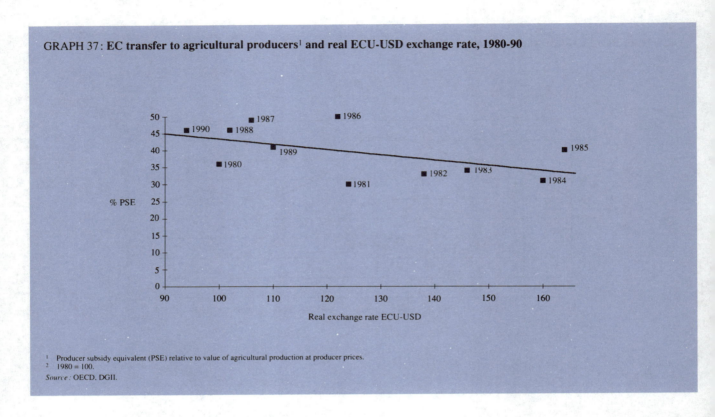

GRAPH 37: **EC transfer to agricultural producers[1] and real ECU-USD exchange rate, 1980-90**

[1] Producer subsidy equivalent (PSE) relative to value of agricultural production at producer prices.
[2] 1980 = 100.
Source: OECD, DGII.

Only 55% of the variation in the PSE over time is explained by EXP and RI and PSE*. This is not surprising given that the yearly variations reflect a complicated adjustment process which we have tried to capture in order to avoid biased estimates of the effect of EXP and RI on PSE. The year-to-year variations in EXP and RI on average explain 21% of the variation in PSE, with one of the best fits for the United States at 66%. The adjustment process in the US is less than in other countries complicated by exchange-rate fluctuations and the model in this case explains 60% of the variation in PSE over time.

Graphs 38 and 39 illustrate the evolution of estimated and actual PSE for 1979-90 for the US and EC respectively. The estimated model traces the evolution over time very well. However, the prediction of year-to-year variations is not accurate, suggesting that the dynamics of adjustment in the level of support are more complicated than those modelled.

5. Development of EC agricultural policy

The public finance analysis presented above provides an explanation of why market price support was adopted as the core element of EC agricultural policy and why this policy has come under increasing pressure.

At the time the common agricultural policy was created, all original six Member States to a varying degree, as predicted by the model estimated above, provided their agricultural sectors with market price support. The level of support was highest in Germany which was the largest importer of agricultural products, smaller in France which at that time was still a net importer, though almost self-sufficient, and smallest in the Netherlands which was a significant exporter. Harmonization of the market price support policies in the Member States was needed in order to create a customs union for agricultural products as for other commodities.

The theory presented above explains why the principle of market price support was also adopted as the core element in the EC common agricultural policy.

As explained above, the situation in the EC at the time the original six Member States created the CAP was characterized by many of the features which favoured the adoption of market price support. It was a period of strong economic growth. The EC had a relatively low level of self-sufficiency in agricultural products, although a large part of the labour force was employed in a farm sector dominated by many small and medium-sized farms with owner-operators. With a still primitive transport infrastructure, the agricultural labour force was rather immobile. In most Member States, the social

GRAPH 38: **EC: predicted, optimal and actual PSE for 1980-90**

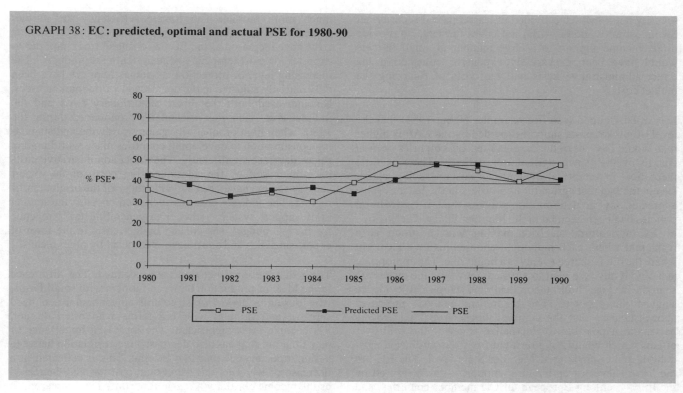

GRAPH 39: **US: predicted, optimal and actual PSE for 1980-90**

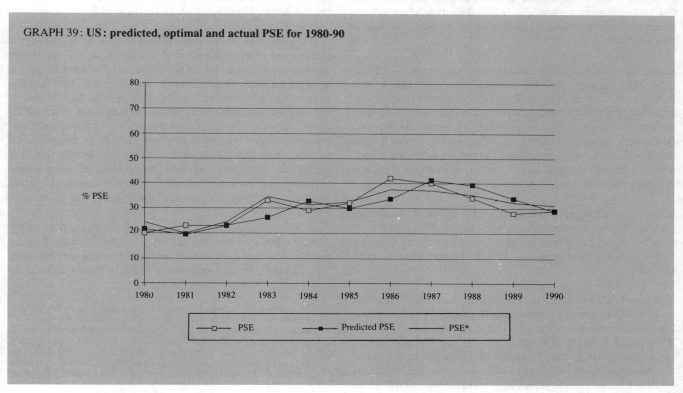

security net — which provided at least a partial security net for industrial workers — did not cover farmers. To provide direct income support to a large number of small farmers would have been excessively expensive considering the direct administrative costs and the costs of financing the budget costs.

It is often claimed (see, for example, Nello, 1984) that the level of market price support provided by the CAP is higher than would have been the case had the EC countries been in charge of their own agricultural policies. There is little theoretical or empirical evidence to sustain such a claim, except the fact that agricultural ministers in the EC may have a greater say in determining policies than if agricultural policies had been decided in the Member States. The analogy of EC agricultural decision-making with a group at a restaurant where each individual chooses his own meal but where the bill is shared evenly is a bogus one. The appropriate analogy, if any, is a visit to a restaurant where the dishes are shared. In fact, both theoretical and empirical evidence suggest the opposite. The theoretical analysis presented above suggests that the common decision-making process has made it possible to internalize some of the spill-over effects which would have resulted from uncoordinated agricultural policy-making at Member State level. The EC has the lowest level of agricultural support — as measured by the PSE — among European OECD member countries, and one of the lowest among all OECD countries when differences in export intensity and relative income are taken into account.

However, the situation has changed in many ways since the CAP was created, making market price support a less attractive instrument for providing income support. Generally speaking, the transfer efficiency (i.e. the decrease in the real income for the rest of society needed to increase the income of farmers by one ecu) of the price support system has decreased, the redistributional benefits have declined, whereas the cost-benefit ratio for alternative support instruments has become more favourable.

Many of the changes can be expressed in terms of changes in the parameters of the model analysed above. The model may thus be used to demonstrate pressure which these changes have created for a shift away from the market price support system.

The direct distortionary costs have increased, as reflected in an increase in the agricultural supply elasticity, E^S, as have the direct transaction costs, E^i, and the indirect costs due to the increase in the budget costs $(p - p^W)Z$. The increase in the supply elasticity may be attributed to the increased use of intermediate inputs and capital services and to the improved transport infrastructure which has made labour in rural areas

much more mobile. The transfer efficiency has further decreased because the direct transaction costs and the indirect costs have increased as the EC has changed from importer to exporter for most temperate zone agricultural products.[1] The increasing level of protection, as domestic prices have been only partially adjusted to the decrease in world market prices, has increased both the direct distortionary costs and the indirect cost. This was particularly pronounced during the 1980s when high productivity gains worldwide and stagnating consumption in developing countries made world market prices decrease significantly. The direct administrative costs have increased as the administrative costs of an export subsidy regime have been added to those of the original tariff regime. The indirect cost has increased because the market price support system, rather than generating tariff revenue for the EC budget, has created budget costs in the form of export subsidies and subsidies for disposal by other means.

The redistributional benefits have declined. The difference in the level of production between farmers with small farms, who during a period of structural adjustment often need support, and farmers with big farms who often do not, has become more significant. The increased importance of part-time farming has also decreased the correlation between agricultural revenue and low income. This is reflected in a decrease of R_Y. The redistributional cost has also increased as the income elasticity of basic foodstuffs has decreased. In the model this is reflected by an increase in R^X.

Finally, the cost of alternative instruments to support farm income has decreased, reflected in a decrease in E^i for direct income support schemes. The increased efficiency of public administration, combined with the fact that the farming population has become much smaller and that a social security net in many Member States has been extended to cover farmers, has decreased the costs of providing direct income support especially to those farmers in most need of it. The evolution of modern information technology has simplified the gathering and processing of information necessary for the implementation and enforcement of a direct payment system to compensate farmers for lower prices.

The market price support system has also come under pressure due to developments which are not reflected in the model. The negative effects on the physical environment have become more pronounced as the use of intermediate

---

[1]   The shift from importer to exporter has meant that the relevant opportunity cost price for a marginal increase in the supply of agricultural products to the EC market has changed from being the cif price to being the fob price. The decrease in the world market price to be taken into account in the model is therefore the combination of the decrease in the price on world markets and the shift of the opportunity cost price for excess agricultural production from the cif price to the fob price.

inputs and capital has increased. The positive externalities associated with an agriculture in the form of social cohesion in rural communities has also been reduced as agricultural production has become more industrialized.

The existence of positive externalities due to R&D provides an argument for market price support which is not captured by the model in its present form. However, this reason for market price support has also been weakened as targeted support has become more economical.

6. Summary and concluding remarks

The basic assumption for the current analysis has been that sectoral policies including market price support, at least as a first approximation, may be understood as the outcome of the maximization, in a second-best environment, of a political preference function defined as a social welfare function, on the real income of all groups in society. The different weights attached to the income of different social groups in the revealed preference function of the political system are assumed to reflect egalitarian value judgments. These preferences may be motivated by altruistic preferences among the members of society, but may also be motivated by the desire of the political élite to maintain social peace.

Emphasizing the importance of the transaction costs associated with government intervention and the importance of the short time horizon implicit in political decision-making, the analysis demonstrates that the political system, under certain circumstances, is likely to choose market price support to transfer income to farmers.

Economic development favours support instruments with relatively high 'transaction costs' and relatively low 'direct distortion costs'. Market price support therefore becomes less attractive as an instrument of support as economies reach a very high level of economic development.

The analysis suggests that a high level of market price support will be particularly attractive if the degree of self-sufficiency in the sector is low such that the market price support policy generates government revenue and if the relative income in the sector is low. Combined cross-section time series analyses of data on PSE, export intensity and relative income of agriculture for 1979-90 for the OECD countries provide strong empirical evidence for this theoretical explanation.

Finally, the analysis highlights a dilemma which economists who wish to assist in the formulation of agricultural or other sectoral policies have to face.

The analysis suggests that the inherent preferences in the political decision-making process, in particular time preferences, may very well conflict with the value judgments which economists may hold, either professionally or personally, and may have important implications for what appears to be the optimum solution. Different value judgments may in particular lead to quite different conclusions with respect to the most cherished tenet of the economic profession, that of free trade.

The economist may contemplate either advising the political apparatus on the basis of his professional value judgments — in which case he runs the risk that his advice will be considered irrelevant — or he may adopt the implicit value judgments of the political system, perhaps thereby advocating courses of action which he himself considers undesirable.

The political apparatus may indeed have limited leeway in adopting policies which are not consistent with the implicit value judgments of the political system. If a politician does not adopt a short time horizon, he may not be re-elected, and others who do, may come to power. In the interests of efficiency, it seems reasonable to require that, in providing advice to the political apparatus, the economist base his advice on the value judgments inherent in the political system although they may be at variance with his own.

However, although not members of the political apparatus, most economists aspire to influencing the direction of policies rather than merely helping to achieve goals decided by others. Economists have little direct influence on the functioning of the political apparatus — with good reason, some would say. The economist may, however, disseminate information to the grass roots of the political system on the likely outcome of government actions and on suggestions for change in institutional arrangements. He may thereby indirectly influence the policy-making process by changing the constraints under which the political apparatus operates.

References

Anderson, K. and Hayami, Y. *The political economy of agricultural protection: East Asia in international perspective,* London, Allen and Unwin, 1986.

Atkinson, A. B., Stiglitz, J. E. *Lectures on public economics,* London, McGraw-Hill, 1980.

Becker, G. S. 'A theory of competition among pressure groups for political influence', *Quarterly Journal of Economics,* Vol. 68, 1983, pp. 371-400.

Becker, G. S. 'Public policies, pressure groups, and deadweight costs', *Journal of Political Economy,* Vol. 28, 1985, pp. 329-347.

Crawford, V. P. 'Long-term relationships governed by short-term contracts', *American Economic Review,* Vol. 78, No 3, 1988, pp. 485-499.

EEC. 'The future of rural society', COM(88) 501, Brussels, 1988.

EEC. 'The development and future of the CAP', COM(91) 100, Brussels, 1991.

De Gorter, H. and Swinnen, J. 'The economic polity of farm policy in Europe and the United States', paper presented at the International Conference on 'New dimensions in North American-European agricultural trade relations' in Italy, 1993.

Downs, A. *An economic theory of democracy,* New York, Harper and Rowe, 1957.

Gardner, B. L. *The economics of agricultural policies,* Macmillan Publishing Company, New York, 1987.

Gardner, B. L. 'Economic theory and farm politics', *American Journal of Agricultural Economics,* Vol. 71, 1989, pp. 1165-1171.

Gardner, B. L. 'Changing economic perspectives on the farm problem', *Journal of Economic Literature,* Vol. XXX, 1992, pp. 62-101.

Guyomard, H., Mahé, L.-P., Munk, K. J. and Roe, T. 'Agriculture in the GATT: The basic conflict between the EC and the US', *Journal of Agricultural Economics,* Vol. 44, No 2, 1993, pp. 245-263.

Hayami, Y. *Japanese agriculture under siege: the political economy of agricultural policies,* New York, St. Martin's Press, 1988.

Hill, B. 'Total income of agricultural households: 1992 Report', Eurostat, Luxembourg, 1992.

Honma, M. and Hayami, Y. 'The determinants of agricultural protection levels: an econometric analysis', in Anderson, K. and Hayami, Y. with associates, *The political economy of agricultural protection: East Asia in international perspective,* London, Allen and Unwin, 1986, pp. 39-49.

Just, R. 'Making economic welfare analysis useful in the policy process: implication of the public choice literature', *American Journal of Agricultural Economics,* Vol. 70, No 2, 1988, pp. 448-453.

Krueger, A., Schiff, M. and Valdes, A. 'Agricultural incentives in developing countries: measuring the effect of sectoral and economywide policies', *The World Bank Economic Review,* Vol. 2, No 3, 1988, pp. 255-271.

Lindert, P. H. 'Historical patterns of agricultural policy' in Timmer, C. P. (ed.) *Agriculture and the State,* 1991.

Munk, K. J. 'Optimal public sector pricing taking the distributional aspect into consideration', *Quarterly Journal of Economics,* Vol LXXXXI, No 4, 1977, pp. 635-650.

Munk, K. J. 'Optimal taxation with some non-taxable commodities', *Review of Economic Studies,* Vol XXXXVII, No 1, 1980, pp. 755-766.

Munk, K. J. 'Price support to the EC agricultural sector: an optimal policy?', *Oxford Review of Economic Policy,* Vol. 5, No 2, 1989, pp. 76-89.

Nello Sr., S. 'An application of public choice theory to the question of CAP reform', *European Review of Agricultural Economics,* Vol. 11, No 3, 1984, pp. 261-283.

Knudsen, O. and Nash, J. 'Domestic price stabilization schemes in developing countries,' *Economic Development and Cultural Change,* 1990.

Newbery, D. and Stiglitz, J. 'The theory of commodity price stabilization: a study in the economics of risk', Oxford, Claradon Press, 1981.

Newbery, D. 'The theory of agricultural taxation for developing countries', in Newbury, D. and Stern, N. (eds.) *The theory of taxation for developing countries,* 1987.

Olson, M. 'The logic of collective action', Cambridge, Massachusetts, Harvard University Press, 1965.

Reutlinger, S. in Gittinger, J. P., Leslie, J. and Hoisington, C. (eds.) *Food policy,* Baltimore, The John Hopkins University Press, 1987.

Sah, R. and Stiglitz, J. 'The taxation and pricing of agriculture and industrial goods in developing economies', in Newbury, D. and Stern, N. (eds.) *The theory of taxation for developing countries,* Oxford University Press, 1987.

Sen, A. 'Poverty and entitlement', in Gittinger, J. P., Leslie, J. and Hoisington, C. (eds.) *Food policy,* Baltimore, The John Hopkins University Press, 1987.

Stiglitz, J. 'Some theoretical aspects of agricultural policies', *The World Bank Research Observer,* 1987.

Swinnen J. *Essays on the political economy of agricultural policies,* dissertation presented to the Faculty of the Graduate School of Cornell University in partial fulfillment of the requirements for the Degree of Doctor of Philosophy, 1992.

Swinnen, J. and van der Zee, F. A. 'The new political economy of agricultural policies: a survey', *European Review of Agricultural Economics,* Vol. 20, No 3, 1994, pp. 261-290.

Swinnen, J. 'The development of agricultural policies in Central and Eastern Europe: an endogenous policy theory perspective', in *Food policy,* June 1993, pp. 187-191.

Swinnen, J. 'A positive theory of agricultural protection', *American Journal of Agricultural Economics* Vol. 76, No 1, 1994, pp. 1-14.

Swinnen, J. and de Gorter H. 'Why small groups and low income sectors obtain subsidies: the 'altruistic' side of a 'self-interested' government', *Economics and Politics,* 1993, Vol. 5, No 3, pp. 285-296.

Tracy, M. *Government and agriculture in Western Europe 1980-1988,* 3rd ed., Harvester Wheatsleaf, 1989.

Appendix: A partial equilibrium model for analysing the choice of the form and the level of support

1. Introduction

The purpose of this appendix is to provide a relatively simple, formalized framework for representing the basic trade-off between equity and efficiency which governments (or the political systems) face in deciding on which instruments to use and at what level to provide support to sectors with structural adjustment problems.

2. Notations and assumptions

(a) Notation

p^w: World market price of agricultural good
p: Producer price of agricultural good
q: Consumer price of agricultural good
t^p: Price wedge between world market price and producer price
t^c: Price wedge between world market price and consumer price
p_z: Producer price of agricultural factors of production
w: Factor price of agricultural factors of production
t_z: Price wedge between producer prices and factors price
y^h: Production of agricultural output of household h
Y: Aggregate production
x^h: Consumption of agricultural good
X: Aggregate consumption
l^h: Primary factor of household h
L: Aggregate factors
Z: Net export of agricultural goods
I^h: Net income of household h
π^h: Agricultural producer surplus of household h
L^h: Net transfer of household h
O^h: Other incomes of household h
Θ^h: Income tax of household h
N: Net lump-sum transfers
T: Tax revenue
$k_1 - 1$: Distortional costs of raising extra general tax revenue
$k_2 - 1$: Transaction costs of raising extra general tax revenue
E^i: Transaction costs of agricultural policies under regime i

$B(q,p) = \Sigma \beta^h S^h(q) + \Sigma \beta^h \pi^h(p)$: Gross benefits function

$C(\tau) = \Sigma \beta^h \theta^h(t)$: Gross costs function

$R_X = \Sigma \beta^h x^h / X$: Distributional characteristics of consumption of an agricultural commodity

$R_\tau = \Sigma \beta^h x^h \dfrac{\partial \theta^h / \partial \tau}{\partial T^h / \partial \tau}$: Distributional characteristics of increase in the alternative tax instrument

$R_Y = \Sigma \beta^h y^h / Y$: Distributional characteristics of production of an agricultural commodity

$E^D = \dfrac{\partial X}{\partial q} / \dfrac{X}{q}$: Elasticity of aggregated demand

$E^S = \dfrac{\partial Y}{\partial p} / \dfrac{Y}{p}$: Elasticity of aggregated supply

$E^Z = \dfrac{\partial Z}{\partial p} / \dfrac{Z}{p}$: Elasticity of net export with respect to the domestic price

$\quad = \dfrac{X}{Z} E^D - \dfrac{Y}{Z} E^S$

(b) Behavioural assumptions

Producer behaviour

(i) supply function

$\quad$ (1) $\quad y^h = y(p, z^h)$

(ii) zero profit condition

$\quad$ (2) $\quad p_z = p_z(p)$

Household behaviour

(i) income

$\quad$ (3) $\quad I^h = O^h + \pi^h + L^h - \Theta^h$

(ii) demand function

$\quad$ (4) $\quad x^h = x^h(q, I^h)$

(iii) primary factor supply function

$\quad$ (5) $\quad z^h = z^h(w)$

(iv) tax payment

(6) $\Theta^h = \Theta(I^h, \tau)$

Policy instruments and price equations

(i)   output subsidies

(7) $p = p^w - t^p$

(ii) consumer taxes

(8) $q = p^w + t^c$

(iii) market price support implies

$t^p = -t^c$

(iv) primary factor subsidies

(9) $p_z = w + t_z$

(v)   lump-sum transfers

(10) $L^h = L^h(\zeta)$

Government behaviour

Government behaviour is assumed to be based on the maximization of social welfare defined as the weighted sum of consumers' surplus, producers' surplus and taxpayers' loss.

The consumers' surplus of the hth household may, under approximation usually adopted in a partial equilibrium framework, be written as:

(11) $S^h = S^h(\hat{q}) = \int_{\hat{q}}^{\infty} x^h(q)dq$

and producers' surplus as

(12) $\pi^h = \int_0^{\hat{w}} z^h(w)dw$

$= S^{zh}(w)$

$= S^{zh}(p_z(p) - t_z)$

$= \pi^h(p; t_z)$

and the real income loss due to the payment in taxes of the amount, $\Theta^h(\tau)$, by the hth household as

(13) $C^h = C^h(\tau) = f^h(\Theta_h(\tau))$

where f(.) is an increasing function representing the distortion costs connected with raising the tax revenue, Θ^h, from the hth household.

The net social benefit therefore becomes

(14) $B = B(q, p, t_z, \zeta) = \Sigma \ \beta^h S^h(q) + \Sigma \ \beta^h \pi^h(p, t_z) + \Sigma \ \beta^h L^h(\zeta)$

and the total social costs

(15) $C = C(\tau) = \Sigma \ \beta^h f^h(\Theta^h(\tau))$.

The government's revenue requirement for administration of agricultural support and other expenditures, E^i, is given by

(16) $G = G(q, p, t_z, \zeta)$

$= g(E^i - (q - p^W)X(q) + (p - p^W)Y(p) - (p_z - w)Z(w) + \underset{h}{\Sigma} \ L^h(\zeta))$

where g(.) is an increasing function representing the transaction costs in connection with raising the tax revenue needed to finance the government's revenue requirement for agricultural support and other expenditures (excluding transaction costs). E^i is assumed to depend on which support instrument is used, but to be independent of the level of support. It is assumed to be higher for the case where the consumer price is set independently of the producer price than in the case of market price support where the consumer price is equal to the producer price.

The total tax revenue collected by the government at the level of taxation, τ, is

(17) $T = T(\tau) = \Sigma \ \Theta^h(\tau)$.

The government's budget constraint therefore becomes

(18) $f(q, p, t_z, \zeta, \tau) = T(\tau) - G(q, p, t_z, \zeta) = 0$.

We assume that the government adheres to the following basic welfare economic value judgment:

A1: Social welfare should be maximized.

The government's maximization problem is

(19) $\underset{q, p, t_z, \zeta, \tau}{\text{Max NB}} = B(q, p, t_z, \zeta) - C(\tau)$ subject to

$T(\tau) - G(q, p, t_z, \zeta) = 0$

We further assume that the government has distributional objectives, i.e. that it bases its behaviour on the following value judgment:

A2: The marginal social welfare of income to a household is falling when income increases and is the same for all households with the same income, i.e. $\beta^h = \beta(Y^h), \dfrac{\partial \beta}{\partial Y} < 0$

Furthermore, to simplify the analysis we assume:

A3: The consumption of the agricultural products across households is increasing with household income, i.e. $x^h = x(Y^h,q) = x^h(q)$ where $x(.)$ is an increasing function in Y

A4: The extra tax payment, due to an increase in the level of taxation, τ, is increasing with income, across households, i.e. $\dfrac{\partial \theta^h}{\partial \tau} = \dfrac{\partial \theta}{\partial \tau}(Y^h,\tau) \equiv \dfrac{\partial \theta^h}{\partial \tau}(\tau)$, were $\dfrac{\partial \theta}{\partial \tau}(.)$ is an increasing function in Y

Assumptions A2, A3 and A4 imply that:

(a) the distributional characteristics of the consumption of the agricultural commodity, R_X, is relatively low if the rich use a relatively big share of their income consuming it;

(b) the distributional characteristics of the alternative tax instrument, R_τ, is relatively high if the rich use a relatively big share of their income paying the tax; and

(c) the distributional characteristics of the production of the agricultural commodity, R_Y, is relatively low if the rich produce a relatively big share of the total agricultural production.

Finally we assume that:

A5: The alternative tax instrument involves marginal distortional costs of $(k_1 - 1)$ per unit of gross tax revenue and the marginal transaction costs of $(k_2 - 1)$ per unit of net tax revenue

This assumption implies that (15) now becomes

(20) $C(\tau) = \Sigma \beta^h k_1 \Theta(Y^h,\tau)$

and (16) becomes

(21) $G(q,p,t_z,\zeta) = k_2[E^i - (q - p^w)X(q) + (p - p^w)Y(p) + (p_z - w)Z(w) + \Sigma_h L^h(\zeta)].$

3. The government's maximization problem under various support regimes

In this section we formulate the government's maximization problem in the cases where either:

(i) lump-sum transfer,

(ii) subsidy to the primary factors,

(iii) output subsidies, or

(iv) market price support

is the only support instrument available for the government

The formulation of the government's maximization problem under the various regimes is based on the same basic model. Only the amount of government expenditure including the administrative costs for the support instrument under consideration, E, varies between the scenarios.

(i) Lump-sum transfer

Tax assumptions

$t^p = t^c = t_z = 0$

$L^h = L^h(\zeta)$

Government's budget constraint

$G^4(\zeta,\tau) = T(\tau) + g(E^4 - \Sigma L^h(\zeta))$

This defines

$\tau^4(\zeta)$

The government's maximization problem

$\underset{\zeta}{\text{Max}}\ NB^4 = \Sigma\ \beta^h L^h(\zeta) - \Sigma\ \beta^h C^h(\tau^4(\zeta))$

(ii) Primary factor subsidy

Tax assumptions

$p = q = p^w$
$L = 0$

The government's budget constraint

$G^3(w,\tau) = T(\tau) + g(E^3 + (w - p_z)L)$

This defines

$\tau^3(w)$

The government's maximization problem

$\underset{w}{\text{Max}}\ NB^3(w) = \Sigma\ \beta^h \pi^h(w) - \Sigma\ \beta^h C^h(\tau^3(w))$

(iii) Output subsidy, consumer tax

Tax assumptions

$t_z = 0$,
$L = 0$

Government's budget constraint

$G^2(p,q,\tau) = T(\tau) + g(E^2 - (q-p^w) X(q) + (p - p^w) Y(p))$

This defines

$\tau^2(q,p)$

The government's maximization problem

Max $NB^2(p,q) = \Sigma \; \beta^h S^h \; (pq + \Sigma \; \beta^h \pi^h \; (p) - \Sigma \; \beta^h C^h(\tau^2(p,q))$
p,q

(iv) Market price support

Tax assumptions

$p = q$
$t_z = 0$
$L = 0$

Government's budget constraint

$G^1(p,\tau) = T(\tau) + g(E^1 + (q-p^w)Z(p))$

This defines

$\tau^1(p)$

The government's maximization problem

Max $NB^1(p) = \Sigma \; \beta^h S^h(p) + \Sigma \; \beta^h \pi^h(p) - \Sigma \; \beta^h C^h(\tau^1(p))$
p

4. The choice of the best support instrument

Having formulated the maximization problem for the different support regimes to identify the best support instrument the optimal level of support for each regime would have to be calculated and the level of social welfare compared. This is not done here. The formula for the optimal level of support is only derived for market price support, but the derivation for the other support regime follows the same logic and is therefore straightforward.

5. Derivation of optimal price formulae

In order to represent that consumer prices and producer prices must be equal in the case of price support we substitute p for q in (16). The government's revenue requirement may now be written as

(23) $G = \tilde{G}(p) = g(E + (p - p^w)[Y(p) - X(p)])$,

and the government's budget constraint therefore becomes

(24) $\bar{b}(p,\tau) = T(\tau) - \tilde{G}(p) = 0.$

Using the implicit function theorem and assuming that $\partial \bar{b}/\partial \tau \neq 0$ we can now derive from the government's budget constraint the trade-off between the tax level, τ, and the price support level, p,

(25) $\dfrac{d\tau}{dp} = - \dfrac{\bar{b}_p}{\bar{b}} = \dfrac{G_p}{T\tau} = k_2 [Z + (p - p^w)\dfrac{\partial Z}{\partial q}] / \dfrac{\partial T}{\partial \tau}$

where $Z = Y - X$ is the net export of the agricultural commodity.

The government's problem of choosing an optimal support price may now be formulated as a maximization problem in one variable without constraints.

(26) Max $NB = B(p,p) - C(\tau(p,p))$
p
$= \Sigma \; \beta^h S^h(p) + \Sigma \; \beta^h p^h(p) - \Sigma \; \beta^h k_1 \theta(Y^h,\tau(p,p)).$

The first-order condition for an optimal support price is

(27) $\dfrac{\partial NB}{\partial p} = - \Sigma \; \beta^h x^h + \Sigma \; \beta^h y^h - k_1\Sigma \; \beta^h \dfrac{\partial \theta^h}{\partial \tau} \dfrac{d\tau}{dq} = 0.$

Using the definitions of R_X, R_Y and R_τ and reordering we get

(28) $- R_X X + R_Y Y - k_1 R_\tau \dfrac{\partial T}{\partial \tau} \dfrac{d\tau}{dq} = 0.$

Using (26) we get

(29) $- R_X X + R_Y Y - k_1 k_2 R_\tau \; [Z + (p^* - p^w)\dfrac{\partial Z}{\partial p}] = 0,$

or after reordering and substituting k for $k_1 k_2$

(30) $\dfrac{p^* - p^w}{p^*} = \left[\dfrac{\dfrac{Y}{Z} R_Y - \dfrac{X}{Z} R_X}{k R_\tau} - 1 \right] \dfrac{1}{- E_Z}$

where $E_Z = \dfrac{\partial Z}{\partial p} / \dfrac{Z}{p}.$

Chapter D: Model simulations of consequences of reform[1]

[1] This chapter was prepared by Knud J. Munk, largely based on contributions from Ian Goldin, Herve Guyomard, Michiel Keyzer, Louis Mahé, Dominique Van der Mensbrugghe and Max Mebis.

Chapter D

Model simulations of consequences of reform

1. Introduction

With a view to providing some quantitative assessment of the direction and magnitude of changes likely to occur as a result of different options for reform of the common agricultural policy, a number of the expert papers adopt a modelling approach. The following sections describe the main simulations which have been carried out. Three scenarios have been specified corresponding broadly to a continuation of existing policies, the CAP reform agreed in May of 1992 and a decoupled variant of the May 1992 reform package. The specific assumptions made are presented, together with the initial values for the main variables. The results from the core reference scenarios are described, in addition to the most important problems of interpretation and implementation which have arisen.

The presentation constitutes a synthesis of simulation results produced by the ECAM, the MISS and the RUNS models and differ in detail with results by either of these models, as presented in the background papers.

The models differ in their structure and assumptions. The ECAM model is a general equilibrium model covering nine EC countries. World market prices in this model are specified exogenously. The model allows the real income effect of policy changes to be modelled and the effect on the EC agricultural budget to be calculated in a comprehensive way. The MISS model is a partial equilibrium international trade model covering the EC, US and the rest of the world. The model allows world market prices to be calculated endogenously and also allows calculation of the impact on the budget expenditures which are directly related to price policies. The budget concept is therefore more narrow than for the ECAM model. The RUNS model is a multi-country general equilibrium model designed in particular to assess the effect of agricultural policies on developing countries. It allows calculation of world market effects and real income effects.

The models used here represent, as all models, only certain aspects of reality. For example, the transaction costs and the costs of saving government revenue are not represented in the models. The model results should therefore be interpreted

with due caution. They provide the means to deduce the implication of the assumptions made in a consistent way, rather than reliable estimates of the likely results of the policy changes considered.

2. Specification of scenarios

2.1. The initial situation

The common base year adopted for all the models is the marketing year 1992/93 which, following the usual conventions, will be referred to in the text and in the tables as 1992. As far as possible, data for production, consumption, trade and world market prices have been harmonized. The base data incorporate the price changes included in the 1992/93 price package but do not include the changes to the oilseed regime decided in 1991. For the purposes of the simulations these changes are deemed to be part of the reform package and are, as with all policy changes defined in the scenarios, considered implemented, beginning in 1993.

Commodity balances and nominal rates of protection for the main products are shown in Tables 34 and 35 for the base year 1992. Table 34 confirms the position of the Community as a significant net exporter of grains, dairy products, beef, sugar, and pork and poultry and as a significant net importer of oilcakes, corn gluten feed, manioc and other grain substitutes. Nominal rates of protection (broadly the ratio of domestic and world market prices) vary between 1.9 for oilseeds and 1.2 for pork and poultry and there is zero protection on corn gluten feed. The use of output subsidies in the oilseeds sector means that the nominal rate of protection measured on the consumption side is close to 1.

The green ecu switch-over coefficient is assumed in the base year to be 1.15.

2.2. General assumptions

It has been assumed that constant prices in nominal green ecu terms, with a 4-5% inflation and an inflation in the country with the strongest currency 1-2% lower due to the switch-over mechanism, will result in a 3% price decrease in real terms.

It has in general been assumed that prices of non-agricultural intermediate inputs will remain constant in real terms.

All the three main scenarios consider a unilateral EC policy change, therefore no policy reactions by third countries in response has been assumed. The USD/ECU exchange rate is also assumed unchanged.

Table 34

Commodity balances, initial values, 1992
(in million tonnes)

	Production	Feed use	Other uses	Net trade
Grains[1]	163.9	79.7	49.5	+ 34.7
Oilseeds				
Oilcakes	14.9[2]	41.4	—	– 26.4[3]
Oils	3.9	—	7.1	– 3.2
Corn gluten feed	1.4	9.5	—	– 8.1
Manioc	—	5.8	—	– 5.8
Other grain substitutes	21.5	28.3	—	– 6.8
Beef	8.1	—	7.2	+ 0.9
Pork and poultry	25.6	—	24.0	+ 1.6
Milk	96.7	—	76.2	+ 13.3
Sugar	15.9	—	11.1	+ 4.8
Other agricultural products	73.1	—	84.7	– 11.6

[1] Excluding rice and durum wheat, and without new German *Länder*.
[2] Oilcake equivalent of domestically produced seed, and other vegetable proteins.
[3] Net import of oilcake + net import of oilcake equivalent of net import of oilseeds.
Source: MISS model.

Table 35

Nominal rates of protection
(no protection = 1.00)

	Initial values 1992	
	Output	Input, consumption
Grains	1.68	1.68
Oilseeds	1.93	1.00
Oilcakes	1.00	1.00
Oils	1.10	1.00
Corn gluten feed	1.00	1.00
Manioc	1.00	1.53[1]
Other grain substitutes	1.25	1.25
Beef	1.53	1.49
Pork and poultry	1.20	1.20
Milk	2.03	1.94
Sugar	2.18	2.18
Other agricultural products	1.20	1.10

[1] Tariff equivalent of VER + ordinary tariff.
Source: MISS model.

GNP growth in the EC has been assumed to follow past trends. The assumptions for the development of demand for agricultural products and for the guidelines for CAP budget expenditure are consistent with this assumption.

2.3. Scenario 1: A continuation of pre-reform policies

Purpose of the scenario

This scenario has been formulated in order to assess the impact of a continuation of policies pursued during the 1980s. It serves as a benchmark against which the results of the reform scenarios are assessed.

Domestic price assumptions

The continuation of pre-reform policies is represented principally by an extrapolation, over the period 1993 to 2001, of the changes in producer prices observed during the 1980s. These price changes are presented in Table 36 for the main commodities. They do not incorporate the effect on prices of the stabiliser mechanism introduced in 1988 in the cereals and oilseeds sectors. To do this would result in significantly deeper price cuts. The price assumptions presented in Table 36 and all other price changes reported in this chapter are in real terms. With an assumed annual rate of inflation in the green ecu of 3% (see above) this implies no change in nominal green ecu prices for grains with small nominal price increases for all other commodities.

Table 36

Assumed real price changes, Scenario 1
(in annual percentage rates of change)

	Domestic production prices	World prices
	1992/2001	
Grains	– 3.0	– 0.5
Oilseeds	– 2.5	– 0.9
Oilcake	– 0.9	– 0.9
Oils	– 0.9	– 0.9
Corn gluten feed	– 1.5	– 1.5
Manioc	n.a.	0.0
Other grain substitutes	– 1.5	– 1.5
Beef	– 2.0	– 0.5 (+.8)[2]
Pork and poultry	– 2.7[1]	– 0.5
Milk	– 1.5	– 0.5
Sugar	– 1.0	– 0.5 (+.5)[2]
Other agricultural products	– 1.0	– 0.5

[1] The prices of pork, poultry and eggs are calculated endogenously.
[2] Figures in parenthesis indicate assumptions in MISS model.
Source: MISS model.

Quotas, other assumptions

A number of other assumptions have been specified in Scenario 1. All policy parameters other than support prices are held at their post 1992/93 price package levels. This implies unchanged levels of coresponsibility levies and unchanged quotas for milk and sugar. Voluntary set-aside is assumed to continue.

World market prices

The models have been calibrated according to exogenous world price assumptions for the purposes of Scenario 1. The assumed world price changes are also set out in Table 36. It is assumed that real prices of most commodities will fall by about 0.5% per annum with oilseeds and carbohydrates falling at slightly faster rates of 0.9 and 1.5% respectively.

The price assumptions contrast with the evolution during the 1980s where EC prices decreased by nearly 4% per year and world market prices by more than 6%. There is a considerable uncertainty above this evolution of world price changes over the period examined. However, it is generally thought unlikely that this trend will continue. The end of the green revolution, rising meat consumption, continuing problems of soil deterioration in the developing world are all factors which should allow world prices towards the end of the century to firm somewhat compared to the 1980s. The World Bank even projects real increases in world wheat prices and smaller increases in coarse grains, sugar and beef with other commodities declining only slightly. Given the conceptual framework used here, it is furthermore reasonable to assume that the domestic EC prices in response to the hardening of world market prices over the coming years still will decrease but at a lower pace than during the period of steep decreases in world market prices during the 1980s.

2.4. Scenario 2: Reform of the CAP. The May 1992 reform package

This scenario corresponds to the actual CAP reform package agreed in May 1992.

An important feature of the scenario is, therefore, the introduction of direct payments linked to land use and to number of livestock, and a set-aside provision which is assumed to result in a 9% reduction of the area of arable land.

Domestic price assumptions

All price changes which form part of the reform package are implemented during the three-year period 1993 to 1995. In addition to the nominal changes specified in the May 1992 reform package, all prices are deflated by 3% per annum over the period 1992 to 2001 taking into account the effect of inflation and the switch-over mechanism. In the case of cereals, the reduction is based on the decrease in the target price by 45 green ecu per tonne. All CAP prices specified in the context of the reform package are expressed in green ecu and have been converted to market ecu using a conversion factor of 1.15. The resulting price assumptions, expressed as average annual rates of change in real prices over the subperiod 1992/95 are presented in the first column of Table 37. The price decline indicated for oilseeds reflects the assumption that the changes in the oilseed regime decided in 1991 are an integral part of the reform. Oilseed prices are reduced to world price levels throughout the period of the reform and full compensation is granted. A 2.5% decrease in the intervention price of butter in each of the years 1993 and 1994 is expressed as a 1.3% decline in the nominal producer price of milk. All coresponsibility levies are eliminated. After the reform period, from 1996 and up until the year 2001, it is assumed that price changes for oilseeds and carbohydrates will follow the world market price while for other commodities prices will fall at the same rate as in Scenario 1.

Table 37

Assumed real domestic price changes, Scenarios 2 and 3
(in annual percentage rates of change)

	1992/95	1995/98	1998/2001	1992/2001
Grains	− 11.0	− 3.0	− 3.0	− 5.7
Oilseeds	− 16.0	− 2.5	− 2.5	− 7.0
Oilcakes	− 0.9[1]	− 0.9[1]	− 0.9[1]	− 0.9
Oils	− 0.9[1]	− 0.9[1]	− 0.9[1]	− 0.9
Corn gluten feed	− 1.5[1]	− 1.5[1]	− 1.5[1]	− 1.5
Manioc	− 1.5[1]	− 1.5[1]	− 1.5[1]	− 1.5
Other grain substitutes	− 1.5[1]	− 1.5[1]	− 1.5[1]	− 1.5
Beef	− 7.0	− 2.0	− 2.0	− 3.7
Pork and poultry	[2]	[2]	[2]	[2]
Milk	− 3.9	− 1.5	− 1.5	− 2.3
Sugar	− 1.0	− 1.0	− 1.0	− 1.0
Other agricultural products	—	—	—	—

[1] Follows the world market price. Price changes in ECAM model, endogenously in MISS model.
[2] These prices are determined endogenously.
Source: MISS model.

World price changes

In Scenario 2 world price changes are calculated endogenously.

Other assumptions

Quota changes are those incorporated in the May 1992 reform package. Milk quotas are reduced by 2% over the period 1992/95. There is no change in sugar quota. Voluntary set-aside is assumed to continue at the same level as in Scenario 1. It is assumed that some land will be withdrawn from arable cultivation and will become permanent grassland. The yields of cereals and oilseeds decline relative to Scenario 1 due to reduced inputs of labour and capital, but still increase compared to the base year. Beef yields are also assumed to decline reflecting the extensification requirement for eligibility for direct payments in that sector. Assumptions to this effect are made by changing parameters in the models.

Direct payments to producers

Direct payments to producers are provided during the reform period by ECU 11.5 billion, 13.75 billion and 16 billion in 1993, 1994 and 1995 respectively and maintained constant in real terms during the period 1996-2001. These payments are assumed not be be decoupled from production.

2.5. Scenario 3: Further reform of the CAP. Decoupled compensation

Purpose of the scenario

The intention in defining this scenario has not been to define an optimum reform programme, but a move in a desirable direction in comparison with past policies which at the same time could easily be compared with the May 1992 reform package. Attention has also been paid to the definition of a reform scenario capable of being implemented within the model structures available to ease interpretation. Most of the features of the reference scenario for reform of the CAP correspond to the terms of the reform actually agreed in May 1992. This is the case for the price elements of the reform package, both the level of price changes and the timing around ECU 2 000 million. The US has an interest in CAP compensation to be offered. The major differences are that compensation is entirely decoupled and that it is not assumed that there will be any commitment to set-aside.

Direct payments to producers

Direct payments to producers are provided during the reform period at the same level as provided for under the May 1992 reform package. These payments are kept constant in real terms but will, however, be made available only to those engaged in agriculture in 1993 on the basis of some historical criterion which the recipients are unable to influence. Payments, therefore, are not dependent on the recipient remaining in agriculture. Payments may not be inherited and are therefore reduced according to the mortality rates of the original recipient population. On this basis it has been estimated that total payments will decline at an average annual rate of 1.6% over the period 1996 to 2001.

3. The effect on prices and quantities

3.1. Continuation of pre-reform policies. The results of Scenario 1

Prices and nominal rates of protection

Domestic and world market prices have, as mentioned above, been set exogenously for virtually all commodities and it is these assumptions which determine the evolution of nominal rates of protection. As domestic prices fall more rapidly than world market prices, rates of protection decline. The rates prevailing by the end of the simulation period are presented in Table 38.

Table 38

Nominal rates of protection, Scenario 1
(no protection = 1.00, annual percentage rates of change)

	1992	2001	1992/2001 %
Grains	1.68	1.36	− 2.3
Oilseeds	1.93	1.68	− 1.5
Oilcakes	1.00	1.00	0.0
Oils	1.10	1.00	− 1.1
Corn gluten feed	1.00	1.00	0.0
Manioc	1.53	1.00	− 4.6
Other grain substitutes	1.25	1.00	− 2.4
Beef	1.53	1.18	− 2.8
Pork and poultry	1.20	1.00	− 2.0
Milk	2.03	1.88	− 0.8
Sugar	2.18	1.89	− 1.6
Other agricultural products			

Source: MISS model.

Commodity balances

The most consistent trend to emerge from the simulations of a continuation of pre-reform policies is a continuing significant expansion in production in virtually all commodities except those constrained by quotas. Table 39 illustrates this outcome. Production growth is most marked in the grain sector with an average annual increase of around 2%, in oilseeds with around 3% and in pork and poultry with 2-3% depending on the assumption made concerning the potential for export growth.

The use of domestically-produced feed expands significantly. The 1980s were characterized by a substantial shift from grains to oilcakes and grain substitutes. This trend does not continue in the base-run scenario. This is due to the assumed evolution of the grain prices. EC grain prices decrease by 3% per year whereas the world price of oilcakes decrease at a substantially lower rate of 0.9% per year.

Final consumption changes little over the period although established trends away from dairy products, beef and sugar and towards pork and poultry are confirmed. The impact on trade is that the Community increases exports of all commodities for which it was already a net exporter in 1992 and increases net imports for all commodities for which it was a net importer. Grain exports expand at an average annual rate of about 7% to double by the end of the simulation period compared with the 1992 level. Pork and poultry exports almost treble and beef exports double to almost 1.5 million tonnes as domestic consumption falls and production increases. Imports of all non-grain feeds increase significantly except those of manioc, which are constrained by a voluntary export restraint.

3.2. Reform of the CAP.
The May 1992 reform package.
The results of Scenario 2

Prices and nominal rates of protection

Domestic prices reflect the terms of the May 1992 reform of the CAP and are presented in Table 37. Steep price reductions, (16% per annum for oilseeds, 11% for grains, 7% for beef and smaller reductions for other commodities) are implemented during a three-year period beginning in 1993. The direct payments to compensate for the price decreases, which in this scenario are not entirely decoupled, are assumed to have a positive effect on supply.

Table 39

Commodity balances, Scenario 1
(in million tonnes, annual percentage rates of change)

	1992	2001	1992/2001 %
Production			
Grains	163.9	194.5	1.9
Oilseeds			
Oilcakes	14.9	18.9	2.7
Oils	3.9		
Other grain substitutes	21.5		
Beef	8.1	8.2	0.1
Pork and poultry	25.6	31.9	2.2
Milk	96.7	96.7	0.0
Sugar	15.9	15.9	0.0
Other agricultural products			
Feed use			
Grains	79.7	85.9	0.8
Oilcakes	41.4	42.0	0.2
Corn gluten feed	9.5	12.2	2.8
Manioc	5.8	5.8	0.0
Other grain substitutes	28.3	32.7	1.6
Other uses			
Grains	49.5	47.4	− 0.5
Oils	7.1	6.4	− 1.1
Beef	7.2	6.6	− 1.0
Pork and poultry	24.0	26.2	1.0
Milk	76.2	75.6	− 0.1
Sugar	11.1	10.4	− 0.7
Other agricultural products			
Net trade			
Grains (E)	+ 34.7	+ 61.1	6.5
Oilseeds			
Oilcakes (I)	− 26.4	− 23.1	− 1.5
Oils (I)	− 3.2		
Corn gluten feed (I)	− 8.1	− 10.8	+ 3.2
Manioc (I)	− 5.8	− 5.8	0.0
Other grain substitutes (I)	− 6.8	+ 1.1	[1]
Beef (E)	+ 0.9	+ 1.5	5.8
Pork and poultry (E)	+ 1.6	+ 5.7	15.2
Milk (E)	+ 13.3	+ 13.9	0.5
Sugar (E)	+ 4.8	+ 5.5	1.5
Other agricultural products			

[1] Not defined (switch from import to export) see Table 34.
Source: MISS model.

After the end of the reform period, prices continue to decline at the same rate as assumed in Scenario 1. Overall, the total price decrease over the simulation period up to 2001 is significantly greater than in Scenario 1. Some domestic prices are determined endogenously by the models. This is the case for pork and poultry whose prices generally follow the trend in domestic prices of feed and for oilseed prices which follow world market prices. In the ECAM model, pork and poultry exports have been assumed constant and the evolution of domestic prices is therefore entirely determined by domestic supply and demand conditions. In the MISS model, the export is endogenous and domestic prices therefore follow world market prices in the post-reform period.

The outcome of this scenario in terms of changes in world prices is determined essentially by changes in the level of the Community's net exports. Interesting differences emerge between subperiods. (See Table 40) The reform period itself is characterized by a strengthening in world markets as prices for some commodities increase (grains, beef, milk, sugar), while the rate of decline is reduced for most other commodities (pork and poultry and non-grain feeds). However, in subsequent years, a downward trend is re-established for all commodities except beef and sugar. World market prices increase or decrease more slowly in the reform period than under continuation of existing policies.

Table 40

World market prices, Scenario 2
(in annual percentage rates of change)

	1992/95	1995/98	1998/2001	1992/2001
Grains	1.0	− 0.3	− 0.5	0.0
Oilseeds	—	—	—	—
Oilcakes	− 1.8	− 0.8	− 1.0	− 1.2
Oils	− 0.2	− 1.0	− 1.2	− 0.8
Corn gluten feed	− 5.9	− 1.3	− 0.5	− 2.6
Manioc	0.1	0.2	0.3	0.2
Other grain substitutes	− 1.2	− 1.3	− 0.8	− 1.1
Beef	2.7	0.8	0.6	1.3
Pork and poultry	− 0.3	− 1.1	− 0.9	− 0.7
Milk	0.2	− 0.7	− 0.7	− 0.4
Sugar	0.5	0.5	0.5	0.5
Other agricultural products	0.1	0.2	0.3	0.2

Source: MISS model.

Nominal rates of protection fall, in general, as domestic prices fall throughout the entire period and world prices either increase or decrease more slowly than domestic prices. The results are presented in Table 41. During or shortly after the initial reform period, the price gap is eliminated for grains, oilseeds, beef, pork and poultry and this situation is maintained up to the end of the period. Even in those sectors which are constrained by quotas and in which relatively small price cuts have been implemented (milk and sugar), world market prices fall more slowly and the nominal rates of protection fall somewhat.

Table 41

Nominal rates of protection, Scenario 2
(no protection = 1.00, annual percentage rates of change)

	1992	1995	1998	2001	1992/ 2001 %
Grains	1.68	1.09	1.00	1.00	− 5.6
Oilseeds	1.93	1.00	1.00	1.00	− 7.0
Oilcakes	1.00	1.00	1.00	1.00	0.0
Oils	1.00	1.00	1.00	1.00	0.0
Corn gluten feed	1.00	1.00	1.00	1.00	0.0
Manioc					
Other grain substitutes					
Beef	1.53	1.08	1.00	1.00	− 4.6
Pork and poultry	1.20	1.00	1.00	1.00	− 2.0
Milk	2.03	1.81	1.77	1.72	− 1.8
Sugar	2.18	2.08	1.98	1.89	− 1.6
Other agricultural products					

Source: MISS model.

Commodity balances

The main results are presented in Tables 42, 43 and 44 which present the changes in production, consumption and trade in absolute terms, in terms of average annual rates of change by subperiod and by comparison with the first scenario, respectively.

Table 42

Commodity balances, Scenario 2
(in million tonnes)

	1992	1995	1998	2001
Production				
Grains	163.9	152.4	155.6	158.4
Oilseeds	—	—	—	—
Oilcakes	14.9	14.0	14.5	16.1
Oils	—	—	—	—
Other grain substitutes	21.5	—	—	—
Beef	8.1	7.9	7.9	7.9
Pork and poultry	25.6	27.9	31.0	34.0
Milk	96.7	94.7	94.7	94.7
Sugar	15.9	15.9	15.9	15.9
Other agricultural products	—	—	—	—
Feed use				
Grains	79.7	87.1	91.5	92.9
Oilcakes	41.4	37.3	38.1	39.7
Corn gluten feed	9.5	10.0	10.6	11.8
Manioc	5.8	5.9	6.0	6.4
Other grain substitutes	28.3	29.5	31.2	33.6
Other uses				
Grains	49.5	52.7	52.0	50.8
Oils	7.1	7.0	6.7	6.5
Beef	7.2	7.5	7.3	7.0
Pork and poultry	24.0	25.5	26.3	27.1
Milk	76.2	76.2	76.1	76.0
Sugar	11.0	10.8	10.6	10.4
Other agricultural products	—	—	—	—
Net trade				
Grains	+ 34.7	+ 12.5	+ 12.1	+ 14.7
Oilseeds	—	—	—	—
Oilcakes	− 26.4	− 23.2	− 23.6	− 23.6
Oils	—	—	—	—
Corn gluten feed	− 8.1	− 8.4	− 9.3	− 10.4
Manioc	− 5.8	− 5.9	− 6.0	− 6.4
Other grain substitutes	− 6.8	− 4.9	− 2.6	− 0.3
Beef	+ 0.9	+ 0.3	+ 0.5	+ 0.8
Pork and poultry	+ 1.6	+ 2.3	+ 4.0	+ 7.0
Milk	+ 13.3	+ 11.3	+ 11.5	+ 11.6
Sugar	+ 4.8	+ 5.1	+ 5.3	+ 5.5
Other agricultural products	—	—	—	—

NB: See notes in Table 34.
Source: MISS model.

Table 43

Commodity balances, Scenario 2
(in annual percentage rates of change)

	1992/1995	1995/1998	1998/2001	1992/2001
Production				
Grains	− 2.4	+ 0.7	+ 0.6	− 0.4
Oilseeds	—	—	—	—
Oilcakes	− 2.1	+ 1.2	+ 3.6	+ 0.9
Oils	—	—	—	—
Beef	− 0.8	0	0	− 0.3
Pork and poultry	+ 2.9	+ 3.6	+ 3.1	+ 3.2
Milk	− 0.7	0	0	− 0.2
Sugar	0	0	0	0
Other agricultural products	—	—	—	—
Feed use				
Grains	+ 3.0	+ 1.7	+ 0.5	+ 1.7
Oilcakes	− 3.4	+ 0.7	+ 1.4	− 1.4
Corn gluten feed	+ 1.7	+ 2.0	+ 3.6	+ 2.4
Manioc	+ 0.6	+ 0.6	+ 2.1	+ 1.1
Other grain substitutes	+ 1.4	+ 1.9	+ 2.5	+ 1.9
Other uses				
Grains	+ 2.1	− 0.4	− 0.8	+ 0.3
Oils	− 0.5	− 1.4	− 1.0	− 1.0
Beef	+ 1.4	− 1.0	− 1.4	− 0.3
Pork and poultry	+ 2.0	+ 1.0	+ 1.0	+ 1.4
Milk	0	0	− 0.1	− 0
Sugar	− 0.9	− 0.6	− 0.6	− 0.7
Other agricultural products	—	—	—	—
Net trade				
Grains (E)	− 28.8	− 1.0	+ 6.7	+ 9.1
Oilseeds	—	—	—	—
Oilcakes (I)	+ 4.2	− 0.6	0	+ 1.2
Oils	—	—	—	—
Corn gluten feed (I)	− 1.2	− 3.4	− 3.8	− 2.8
Manioc (I)	− 0.6	− 0.6	− 2.1	− 1.1
Other grain substitutes (I)	+ 10.3	+ 19.0	+ 51.3	+ 29.3
Beef (E)	− 30.6	+ 18.6	+ 17.0	− 1.3
Pork and poultry (E)	+ 12.9	+ 20.2	+ 20.5	+ 17.8
Milk (E)	− 5.3	+ 0.6	+ 0.3	− 1.5
Sugar (E)	+ 2.0	+ 1.3	+ 1.2	+ 1.5
Other agricultural products	—	—	—	—

NB: See notes in Table 34.
Source: MISS model.

Table 44

Commodity balances, Scenario 2

(in percentage of Scenario 1)

	1995	1998	2001
Production			
Grains	87.8	84.7	81.4
Oilseeds			
Oilcakes	87.0	82.9	85.2
Oils			
Other grain substitutes			
Beef	97.5	97.5	96.3
Pork and poultry	101.5	106.5	106.6
Milk	97.9	97.9	97.9
Sugar	100.0	100.0	100.0
Other agricultural products			
Feed use			
Grains	106.7	109.3	108.1
Oilcakes	89.9	91.4	94.5
Corn gluten feed	97.1	94.6	96.7
Manioc	101.7	103.4	110.3
Other grain substitutes	99.7	100.3	102.8
Other uses			
Grains	108.0	108.1	107.2
Oils	101.4	101.5	101.6
Beef	107.1	107.4	106.1
Pork and poultry	103.2	103.1	103.4
Milk	100.3	100.4	100.5
Sugar	100.0	100.0	100.0
Other agricultural products			
Net trade			
Grains	29.0	23.3	24.1
Oilseeds			
Oilcakes	91.3	97.1	102.2
Oils			
Corn gluten feed	94.4	94.9	96.3
Manioc	101.7	103.4	110.3
Other grain substitutes	106.5	130.0	– 27.3
Beef	27.3	38.5	533.3
Pork and poultry	82.1	97.6	122.8
Milk	83.7	83.9	83.5
Sugar	102.0	101.9	100.0
Other agricultural products			

N.B.: See notes in Table 34.
Source: MISS model.

Production of the main commodities not constrained by quota falls during the reform period. The downward pressure on production resulting from the statutory 15% set-aside requirement (9% effective) is offset somewhat by the production-enhancing effect of the requirement that the remaining arable land (some of which at the cereal price, which in this scenario is much lower than in Scenario 1, otherwise would have gone out of rotation) must be kept in production in order to qualify for compensation.

One would expect the positive effect on production of retaining primary factors in the agricultural sector by the compensation scheme to become relatively more important than the negative effect of the set-aside provision as time goes on and the scope for primary factor adaptation increases. This is, however, not fully reflected in the structure of the models, and hence neither in the model results.

Relative prices move in favour of domestically-produced grains for animal feed during this initial reform period and use of grains for feed increases significantly. Protein cakes become much less competitive relative to grains which is reflected in large substitution of domestic grains for cakes. This contrasts with the results for grain substitutes where the price follows the decline in EC grain prices, grain substitutes in general being by-products and hence having low supply elasticities. As a result, the substitution of grains for grain substitutes is much less than in the case of oilcakes.

Final consumption increases for most products in response to price cuts and net exports decline significantly except for sugar, where the price has not been reduced, and for pork and poultry where net exports increase substantially.

Following the initial reform period 1993-95, the same trends as in Scenario 1 in prices, production, consumption and trade re-emerge. The growth in production resumes for all commodities which are not constrained by quotas and remains particularly strong for pork and poultry. The demand grows for all feedstuff ingredients, the use of corn gluten feed expands rapidly and the decline in the use of oilcakes during the reform period is reversed. Final consumption tends, in the post-reform period, to decline slightly for most commodities, except pork and poultry. By the end of the period, net exports of grains again expand at a rapid rate. Net imports of oilcakes are lower than their initial levels, but corn gluten feed imports show a strong increase. Beef exports again reach the initial levels, having been virtually eliminated during the reform period. Dairy exports remain at the 1995 levels, whereas pork and poultry exports continue to grow rapidly.

These differences in the outcome between the reform period and the post-reform period suggest that the reform will be quite effective in curbing production and hence export growth initially, but if not sustained will not in the subsequent period be able to offset the impact of continuing technological progress, despite the fact that the growth in production due to technological progress has been assumed to have been reduced due to the sharp reduction in prices.

The main difference between the outcomes in Scenarios 1 and 2 occurs in the period of the reform itself, reflecting the incidence of the price reductions.

That the primary factors adjust only gradually to the sharp reduction in product prices during the reform period has not been taken into account in the model simulations. The results may therefore overestimate the effects during the reform period and underestimate the effects in the following period.

3.3. Reform of the CAP.
Decoupled compensation.
The results of Scenario 3

The reform implemented in this scenario contains many of the elements of the reform agreed in May of 1992. The main additional feature of this scenario is that the compensation granted is decoupled and not contingent on land being set aside.

Prices and nominal rates of protection

The evolution in domestic prices is similar to that in Scenario 2 as presented in Table 37. The evolution of world market prices is shown in Table 45. As in the CAP reform scenario, the decoupled run has a significant impact on world prices with noticeable differences between the first subperiod when price changes are implemented and the two following subperiods.

Table 45

World market prices, Scenario 3
(in annual percentage rates of change)

	1992/95	1995/98	1998/2001	1992/2001
Grains	1.7	– 0.5	– 0.8	0.1
Oilseeds	—	—	—	—
Oilcakes	– 0.9	– 0.8	– 0.5	– 0.7
Oil	0.6	– 1.0	– 1.0	– 0.5
Corn gluten feed	– 6.4	– 1.3	– 0.2	– 2.6
Manioc	0.2	0.2	0.3	0.2
Other grain substitutes	– 1.9	– 1.3	-- 0.6	– 1.3
Beef	3.1	– 0.7	0.2	1.3
Pork and poultry	– 0.4	– 1.1	– 0.8	– 0.8
Milk	0.3	– 0.8	– 0.7	– 0.4
Sugar	0.5	0.5	0.5	0.5
Other agricultural products	0.0	0.2	0.3	0.2

Source: MISS model.

Nominal rates of protection fall, in general, as domestic prices fall throughout the entire period and world prices either increase or decrease more slowly than domestic prices. The results are presented in Table 46. As in the CAP reform scenario, the world/domestic price gap is eliminated for grains, oilseeds, beef, pork and poultry after 1996.

Table 46

Nominal rates of protection, Scenario 3
(no protection = 1.00, annual percentage rates of change)

	1992	1995	1998	2001	1992/ 2001 %
Grains	1.68	1.08	1.00	1.00	– 5.6
Oilseeds	1.93	1.00	1.00	1.00	– 7.0
Oil					
Oilcakes					
Corn gluten feed	1.00	1.00	1.00	1.00	0.0
Manioc					
Other grain substitutes					
Beef	1.53	1.08	1.00	1.00	– 4.6
Pork and poultry	1.20	1.00	1.00	1.00	– 2.0
Milk	2.03	1.80	1.76	1.72	– 1.8
Sugar	2.18	2.08	1.98	1.89	– 1.6
Other agricultural products					

Source: MISS model.

Commodity balances

The decoupled nature of the reform implemented in this scenario is such that the prices determining production, intermediate and final consumption fall significantly. The main difference between the outcomes in Scenarios 1 and 3 occurs in the period of the reform itself, reflecting the incidence of the price reductions. The main results are presented in Tables 47, 48 and 49 which present the changes in production, consumption and trade in absolute terms, in terms of average annual rates of change by subperiod and by comparison with the first scenario respectively.

Table 47

Commodity balances, Scenario 3
(in million tonnes)

	1992	1995	1998	2001
Production				
Grains	163.9	140.2	143.2	151.9
Oilseeds	—	—	—	—
Oilcakes	14.9	10.3	11.2	12.0
Oils	—	—	—	—
Other grain substitutes	—	—	—	—
Beef	8.1	7.7	7.7	7.9
Pork and poultry	25.6	28.4	31.6	34.5
Milk	96.7	94.7	94.7	94.7
Sugar	15.9	15.9	15.9	15.9
Other agricultural products	—	—	—	—
Feed use				
Grains	79.7	86.6	90.8	93.2
Oilcakes	41.4	36.2	37.0	38.5
Corn gluten feed	9.5	9.7	10.6	11.7
Manioc	5.8	5.9	6.1	6.4
Other grain subsitutes	28.3	29.4	31.2	33.7
Other uses				
Grains	49.5	52.7	51.9	50.9
Oils	7.1	6.9	6.6	6.4
Beef	7.2	7.5	7.3	7.0
Pork and poultry	24.0	25.6	26.3	27.0
Milk	76.2	76.3	76.2	76.1
Sugar	11.0	10.8	10.6	10.4
Other agricultural products	—	—	—	—
Net trade				
Grains	+ 34.7	+ 0.9	+ 0.5	+ 7.8
Oilseeds	—	—	—	—
Oilcakes	− 26.4	− 25.9	− 25.8	− 26.5
Oils	—	—	—	—
Corn gluten feed	− 8.1	− 8.3	− 9.2	− 10.3
Manioc	− 5.8	− 6.0	− 6.1	− 6.4
Other grain substitutes	− 6.8	− 4.2	− 2.0	+ 0.2
Beef	+ 0.9	+ 0.2	+ 0.4	+ 0.9
Pork and poultry	+ 1.6	+ 2.8	+ 5.3	+ 7.4
Milk	+ 13.3	+ 11.3	+ 11.4	+ 11.5
Sugar	+ 4.8	+ 5.1	+ 5.3	+ 5.5
Other agricultural products	—	—	—	—

NB: See notes in Table 34.
Source: MISS model.

Table 48

Commodity balances, Scenario 3
(in annual percentage rates of change)

	1992/1995	1995/1998	1998/2001	1992/2001
Production				
Grains	− 5.1	+ 0.7	+ 2.0	− 0.8
Oilseeds	—	—	—	—
Oilcakes	− 11.6	+ 2.8	+ 2.3	− 2.4
Oils	—	—	—	—
Other grain substitutes	—	—	—	—
Beef	− 1.6	+ 0.0	+ 0.9	− 0.3
Pork and poultry	+ 3.5	+ 3.6	+ 3.0	+ 3.4
Milk	− 0.7	0.0	0.0	− 0.2
Sugar	0.0	0.0	0.0	0.0
Other agricultural products	—	—	—	—
Feed use				
Grains	+ 2.8	+ 1.6	+ 0.9	+ 1.8
Oilcakes	− 4.4	+ 0.7	+ 1.3	− 0.8
Corn gluten feed	+ 0.7	+ 3.0	+ 3.4	+ 2.3
Manioc	+ 0.6	+ 1.1	+ 1.6	+ 1.1
Other grain substitutes	+ 1.3	+ 2.0	+ 2.6	+ 2.0
Other uses				
Grains	+ 2.1	− 0.5	− 0.7	− 0.3
Oils	− 1.0	− 1.5	− 1.0	− 1.2
Beef	+ 1.4	− 0.9	− 1.4	− 0.3
Pork and poultry	+ 2.2	+ 0.9	+ 0.9	+ 1.3
Milk	+ 0.0	− 0.0	− 0.0	0.0
Sugar	− 0.9	− 0.6	− 0.6	− 0.7
Other agricultural products	—	—	—	—
Net trade				
Grains (E)	− 70.4	− 17.8	+ 149.9	+ 15.3
Oilseeds	—	—	—	—
Oilcakes (I)	− 0.6	− 0.1	+ 0.9	0.0
Oils	—	—	—	—
Corn gluten feed (I)	+ 0.8	+ 3.5	+ 3.8	+ 2.7
Manioc (I)	+ 1.1	+ 0.6	+ 1.6	+ 1.1
Other grain substitutes (I)	− 14.8	+ 21.2	[1]	[1]
Beef (E)	− 39.4	+ 25.9	+ 31.0	0.0
Pork and poultry (E)	+ 20.5	+ 23.7	+ 11.8	18.6
Milk (E)	− 5.3	+ 0.3	+ 0.3	− 1.6
Sugar (E)	+ 2.0	+ 1.3	+ 1.2	+ 1.5
Other agricultural products	—	—	—	—

[1] Not defined (switch from import to export). Other notes: see Table 34.
Source: MISS model.

Table 49

Commodity balances, Scenario 3
(in percentage of Scenario 1)

	1995	1998	2001
Production			
Grains	80.8	78.0	78.1
Oilseeds			
Oilcakes	64.0	64.0	63.5
Oils			
Other grain substitutes			
Beef	95.1	95.1	96.3
Pork and poultry	103.3	108.6	108.2
Milk	97.9	97.6	97.9
Sugar	100.0	100.0	100.0
Other agricultural products			
Feed use			
Grains	106.1	108.5	108.5
Oilcakes	87.2	88.7	91.7
Corn gluten feed	94.2	94.6	95.9
Manioc	101.7	105.2	110.3
Other grain substitutes	99.3	100.3	103.1
Other uses			
Grains	108.0	107.9	107.4
Oils	100.0	100.0	100.0
Beef	107.1	107.4	106.1
Pork and poultry	103.6	103.1	103.1
Milk	100.4	100.5	100.7
Sugar	100.0	100.0	100.0
Other agricultural products			
Net trade			
Grains	2.1	1.0	12.8
Oilseeds			
Oilcakes	102.0	106.2	114.7
Oils			
Corn gluten feed	93.3	93.9	95.4
Manioc	103.4	105.2	110.3
Other grain substitutes	91.3	100.0	18.2
Beef	18.2	30.8	60.0
Pork and poultry	100.0	129.3	129.8
Milk	83.7	83.2	82.7
Sugar	102.0	101.9	100.0
Other agricultural products			

NB: See notes in Table 34.
Source: MISS model.

During the reform period, production of grains and oilseeds fall at average annual rates of 5 and 12% respectively. Beef production also declines as does milk as a direct consequence of the imposition of a quota cut. Pork and poultry production expand rapidly as a result of falling feedstuff prices and a strong substitution effect away from commodities whose prices are falling more rapidly. During this period relative prices move strongly in favour of grains which increase their share of total feed utilization. Use of oilcakes for feed actually declines in absolute terms at an average annual rate in excess of 4% per annum. The expansion effect from increase in meat production is not sufficient to neutralize the negative substitution effect. Final consumption of most commodities increases in response to the price changes with grains, beef, pork and poultry experiencing the largest increases. The effect on net exports in this initial period is quite dramatic. Large declines occur for those commodities such as grains and beef with falling production and rising consumption. There is a slight decrease in net imports of oilcakes and a big decline in imports of other grain substitutes. Net exports of milk fall while there is rapid expansion in exports of pork and poultry.

The EC returns to self-sufficiency for grains in 1996 because the price cut has now its full impact on production since the decoupled payments do not keep marginal land in production. Feed use of grains increases substantially due to a better price competitiveness with respect to oilcakes and, to a much smaller extent, to grain substitutes. Production of animal products is nearly the same in the two reform scenarios.

As regards the two following subperiods, the global picture of the decoupled CAP reform does not differ from the one derived from the CAP reform scenario. The price assumptions are the same and there is a re-assertion of previous trends in production, consumption and trade in the post-reform period.

4. The effects of CAP reform within the EC: comparison of scenarios

4.1. Comparison of production, consumption and trade effects between scenarios

The major difference between Scenario 1 on the one hand and Scenario 2 and 3 on the other hand is illustrated in Table 50. The EC achieves through the reform of the CAP the rebalancing which has for long been an important objective of EC agricultural trade policy, i.e. the equalization of the rate of protection for different feed ingredients. This is, however, achieved by a decrease in the price of cereals rather than an increase in the domestic price of imported feedstuff, as had previously been envisaged. For the feed utilization the effect is basically the same, whatever way the rebalancing is being achieved, whereas the production effects naturally are different. In Scenario 2 and 3 there is a significant increase compared with Scenario 1 in the use of cereals for feed and a corresponding decrease in the use of oilcakes and other imported feedstuff. Cereals and oilseed production is significantly lower in Scenario 2 and 3 compared with Scenario 1. Also beef production falls significantly compared to Scenario 1, whereas the increase in the production of pork and poultry are almost the same in all scenarios.

Table 50

Changes in production, feed use, final consumption and trade (in annual rates of change)

	Scenario 1	Scenario 2	Scenario 3
Production			
Grains	1.9	– 0.4	– 0.8
Oilcakes[1]	2.7	0.9	– 2.4
Beef	0.1	– 0.3	– 0.3
Pork and poultry	2.2	3.2	3.4
Feed use			
Grains	0.8	1.7	1.8
Oilcakes	0.2	– 1.4	– 0.8
Corn gluten feed	2.8	2.4	2.3
Other uses			
Grains	– 0.5	0.3	0.3
Beef	– 1.0	– 0.3	– 0.3
Pork and poultry	1.0	1.4	1.3
Net trade			
Grains (E)	6.5	– 9.1	– 15.3
Oilcakes[2] (I)	– 1.5	+ 1.2	0.0
Beef (E)	5.8	– 1.3	0.0
Pork and poultry (E)	15.2	17.8	18.6

NB: See notes in Table 34.
Source: MISS model.

The consumption of agricultural products is not much different in the three scenarios. The difference in production and feed use between Scenario 1 on the one hand and Scenario 2 and 3 on the other hand are therefore reflected in differences in net trade. The EC cereal net exports are significantly reduced in Scenario 2 and 3 compared with Scenario 1, whereas import of oilseed remains at roughly the same level.

The price changes are the same in the 1992 reform scenario (Scenario 2) and the decoupled scenario (Scenario 3) and therefore differ not much with respect to production, consumption and trade. However, cereals and oilseed production is, according to the MISS model, bigger in the 1992 reform

scenario than in the decoupled scenario. This reflects that the negative effects on production of the set-aside provision in the 1992 reform are less important than the positive effects on production because the direct payment requires the remaining land to be cultivated. The differences in production are reflected in smaller grains export and greater oilseed import in the decoupled scenario than in the 1992 reform scenario.[1]

4.2. The effect on the EC budget

Scenario 1 *Continuation of existing policies*

The budgetary consequences of a continuation during the 1990s of the agricultural policies of the 1980s would, according to the model results, have been less dramatic than is generally believed. The main explanation of this is that world market prices have been assumed to develop during the 1990s at a much more favourable rate than was the case during the 1980s whereas domestic prices are decreased at almost the same rate as in the 1980s. The justification for this assumption has been provided above. Despite large increases in export for several commodities, the costs in real terms of export subsidies therefore decline. This is the case for grains, beef, pork and poultry where the nominal protection is either sharply reduced or totally eliminated. The export subsidies in the milk and sugar sectors are constrained by quotas. As a result, the budgetary transfers fall by ECU 1 500 million from 1992 to 2001.[2]

The costs of storage are increased, however, by ECU 1 200 million. Total EAGGF Guarantee outlays therefore increase by around 0.3% a year in real terms for 1992-2001.

Scenario 2 *1992 CAP reform*

The budget transfer payments increase under the 1992 CAP reform scenario by around ECU 4 200 million from 1992 to 2001.[3] Exports decrease sharply due to the decrease in beef prices and the steep decrease in grain prices, but the increase in direct payments is greater than the savings in export refunds.

---

[1]   This contrasts with the results in the ECAM model where cereals and oilseed production is higher in the decoupled scenario than in the 1992 reform scenario.

[2]   The ECAM model projects that the budgetary transfer will fall by 0.7% per year and the MISS model by Y% a year.

[3]   The annual rates of increase are 1.8% and Y% according to the ECAM and the MISS models, respectively.

The cost of storage increases by ECU 750 million. In real terms the total EAGGF Guarantee budget increases by around ECU 7 000 million, i.e. by 2.3% per year for 1992-2001.

Scenario 3 *Decoupled CAP reform*

The decoupled reform scenario results in an increase in budget transfer payments in 2001 of around ECU 1 900 million compared to 1992,[1] which takes into account a

reduction of user's subsidies by almost ECU 1 300 million. Export subsidies decline, but the decline is, as in Scenario 2, more than compensated for by the increase in direct payments.

The storage costs increase according to the ECAM model by ECU 1 300 million. The total annual rate of increase in EAGGF Guarantee outlays is 1.3% per year for 1992-2001.

---

[1]   The annual rates of increase are 0.8% and Y% according to the ECAM and the MISS models, respectively.

Table 51A

FEOGA Guidance budget expenditures
(in million ECU, 1992 value)

Scenario 1

	1992	1995	1998	2001
A. Transfers to producers EUR-12	19 091	18 230	17 905	17 552
of which				
refunds on agricultural trade EUR-9	6 446	6 389	5 883	5 300
output subsidies EUR-9	4 238	3 643	3 666	3 685
input subsidies EUR-9	2 189	2 114	2 112	2 123
direct payments EUR-9	3 242	2 863	2 826	2 816
transfers to producers EUR-3	2 976	3 221	3 418	3 628
B. Transfers to users EUR-12	2 736	2 715	2 744	2 794
of which				
consumer subsidies EUR-9	1 600	1 571	1 574	1 591
subsidies to processors EUR-9	730	705	704	708
transfers to users EUR-3	406	439	466	495
Total: A + B	21 827	20 945	20 649	20 346
C. Non-transfer expenditure EUR-12	9 829	10 756	11 335	12 214
of which				
interest and storage EUR-9	3 270	3 855	4 091	3 503
stock devaluation EUR-9	204	21	– 56	– 36
EUR-9 miscelleneous	2 915	3 156	3 349	3 554
non-transfer expenditure EUR-3	3 440	3 724	3 951	4 193
Total: A + B + C	31 656	31 701	31 984	32 560

Source: ECAM model.

Table 51B

FEOGA Guidance budget expenditures 1992-2001

(annual rates of change)

	Scenario 1	Scenario 2	Scenario 3
A. Transfers to producers	− 0.93	2.19	− 10.2
of which			
refunds on agricultural trade EUR-9	− 2.14	− 8.56	− 6.60
output subsidies EUR-9	− 1.51	− 1.89	− 2.37
input subsidies EUR-9	− 0.34	− 0.51	− 10.8
direct payments EUR-9	− 4.61	17.09	[1]
transfers to producers EUR-3	2.23	3.39	1.55
B. Transfers to users	0.23	0.40	− 7.07
of which			
consumer subsidies EUR-9	− 0.06	− 0.16	[1]
subsidies to processors EUR-9	− 0.34	− 0.51	2.95
transfers to users EUR-3	2.23	3.39	1.55
Total: A + B	− 0.77	1.98	− 9.7
C. Non-transfer expenditure EUR-12	2.44	2.81	2.15
of which			
interest and storage EUR-9	3.63	3.67	4.64
stock devaluation EUR-9	− 22.3	− 7.24	− 26.4
EUR-9 miscelleneous	2.23	3.39	1.55
non-transfer expenditure EUR-3	2.23	3.39	1.55
D. Compensation payments	[1]	[1]	[1]
Total: A + B + D	− 0.77	1.98	0.92
Total: A + B + C + D	0.31	2.25	1.31

[1] Not defined.
Source: ECAM model.

Table 51C

FEOGA Guidance budget expenditure in percentage of Scenario 1 in 2001

	Scenario 2	Scenario 3
A. Transfers to producers	132	41
of which		
refunds on agricultural trade EUR-9	50	61
output subsidies EUR-9	97	− 0
input subsidies EUR-9	98	30
direct payments EUR-9	386	[1]
transfers to producers EUR-3	111	94
B. Transfers to users	102	51
of which		
consumer subsidies EUR-9	100	0
subsidies to processors EUR-9	98	134
transferts to users EUR-3	111	94
Total: A + B	128	43
C. Non-transfer expenditure EUR-12	103	97
of which		
interest and storage EUR-9	89	102
stock devaluation EUR-9	− 90	15
EUR-9 miscelleneous	111	94
non-transfer expenditure EUR-3	111	94
D. Compensation payments	[1]	[1]
Total: A + B + D	128	116
Total: A + B + C + D	119	109

[1] Not defined.
Source: ECAM model.

Comparison of scenarios

The budget implication of the three scenarios are rather similar. The 1992 CAP reform (Scenario 2) has in 2001 the highest budget costs followed by the decoupled CAP reform (Scenario 3). The transfer payments in the 1992 CAP reform are around ECU 5 700 million higher than under the continuation of existing policies (Scenario 1), and around ECU 2 300 million higher than in the decoupled CAP reform.

The export subsidies are ECU 600 million higher in Scenario 3 compared with Scenario 2 according to the

ECAM[1] model. The direct payments are in Scenario 2 reduced by the green ecu inflation whereas in Scenario 3 they are reduced by the death rate of farmers. Storage costs are ECU 600 million higher in Scenario 3 than in Scenario 2, but reduction in user subsidies and in other budget expenditures make total EAGGF Guarantee expenditures in Scenario 3, ECU 3 000 million lower than in Scenario 2.

The total EAGGF Guarantee expenditures are in all scenarios, assuming 2.5% EC GNP growth, within the 1988 guidelines and in the case of Scenario 1 comfortably so.

The 1992 CAP reform and the decoupled CAP reform imply a shift of transfers from consumers and other users to transfers from taxpayers. It is therefore not surprising that these scenarios imply an increase in budget costs. It is, maybe, more surprising that the increase in budget costs is so relatively small. The reason for this is that the agricultural sector is a major user of cereals which have the most severe price cut, such that the decrease in grain prices makes it possible to reduce the prices for animal products without decreasing the income of animal producers.

4.3. Effects on primary factors use and on farm income

Land use

Land use is the same under the continuation of existing policies (Scenario 1) and under the 1992 CAP reform scenario (Scenario 2). Land use is, under these scenarios, reduced by around 0.3% a year. Under the decoupled CAP reform scenario (Scenario 3), land use is reduced by 0.5% a year. This stronger decrease reflects that the reduction of land use, under the 1992 reform due to the set-aside provisions, will be less than the increase in land use due to the fact that direct payments require land to be kept under cultivation. The differences in aggregate land use under the different scenarios are, however, to some extent misleading because the composition of the land will be different. Under the 1992 reform, both fertile and less fertile land are retired from production due to the set-aside, whereas under the decoupled scenario only the less fertile land will be taken out of production.

Employment

The decrease in employment under the three scenarios mainly reflects the reduction of the labour force due to demographic factors, i.e. the large percentage of older farmers in the

agricultural labour force. Employment decreases by 2.6% a year in Scenarios 1 and 2. The decrease in Scenario 3 is greater, 2.9% a year. This reflects that the use of inputs in general under this scenario is reduced compared with the two other scenarios.

Farm income

The value-added and transfer payments in the agricultural sector will decline most in Scenario 1, by 0.7% a year in real terms, by 0.4% in Scenario 2 and increase by 0.1% in Scenario 3. This corresponds, per person employed, to increases of 1.7, 2.2 and 3% a year in Scenario 1, Scenario 2 and Scenario 3, respectively. Whereas this in the case of Scenario 1 represents a decrease of income relative to that in other sectors in the economy, assuming a 2.5% GNP growth, it is in the case of Scenario 3 likely to represent increase above that in other sectors. The fact that the income in Scenario 3 is higher than in Scenario 2, the price decrease being the same, reflects that the use of resources is more efficient in the agricultural sector in Scenario 3 than in Scenario 2, and that the direct income payments are greater.

Table 52

Agricultural employment and agricultural income — EUR-9
(in annual rates of change)

	1992/95	1995/98	1998/2001	1992/2001
Employment				
Scenario 1	− 2.5	− 2.6	− 2.8	− 2.6
Scenario 2	− 2.6	− 2.6	− 2.7	− 2.6
Scenario 3	− 2.9	− 3.0	− 2.9	− 2.9
Value-added				
Scenario 1	− 1.1	− 0.9	− 0.1	− 0.7
Scenario 2	− 0.6	0.1	0.6	0.0
Scenario 3	− 2.2	0.9	1.1	− 0.1
Value-added + compensation				
Scenario 3	− 0.3	0.5	0.6	0.3

Source: ECAM model.

4.4. Real income effects

The decrease in prices will reduce distortion costs both for consumers and producers. The ECAM model indicates that the improvement in aggregate real income in 2001 in Scenario 2 and Scenario 3 compared with Scenario 1 is ECU 5 700 million and ECU 6 800 million respectively.

These figures do not take into account the costs of administrating the CAP policies nor of tax collection. Taking such

---

[1] The difference with respect to exports between the ECAM and the MISS models has only a marginal impact for the budget projections due to the low level of protection which is assumed to prevail for grains by the year 2001.

costs into account is likely to reduce the aggregate real income gains compared to Scenario 1, in particular in the case of Scenario 2. The reduction in storage costs which is expected due to the simplification of the intervention arrangements for cereals is not reflected in the model results. Such a reduction would on the other hand increase the aggregate real income gain of reform.

The results are consistent with the expectation on theoretical grounds that a switch from market price support to direct income payments will increase aggregate real income. The real income gains are, however, rather small.

The RUNS model predicts negative effects on aggregate real income. This is not entirely surprising. The CAP reform implies a reduction in the level of support in the crop sector with a similar reduction in the animal sector, resources are different and are therefore stronger from the crop sector to use in the animal sector where they have a lower opportunity value. This dominates in the RUNS model simulation the increase in real income due to resources being shifted out of agriculture altogether.

4.5. Effects on Member States

The ECAM results suggest that the effect of reform on employment and income does not differ significantly between Member States. Also the effect on aggregate real income is very similar. Only in Ireland are the gains per capita significantly greater than in other countries.

Table 53

Change in value-added per person employed in agriculture for Member States (EUR-9)

(in annual rates of change)

	Scenario 1	Scenario 2	Scenario 3
Belgium + Luxembourg	1.2	2.0	2.5
Denmark	3.3	3.3	4.8
Germany	− 0.1	0.45	1.6
France	2.4	3.0	4.1
Ireland	3.2	4.3	5.3
Italy	2.8	2.9	3.6
Netherlands	1.4	1.7	1.7
United Kingdom	− 0.0	0.7	1.6
EUR-9	1.7	2.2	3.0

Source: ECAM model.

Table 54

Direct payments in Scenarios 2 and 3 for the Member States in 1995

Belgium + Luxembourg	
share of GNP	0.2
share of value of agricultural production	4.5
share of agricultural value-added	10.2
ECU per person employed in agriculture	1 320
Denmark	
share of GNP	0.8
share of value of agricultural production	11.1
share of agricultural value-added	17.4
ECU per person employed in agriculture	3 760
Germany	
share of GNP	0.2
share of value of agricultural production	8.7
share of agricultural value-added	17.3
ECU per person employed in agriculture	962
France	
share of GNP	0.5
share of value of agricultural production	10.7
share of agricultural value-added	24.4
ECU per person employed in agriculture	2 137
Ireland	
share of GNP	1.5
share of value of agricultural production	12.0
share of agricultural value-added	19.4
ECU per person employed in agriculture	1 617
Italy	
share of GNP	0.6
share of value of agricultural production	9.6
share of agricultural value-added	15.0
ECU per person employed in agriculture	1 017
Netherlands	
share of GNP	0.2
share of value of agricultural production	3.8
share of agricultural value-added	5.7
ECU per person employed in agriculture	808
United Kingdom	
share of GNP	0.3
share of value of agricultural production	11.8
share of agricultural value-added	24.2
ECU per person employed in agriculture	2 306
EUR-9	
share of GNP	0.4
share of value of agricultural production	9.5
share of agricultural value-added	17.7
ECU per person employed in agriculture	1 424

Source: ECAM database.

5. Effects outside the EC

5.1. Effect on world market prices

The 1992 CAP reform has, as expected, a positive impact on world market prices for cereals. Prices in 2001 are, in Scenario 2, 7.1% higher than in Scenario 1. The effect of the 1992 CAP reform on the world market price for oilcakes is, however, modest. The reason for this is that the decrease in domestic production is accompanied by a decrease in feed use of a similar amount, leaving net trade at the same level as in Scenario 1. The prices of by-products are, on the other hand, strongly affected by the reform. World market prices for these products fall in line with the fall in the domestic EC prices. These products are in general by-products and therefore have low supply elasticities.

The prices for beef and dairy products are higher in Scenario 2 than in Scenario 1 due to reduced EC export, but are lower for pork and poultry as a consequence of expanded EC export.

The world market prices in Scenario 3 are in general very similar to those in Scenario 2. However, cereal prices and in particular oilseed prices, are higher than in Scenario 2. The reason for this is that the net effect of abolishing the system of set-aside and direct payments linked to area use in the MISS model decreases production of cereals and oilseeds. The effect is particular strong for oilseeds.

Table 55

World market price effects
(in annual rates of change)

	1992/95	1995/98	1998/2001	1992/2001
Scenario 1				
Grains[1]	− 0.8	− 0.7	− 0.8	− 0.7
Oilseeds				
Oilcakes[2]	− 1.1	− 1.0	− 1.0	− 1.0
Oils	− 1.0	− 0.9	− 0.9	− 0.9
Corn gluten feed	− 1.5	− 1.6	− 1.6	− 1.6
Manioc	0.0	0.0	0.0	0.0
Other grain substitutes	− 1.6	− 1.6	− 1.6	− 1.6
Beef	0.8	0.8	0.8	0.8
Pork and poultry	− 0.7	− 0.7	− 0.7	− 0.7
Milk	− 0.7	− 0.7	− 0.7	− 0.7
Sugar	0.5	− 0.5	0.5	0.5
Other agricultural products				
Scenario 2				
Grains[1]	1.0	− 0.3	− 0.5	0.0
Oilseeds				
Oilcakes[2]	− 1.8	− 0.8	− 1.0	− 1.2
Oils	− 0.2	− 1.0	− 1.2	− 0.8
Corn gluten feed	− 5.9	− 1.3	− 0.5	− 2.6

	1992/95	1995/98	1998/2001	1992/2001
Manioc	0.1	0.2	0.3	0.2
Other grain substitutes	− 1.2	− 1.3	− 0.8	− 1.1
Beef	2.7	0.8	0.6	1.3
Pork and poultry	− 0.3	− 1.1	− 0.9	− 0.7
Milk	0.2	− 0.7	− 0.7	− 0.4
Sugar	0.5	0.5	0.5	0.5
Other agricultural products	0.1	0.2	0.3	0.2
Scenario 3				
Grains[1]	1.7	− 0.5	− 0.8	0.1
Oilseeds				
Oilcakes[2]	− 0.9	− 0.8	− 0.5	− 0.7
Oils	0.6	− 1.0	− 1.0	− 0.5
Corn gluten feed	− 6.4	− 1.3	− 0.2	2.6
Manioc	0.2	0.2	0.3	0.2
Other grain substitutes	− 1.9	− 1.3	− 0.6	1.3
Beef	3.1	− 0.7	0.2	1.3
Pork and poultry	− 0.4	− 1.1	− 0.8	− 0.8
Milk	0.3	− 0.8	− 0.7	− 0.4
Sugar	0.5	0.5	0.5	0.5
Other agricultural products	0.0	0.2	0.3	0.2

NB: See notes in Table 34.
Source: MISS model.

Table 56

World market price relative to Scenario 1

	1995	1998	2001
Scenario 2			
Grains[1]	1.053	1.064	1.071
Oilseeds	—	—	—
Oilcakes[2]	0.997	0.984	0.986
Oils	1.025	1.023	1.014
Corn gluten feed	0.857	0.869	0.899
Manioc	1.002	1.006	1.014
Other grain substitutes	1.009	1.017	1.043
Beef	1.055	1.052	1.045
Pork and poultry	1.012	1.000	0.995
Milk	1.027	1.027	1.027
Sugar	1.000	1.000	1.000
Other agricultural products	—	—	—
Scenario 3			
Grains[1]	1.075	1.083	1.081
Oilseeds	—	—	—
Oilcakes[2]	1.006	1.014	1.030
Oils	1.047	1.045	1.043
Corn gluten feed	0.845	0.852	0.889
Manioc	1.004	1.008	1.016
Other grain substitutes	0.988	0.996	1.027
Beef	1.065	1.062	1.045
Pork and poultry	1.010	0.998	0.994
Milk	1.031	1.029	1.029
Sugar	1.000	1.000	1.000
Other agricultural products	—	—	—

N.B.: See notes in Table 34.
Source: MISS model.

5.2. Effect on the United States

EC agriculture policies affect the US through their effect on world market prices, either by changing prices to US farmers and consumers or by affecting the US government spending on farm programmes.

Who is affected depends on to what extent US domestic policies modify the price signals coming from the world market, which differs from product to product. Changes in EC policies which increase world market prices will, where the US is an exporter, as is the case for grains, provide the US with a gain in aggregate real income.

The effect on the US of CAP reform is mainly through the increase in the world market price of cereals. Farm income is almost unaffected by CAP reform since US farmers under the target price programme are assumed to be isolated from changes in the world market price for cereals. The US government budget does, however, benefit from the increase in the world market price of grain. Grain subsidies decrease by around ECU 2 000 millioon. The US has an interest in CAP reform, but the MISS model results suggest that the benefits to the US, compared with a continuation of existing policies, are relatively modest.

5.3. Effect on developing countries

The RUN model simulations show that the 1992 CAP reform will decrease the aggregate real income of a number of low-income developing countries, especially in Africa. The loss is, however, relatively small, in the order of 0.3% of GNP. Certain food-exporting countries in Latin America and India will benefit, together with Australia and New Zealand.

References

Goldin, I., Van der Mensbrugghe, D. and Cordella, A. 'The consequences of CAP reform for developing countries'.[1]

Mahé, L. P. and Guyomard, H. 'EC-US trade relations in the context of the GATT negotiations and of the reform of the CAP'.[1]

Keyzer, M. A., Folmer, C., Merbis, M. D., Stolwijk, H. J. J. and Veenendaal, P. J. J. 'CAP reform and its differential impact on Member States'.[1]

---

[1] Forthcoming in 'The economics of the CAP', *European Economy,* No 5, 1994.

List of contents of European Economy

17, September 1983	— *The borrowing and lending activities of the Community in 1982*
18, November 1983	— *Annual Economic Report 1983-84* — *Annual Economic Review 1983-84*
19, March 1984	— *Economic trends and prospects* — *Industrial labour costs* — *Medium-term budget balance and the public debt* — *The issue of protectionism*
20, July 1984	— *Some aspects of industrial productive performance in the European Community: an appraisal* — *Profitability, relative factor prices and capital/labour substitution in the Community, the United States and Japan, 1960-83* — *Convergence and coordination of macroeconomic policies: some basic issues*
21, September 1984	— *Commission report to the Council and to Parliament on the borrowing and lending activities of the Community in 1983*
22, November 1984	— *Annual Economic Report 1984-85* — *Annual Economic Review 1984-85*
23, March 1985	— *Economic trends and prospects 1984-85*
24, July 1985	— *The borrowing and lending activities of the Community in 1984*
25, September 1985	— *Competitiveness of European industry: situation to date* — *The determinants of supply in industry in the Community* — *The development of market services in the European Community, the United States and Japan* — *Technical progress, structural change and employment*
26, November 1985	— *Annual Economic Report 1985-86* — *Annual Economic Review 1985-86*
27, March 1986	— *Employment problemsfi: views of businessmen and the workforce* — *Compact —A prototype macroeconomic model of the European Community in the world economy*
28, May 1986	— *Commission report to the Council and to Parliament on the borrowing and lending activities of the Community in 1985*
29, July 1986	— *Annual Economic Review 1986-87*
30, November 1986	— *Annual Economic Report 1986-87*
31, March 1987	— *The determinants of investment* — *Estimation and simulation of international trade linkages in the Quest model*
32, May 1987	— *Commission report to the Council and to Parliament on the borrowing and lending activities of the Community in 1986*

Special editions

Special issue 1979	— *Changes in industrial structure in the European conomies since the oil crisis 1973-78* — *Europe — its capacity to change in question!*
Special edition 1990	— *The impact of the internal market by industrial sector: the challenge for the Member States*
Special edition No 1/91	— *The economics of EMU*
Special edition No 2/91	— *The path of reform in Central and Eastern Europe*
Special edition No 1/92	— *The economics of limiting CO_2 emissions*

Reports and studies

1-1993	— *The economic and financial situation in Italy*
2-1993	— *Shaping a market economy legal system*
3-1993	— *Market services and European integration: the challenges for the 1990s*
4-1993	— *The economic and financial situation in Belgium*
5-1993	— *The economic of Community public finance (in preparation)*
6-1993	— *The economic and financial situation in Denmark*
1-1994	— *Applying market principles to government borrowing* — *Growth and employment: the scope for a European initiative*